Reducing the Risk:
Schools as Communities of Support

Education Policy Perspectives

General Editor: **Professor Ivor Goodson**, Faculty of Education, University of Western Ontario, London, Canada N6G 1G7

Education policy analysis has long been a neglected area in the United Kingdom and, to an extent, in the USA and Australia. The result has been a profound gap between the study of education and the formulation of education policy. For practitioners such a lack of analysis of the new policy initiatives has worrying implications particularly at such a time of policy flux and change. Education policy has, in recent years, been a matter for intense political debate — the political and public interest in the working of the system has come at the same time as the consensus on education policy has been broken by the advent of the 'New Right'. As never before the political parties and pressure groups differ in their articulated policies and prescriptions for the education sector. Critical thinking about these developments is clearly necessary.

All those working within the system also need information on policy making, policy implementation and effective day-to-day operation. Pressure on schools from government, education authorities and parents has generated an enormous need for knowledge amongst those on the receiving end of educational policies.

This series aims to fill the academic gap, to reflect the politicalization of education, and to provide the practitioners with the analysis for informed implementation of policies that they will need. It will offer studies in broad areas of policy studies. Beside the general section it will offer a particular focus in the following areas: School organization and improvement (David Reynolds, *University College, Cardiff, UK*); Critical social analysis (Professor Philip Wexler, *University of Rochester, USA*); Policy studies and evaluation (Professor Ernest House, *University of Colorado-Boulder, USA*).

Policy Studies and Evaluation Series
Editor: Professor Ernest House, Center for Policy Studies, School of Education, University of Colorado-Boulder, USA

Flunking Grades: Research and Policy on Retention
Edited by L. A. Shepard and M. L. Smith

Reducing the Risk: Schools as Communities of Support
Gary G. Wehlage, Robert A. Rutter, Gregory A. Smith, Nancy Lesko and Ricardo R. Fernandez

Education Policy Perspectives

Reducing the Risk: Schools as Communities of Support

Gary G. Wehlage,
Robert A. Rutter,
Gregory A. Smith,
Nancy Lesko
and
Ricardo R. Fernandez

The Falmer Press

(A member of the Taylor & Francis Group)
London • New York • Philadelphia

UK   The Falmer Press, Falmer House, Barcombe, Lewes, East Sussex, BN8 5DL

USA   The Falmer Press, Taylor & Francis Inc., 242 Cherry Street, Philadelphia, PA 19106-1906

First published 1989

British Library Cataloguing in Publication Data

Reducing the risk : schools as communities of support.
  1. United States. Secondary Schools. Dropout. Prevention.
I. Title. II. Wehlage, Gary.
373.12′913′0973
ISBN 1-85000-530-3
ISBN 1-85000-531-1 (pbk.)

Library of Congress Cataloging-in-Publication Data

Reducing the risk : schools as communities of support / Gary G. Wehlage . . . [et al.].
  p. cm.—(Education policy perspectives. Policy studies and evaluation series)
  Bibliography p.
  Includes index.
  ISBN 1-85000-530-3.—ISBN 1-85000-531-1 (pbk.)
  1. High school dropouts—United States—Case studies. 2. High school students—Counseling of—United States—Case studies.
I. Wehlage, G. II. Series
LC146.5.R43   1989
373.12′913′0973—dc19   88-32454

Typeset by
Mathematical Composition Setters Ltd, Ivy Street, Salisbury

Jacket design by Caroline Archer

Printed in Great Britain by Taylor & Francis (Printers) Ltd, Basingstoke

Contents

Preface		*vii*
Introduction		1
Chapter 1	Who Is At Risk and Why?	7
Chapter 2	Dropping Out: Can Schools Be Expected to Prevent It?	28
Chapter 3	At-Risk Youth: Uncovering Their Diversity	48
Chapter 4	Diverse Programs for Diverse Students	75
Chapter 5	School Membership	113
Chapter 6	Teacher Culture and School Structure	134
Chapter 7	Effects of School as a Community	151
Chapter 8	Educational Engagement	176
Chapter 9	Continuing Issues	196
Chapter 10	School Reform and Beyond: Policy Implications	221
Appendix A	Fourteen Schools	242
Appendix B	Research Methodology	253
References		261
Index		267

Preface

From the ground up makes good sense for building. Beware of from the top down. (Frank Lloyd Wright)

This book is the product of a complex series of tasks. Early on, our energies focused on selecting schools, visiting classrooms, and talking with teachers and students. Once data had been collected, it was synthesized into a case study of each school; the project's staff spent long hours discussing and evaluating the insights that each school provided. Finally, we were faced with the challenge of presenting our story in a way that would best influence practice and policy. The book had to meet the strict standards of scholarship and yet be readable by all members of the broad group interested in the issues of at-risk youth. Most of the chapters evolved through dialogue and criticism, a process that was occasionally frustrating, but ultimately satisfying. We came to know well the schools, their students and their teachers. Our concrete and theoretical understanding has grown immensely. It is our hope and our intent to communicate much of this understanding to the reader.

Special thanks are due to the schools' teachers and administrators; their cooperation was essential and we are well aware that our presence must have been inconvenient at times. Their candor about their educational views and experiences was invaluable. We also thank the students, who not only were cooperative but who often made us feel at ease as our questions probed for their thoughts and ideas. One school was promised anonymity at the onset of the study, but elsewhere we have used the actual names of schools and educators. We have in all cases changed students' names and masked their identities.

We wish to thank Mary Anne Raywid, Lois Weis, John Mergendoller, Mara Clisby, Susan Fuhrman and Fred Newmann for their useful comments on the manuscript as well as Dianne Paley for her superb editing. Finally, we offer our appreciation to Jean Norman for her help and patience with us throughout the project.

This book was prepared at the National Center on Effective Secondary Schools, Wisconsin Center for Education Research, School of Education, University of Wisconsin-Madison which is supported in part by a grant from the Office of Educational Research and Improvement (Grant No. G008690007). Any opinions, findings, and conclusion or recommendations expressed in this publication are those of the author and do not necessarily reflect the views of this agency or the U.S. Department of Education.

Gary G. Wehlage
Robert A. Rutter
Gregory A. Smith
Nancy Lesko
Ricardo R. Fernandez
September 1988

Introduction

It seems an irony that today, when statistics indicate that the national dropout rate may be approaching the historic low of 25 per cent, public attention has come to rest on the dropout issue. But current concern focuses not so much on the number of dropouts as on their impact on the nation's social and economic future. While the national average appears relatively low, dropout rates are unevenly distributed across communities, and many urban school systems report that 30 to 40 per cent of students leave school before graduation. More serious is the fact that dropouts face a future in which unemployment and low wages are a near certainty. In addition, dropouts can be viewed as a financial drain on society; they detract from the overall well being of a competitive economic system when they become unemployable, under-employed or dependent upon welfare and other social services. Consequently, educators, business leaders, policy makers and the public have issued a call to action. What, if anything, can be done to stem the flow of dropouts from America's schools?

This book suggests answers to this question. We describe the efforts of fourteen secondary schools to prevent students from dropping out. These schools were selected for study because they offered evidence that students typically at risk of dropping out can be kept in school. In studying school efforts clearly aimed at at-risk students we hoped to identify and describe those practices that work to keep students in school.

It was not difficult to locate schools that target the potential dropout, but identifying those that could produce data indicating a track record of effectiveness was another matter. During the spring of 1986 we conducted a national search for 'effective' schools to serve as the basis of our study. Nominations from a variety of key informants across the country produced a list of more than sixty schools that were considered effective or promising in their efforts. These schools submitted data about their programs, including effectiveness based on graduation, attendance and achievement rates. A process of elimination produced a list of about twenty that appeared to meet our criteria and were willing to participate in the study. Investigators visited these schools, and based on established criteria, the list was pared to fourteen.

The participating schools were selected to guarantee a broad range of intervention strategies, as well as diversity among students. While all participating students were categorized as at-risk, they differed in terms of social class, race, ethnicity and geographical location, as well as in the kinds of problems they faced. Clearly the term *at-risk* is an imprecise one. In classifying students, the judgment was partly our own, but we relied heavily on the opinion of the educators at each of the fourteen schools. Some students had problems and characteristics making them more at risk of dropping out than others, and the reader will note this throughout the course of the book. This ambiguity is inherent in research on at-risk students.

The fourteen schools in the study are:

1   *Alcott Alternative Learning Center, Wichita, Kansas* — Alcott is a junior high school serving just over 100 students, all of whom have a history of school failure, truancy or disruption. Generally they are from poor homes; many have experienced serious family problems.

2   *Croom Vocational High School, Upper Marlboro, Maryland* — In existence since 1965, Croom serves 125 black and white urban youth. The curriculum is divided between academic courses and vocational shops that prepare students for employment in the local economy.

3   *Lincoln High School (pseudonym), Atlanta, Georgia* — Lincoln is an inner-city comprehensive high school serving about 900 black students. The intervention focused on approximately fifty students who were judged at-risk, but who nevertheless exhibited academic potential. The program was designed to prepare these students for college.

4   *Media Academy, Fremont High School, Oakland, California* — The Media Academy is a school-within-a-school serving inner-city black and Hispanic youth since the Fall of 1986. The Academy offers an academic curriculum incorporating a variety of first-hand experiences, including the publication of an

award-winning school newspaper and frequent contact with local professionals in radio, television and newspapers.

5   *Minneapolis Federation of Alternative Schools, Minneapolis, Minnesota* — Five privately funded inner-city high schools with various affiliations comprise the federation. They are: Loring-Nicollet; Plymouth Christian Youth Center; Minneapolis Education and Recycling Center; NA-WAY-EE (The Center School); and Minneapolis Street Academy. These schools are affiliated for fund-raising purposes while their clientele and curricula differ widely.

6   *New Futures School, Albuquerque, New Mexico* — In existence since 1970, this four-year public school serves approximately 400 pregnant or mothering girls. In addition to providing health services and day-care, the curriculum includes a focus on parenting skills and information.

7   *School-Within-A-School (SWS), Madison Memorial High School, Madison, Wisconsin* — Established in 1984, this is a two-year academic and vocational program for credit-deficient youth over 16 years of age. The program, which incorporates a variety of community-based experiences, maintains an average enrollment of about 65 students.

8   *Sierra Mountain High School, Grass Valley, California* — Begun in 1980 to provide drop-out prevention and retrieval, this two-year school for ninth and tenth graders now serves an average of 85 rural and small-town youth. This is a school of choice for students who prefer an alternative to a large comprehensive high school.

9   *Two Majors At A Time (TMAT), Orr Community Academy, Chicago, Illinois* — This large comprehensive inner-city high school offers TMAT to 530 ninth and tenth graders, all of whom are black or Hispanic. TMAT provides greater academic focus to a student population that traditionally experiences academic difficulties.

10 *Wayne Enrichment Center (WEC), Wayne Township (Indianapolis), Indiana* — This school began in the early 1970s as a drop-out retrieval program. It now is primarily a prevention effort, serving a diverse population of about 70 credit deficient students with an academic and vocational curriculum. (Appendix A contains more information about each of the schools.)

In choosing successful schools clearly focused on at-risk populations, we hoped to find answers to questions about why some young people drop out. What are their problems? What perceptions do they hold of themselves, school and their future? We also wanted to discover what teaching practices and curriculum strategies are employed in these schools. How did students respond to various programs? What did teachers believe made these practices appropriate and successful with their students?

We hoped to achieve three objectives. One goal was to provide descriptions of good programs in real schools carried out by practicing teachers with students identified as at-risk of dropping out of school. Our intent was to make these descriptions useful to practitioners across the country, not as recipes to be followed blindly, but as examples to stimulate thinking and encourage action.

A second objective was to provide practitioners and researchers with a generalizable, theoretical framework for understanding at-risk students and their schools. A theory of dropout prevention is a very useful tool for bringing practitioners and researchers together in the development of school reforms. It provides the conceptual language for program development, research and evaluation.

Finally, our third purpose was to influence local and state policy-makers in a position to make important decisions about the extent to which schools respond constructively to at-risk youth. Success at this task initially requires that we achieve the first two purposes. It is our hope that the descriptions of schools, students and teacher practices will convince policy makers that it is possible for schools to more successfully retain at-risk students. If our theoretical formulation of the problem is convincing and useful, policy makers will have a framework with which to make judgments about school reforms and initiatives.

The reader should be aware that the book pursues two somewhat different lines of enquiry by describing schools and students on the one hand, and developing theory on the other. Chapter 1 presents a series of vignettes to introduce the reader to some of the students we encountered and the schools they attend. Chapter 2 shifts the subject to offer an historical perspective on the dropout issue and then begins to develop a theory intended to be useful to practitioners concerned with the education of at-risk youth. Chapters 3 and 4 return to the presentation of data by describing the diversity of students and schools we studied. The reader will note that data is presented in such a way as to build the case for our findings and theory.

Chapter 5 presents more data about the characteristics of school programs and further develops our theory about effective practices. This chapter also defines school membership, a concept that is central to our theory. Chapter 6 analyzes the teachers in the fourteen schools and provides a set of generalizations about professional culture and school structure associated with school effectiveness. Chapter 7 presents quantitative and qualitative data describing the impact of the schools on students. The measures of school impact include achievement, attendance, credit accumulation and dropout rates. Chapter 8 returns to the task of theory development by exploring the problem of engaging students in schoolwork, an issue that is particularly troublesome in teaching at-risk youth. This chapter concludes with the theory of dropout prevention developed from our data. Chapter 9 takes a critical stance with respect to our findings about the effectiveness of the fourteen schools in educating at-risk youth. It suggests some of the limitations of the educational strategies employed and the political constraints facing even the best alternative schools. Finally, chapter 10 summarizes our main findings and offers recommendations for policymakers and practitioners. (For an extensive discussion of the methodology used during the research see Appendix B.)

This book is intended to influence educational practice at the school building level. To achieve this goal, we believe it also is necessary to influence policy making at the state and district levels toward reforms benefitting students at risk of dropping out. We believe our data and analysis have much to say to those who offer alternative programs for these students. Our recommendations also are aimed at a systematic strengthening of traditional, mainstream schools for the benefit of the potential dropout.

Beyond this, we are convinced our message is important to the broad educational community. We believe that one can view at-risk students as indicators of the general health of an educational system; dropouts typically are the visible signs of school problems that may affect a much broader group of students. Recommendations developed from our study of dropout prevention efforts will benefit many students who may not be labeled at risk of dropping out. In addition, we believe that what is good for at-risk students is usually good for other students as well; given this, we view the implications of our research as pertinent to the improvement of most schools.

Chapter 1:
Who Is At Risk and Why?

Two girls passed a visitor in the hall and one of them greeted him with a perky, 'Hi, Mr. Wisconsin! What do you *really* think of Alcott? Will you come and visit us in class?'

It was the visitor's first day at Alcott Alternative Learning Center, a school for at-risk junior high students. He had been introduced earlier at an all-school assembly, and obviously the state university he represented had stuck in lieu of his name. As the two girls made their way down the hall through a knot of students, the one he later knew as Melody called out over her shoulder, 'Come and visit me in algebra'. She and her friend laughed and waved as they turned into a classroom.

Melody's friendliness seemed unusual for any junior high student, and the stereotype of at-risk junior high students did not easily accommodate her bright, alert manner. The observer was ready to see signs of wariness, apprehension or boredom that school-phobic teenagers often show in the presence of an adult, especially an adult stranger.

Melody, as it turned out, is somewhat different from many of the at-risk students we met during the year of our research. Unlike many of the students at Alcott, she comes from a middle-class family. In fact, her mother has a college degree and her father is an accountant. Melody's scores on the Iowa Test of Basic Skills are above the 90th percentile in math and reading. By the time she finished eighth grade she had completed algebra I and was beginning algebra II. She and a friend reportedly were writing a play about a fictional rock star. Melody talks confidently about going to college, where she may major in English because she likes to read and write. Such academic ability and interest are characteristic of a model student, but in fact Melody was a junior high dropout.

During conversations with Melody, and with her teachers and Principal, it became clear that she had dropped out of another junior high because of personal and social problems connected to her physical shape and size. The most compelling thing in Melody's life is her size: she is large, particularly for a 14-year-old. Problems with size or weight are traumatic for all adolescents. As a result of her shape, Melody's self-image and self-esteem were negative, and she had experienced problems with her peers. She had hated gym class at her previous school because she occasionally had been ridiculed by students and the teacher because of her appearance. According to Melody, her peers taunted her about her weight so much that she quit school. She had suffered to the breaking point from the indignities that many young adolescents experience. Eventually she was persuaded to enroll at Alcott, where she says she has had a much more positive experience with peers and teachers. 'It is a place where I could find myself', she says.

Melody's presence at Alcott indicates there is great diversity in background among those who are in danger of dropping out of school. Cases such as hers add complexity to the set of factors that make school a hazardous, uncomfortable, often unforgiving place for young people to spend so much of their time. While she is atypical as an at-risk student in that she is above average in academic ability and comes from a professional family, the experiences that drove her to drop out are variations of the experiences of many young people. For some, the indignities result from academic failure; for others it is conflict with peers or adults, loneliness and isolation, and general lack of success in things valued by the school or peer group. Many students go to school each day only to be told in various subtle and direct ways that they are not good at anything. The message is that they are not and cannot be successful. Repeated assaults on their self-esteem make school intolerable. Unfortunately, few of these young people have Melody's personal or family resources; instead they become dropouts who are permanently disadvantaged by their decision to leave school. Moreover, many potential dropouts have no alternative in the form of a school or program designed to help them cope with their difficulties. For many youth, school offers a single disparaging message: 'If you don't fit in, it is your fault; if you don't like things the way they are, move on'.

What, if anything, can schools do to prevent students from dropping out? Should schools be responsible for helping students like Melody deal with problems like being overweight and suffering humiliation at the hands of cruel teenagers and insensitive teachers?

What about problems that interfere with student motivation and achievement, such as drug abuse? What can be done for students who come from homes disrupted by divorce, violence, poverty and unemployment? Is there anything teachers can do to engage adolescents in school work when over the years they have fallen so far behind in achievement that they now consider themselves school losers?

The vignettes that follow suggest in concrete ways how some schools have developed strategies and entire programs to help students who have found success difficult, if not impossible, in conventional settings. These vignettes offer a flavor of the research data gathered in our study of the fourteen schools. They suggest the complexity of the problems educators face and the need to understand schools' efforts on behalf of students. We describe real students who bring to school their individual characteristics and problems. We discuss real schools in which adults interact with students. Without exception, these adults expressed genuine concern about the young with whom they worked. These educators consciously sought to provide experiences that would make a difference in their students' school performance and in their attitudes and behaviors outside of school.

Getting to the Problem

Mrs Gutierrez, the Principal, invites 16-year-old Terry and his mother to sit in the two large easy chairs in her office. Mrs G, as she is affectionately called by students and staff, is a woman in her 50s. She has lived her entire life in Wichita, and knows its diverse population well. According to his mother, Terry has not attended school since the preceding Spring. Their decision that he should enter Alcott Alternative Learning Center, a junior high, is based primarily on the recommendation of one of Terry's friends. At this point in the conversation Mrs G turns directly to Terry and addresses him: 'We are going to meddle in your business. I will know everything about you, even what you were like at age 5'.

She asks about his reading ability and asks Terry to read aloud from a short reading assessment instrument. It is a simple test and he correctly pronounces most of the words and seems to know their meaning. In an upbeat, positive and encouraging tone, Mrs G comments that he is probably reading at the eighth-grade level and that there does not appear to be any reading problem. Despite this, Terry becomes noticeably nervous as Mrs G quizzes him about his previous school. Yes, he was frequently truant and eventually was suspended. One of the reasons he quit attending is that he needs new glasses; he broke the pair he had last year by throwing them at his mother in a fit of anger. Terry's mother refuses to buy him some more until he promises to attend school regularly.

At this point, Mrs G says: 'You hurt yourself by losing control of the situation. Your temper got the best of you then. You will learn to think before you act while you're here at Alcott. You will learn to act in your own self-interest.'

Mrs G then turns to the mother and asks her about the family situation. Terry's mother is remarried with four children; three boys by the first marriage and a much younger girl by the second. She comments that the boys are very difficult and won't obey her. Terry, she says, just sleeps and won't go to school or do anything around the house. She says he has never been examined for special education despite the fact he has been held back twice. Terry's mother explains that part of the problem is a lack of support from her husband, who won't discipline her sons. An older brother is the worst problem because he is a drug and alcohol abuser.

Mrs G confronts Terry with the question, 'Do you use drugs?' After some prodding, he admits he does. His mother looks surprised. 'You told me you didn't use that stuff.' Mrs G looks at Terry and says, 'So you lie to your mother'. He nods and looks down.

Terry's mother now begins to talk rather rapidly and openly. Terry is in trouble with the law because he broke into a neighbor's house. The Judge has required restitution for the money and valuables stolen, and Terry must attend school as a condition of staying out of the reformatory. Mrs G asks Terry why he stole and he confesses that he needed money to buy drugs. Mrs G suggests he enter a drug and alcohol treatment program, but Terry resists, saying he doesn't have a serious problem.

Mrs G tells the mother there is a need for better communication between mother and son. 'He is not old enough to make his own decisions. You're all he has. He needs you to help him or he will make too many mistakes. He may need you till the day he dies.' Terry's mother says she knows this is true, but she is frustrated because she gets no support from her husband or the boys. She talks about the nights when a local bartender calls to tell her to come after her husband, that he is too drunk to drive home. Mrs G suggests that she may be assuming too much responsibility around the house. They discuss the possibility of involving a family counselor to help make changes in their lives.

Mrs G turns to Terry and says, 'I have heard some words here this morning: thief, lazy, hostile, liar. Do these words describe you? Do you lie?' There is a pause, and then Terry responds, 'Yes'. Mrs G smiles. 'Thank you for not lying to a little old lady. You know that little old ladies are next to God.'

The secretary enters the office with results from some written tests Terry had taken earlier. Mrs G says, 'Terry, you are not dumb. Look at these results. If you are this smart, you should be able to avoid going to jail and getting raped. You know that's what will happen to a pretty boy like you, if you go to jail.' Terry is wide-eyed and maybe a bit embarrassed. He looks away and does not comment.

Mrs G continues, 'We expect you to do well here — there is no reason for you not to be successful. You might be able to go to Metro High School at the end of the semester, if you work hard. It's up to you. If you come and work hard you can go to high school.'

'That would be great', says Terry. For the first time he seems pleased and even enthused about the idea of attending Alcott. His mother is surprised and obviously pleased by this optimistic prospect.

As Terry is about to leave to meet the school counselor, Mrs G reminds him that there can be no lies or secrets. She says she will find out what he is doing and tell his mother. 'I'll tattle on you.' He asks if there is anything else he needs to do. Mrs G says, 'Give me a hug'. Terry is visibly shocked at the request. He stumbles toward her, hesitates, then hugs her rather awkwardly. Mrs G says, 'You have to learn to hug now that you're an [Alcott] Eagle'.

As Terry's mother gets up to leave, she expresses her surprise that Terry is a 'dope smoker'. She hugs Mrs G before leaving the office. 'You're a wonderful person. You've helped so much already', she says.

After they have gone, Mrs G explains that Terry's grandmother lives only two doors away from his family. Why is Terry's mother not getting any support from her own mother? Does a request for help in dealing with a difficult home situation signal a failure as mother and wife? Mrs G suggests that the mother may get some satisfaction in stoically facing these problems alone, in being a martyr, and that this attitude is unhealthy. She also suggests that the mother's open contempt for her sons, their father and their stepfather creates an unhealthy situation for the entire family. Terry's home situation may require family counseling if things are to improve. Mrs G says she will see if something can be arranged.

Terry's interview is typical of those she and the school counselor have with each incoming student, Mrs G reports. Young adolescents have fragile egos despite their swagger and street-wise appearance, she says, and much of their behavior is a defense against the negativism they experience in and out of school. Most of the students at Alcott come from homes that are in a constant state of chaos. Their problems are compounded by the school, which is quick to identify their weaknesses with messages of failure and negative labeling. The assault upon adolescents by a hostile school when there are no protective resources in the home produces at-risk students, she says. 'They come to us with hostility as a result of their home and school experiences.' In Mrs G's view, these students are understandably negative toward school and adults.

Reading, Writing and Reporting

From a school that deals with the most difficult junior high students, we move to a high school where the young people apparently have not been traumatized by disruption of their homes or personal lives. Conversations with these students indicate that, for the most part, they have not experienced an especially negative school environment. All students who attend the Media Academy at Fremont High School in Oakland, California are black, Hispanic or recent immigrants from Asia. For some, English is a second language. Most are from working-class homes. Before entering the Media Academy, most of the students found school neither discouraging, nor motivating or satisfying. Most struggled reluctantly with their academic courses. They were only modestly successful in a school system that has been accused of being discouraged with itself and of projecting low expectations for most of its students.

Students at the Media Academy represent that great middle group of 'unspecial' students that populates many urban high schools. Because they are poor and of minority backgrounds, with little support or impetus from their homes, many of these students hold low expectations and aspirations for themselves in terms of education and future careers. Those motivated to continue their education beyond high school exhibit a naivete about the prerequisites for college entrance and the costs involved in a college education. Moreover, many critics say teachers and administrators also have conveyed a message of limited hope for these youth, thereby suppressing in some whatever initiative they might have had. Media Academy students represent a dimension of the student population that is likely to underachieve at best. While they may be less at risk of dropping out than students in some other settings, school is something only marginally attractive, and unexpected events in a student's life can easily tip the balance of interest away from school to the streets, early pregnancy or a low-paying job.

Visit to Harbor Bay Teleport

It is immediately clear that the setting is not a school classroom. The atmosphere suggests professionalism, high technology and success. This is a conference room in a large modern office complex housing a variety of international businesses. The room is plush with heavy furniture, thick carpets and fine drapery. The professionals here move easily, confidently, with purpose. On a large television screen is the face of John Drury, a television anchorman and media personality from the San Francisco Bay area. But instead of the settings's typical audience of middle-aged businessmen in three-piece suits, the conference room is filled with fifty 14- and 15-year-old high school sophomores from the Media Academy. Many wear their standard blue jeans and sweatshirts. They have been brought to the Harbor Bay Teleport, the focal point of which is a satellite communication system used by international businesses to communicate world-wide. Today, the satellite is linking students in Oakland with Mr Drury in his office in San Francisco. The event was made possible through the cooperation of Harbor Bay Teleport Corporation, one of the many community sponsors who have joined forces to help develop the Media Academy.

Six students who are seated at a table with microphones begin to ask Mr Drury questions about his experiences in the media business and his views on the profession. After a few minutes, another group of students moves to the table for its turn. While each student is to have prepared several questions in advance, only those who have volunteered come forward to speak with Mr Drury.

Questions range from the personal to the professional and from the concrete to the abstract. One student asks about Mr Drury's high school background; they are surprised to learn that he graduated from Fremont. Another student enquires about where he gets the stories he reports each day. Another asks about job opportunities in television. A black student asks about opportunities for minorities in the media. As a follow-up, the same student wonders whether the presence of minority reporters and writers changes the stories that are aired on television or published in newspapers.

Maria, a recent immigrant from Mexico, has volunteered to ask questions. Her journalism teacher, Mr O'Donoghue, comments before the session that her participation surprises him because she has been extremely shy in classes during the first weeks of the semester. Because it is her first year in an American school, and because her command of English is tentative, journalism, English and history classes have been particularly difficult for Maria. In preparation, Mr O'Donoghue has helped write her ideas and questions in correct English. When it is her turn, she asks her initial question in carefully measured words, trying to pronounce each correctly: 'Does one have to pass a government examination to become a television reporter?' When Mr Drury completes his answer, Maria asserts her prerogative and asks a follow-up question: 'Is a college degree in journalism required for one to be a television reporter?' As Maria moves away from the table, Mr O'Donoghue catches her eye and raises his hand in a well-done signal.

Near the conclusion of the forty-five minute session, Mr O'Donoghue invites any student with a final question to the table. Maria, who is seated at the very back of the room, winds her way between chairs and students toward the front. Several students have already begun to question Mr Drury. Maria edges between them to get close to a microphone. Time is almost gone, but she finds the appropriate moment to ask a question about the responsibility of the media for encouraging crisis events involving the safety of human lives. 'Does television make more people do things like take hostages because they know television will be there?' For Maria, developing the confidence and initiative to ask her questions was an important event signifying a positive step toward success and achievement in school.

Commenting on Maria's triumph, Mr O'Donoghue says, 'What a breakthrough! What a confidence-builder for her! She can be a real success story! If she works on her English — and she is working hard now — she can be a winner. This program can do a lot for her.'

Learning by Doing

The students at Croom Vocational High School in Upper Marlboro, Maryland are different from those at the Media Academy. While Croom also draws students from a large urban area, they come from much more impoverished homes and generally have a more limited set of life experiences. Student scores on standardized academic tests cluster in the bottom quartile. In response, Croom offers juniors and seniors from several district high schools a combination of vocational and academic course work leading to a high school diploma and/or vocational certification in one of eight areas, including auto mechanics, groundskeeping and office work. The school's expansive campus and numerous buildings provide students with practical opportunities for applying the knowledge and skills learned in the shops. Food-service students prepare the school cafeteria's noon meal each day; classrooms are painted, doors are repaired and new window screens are built; groundskeeping students maintain the lawn, flowers and shrubs; and the auto shop has a constant supply of vehicles from the school staff and local residents.

The twenty-eight acre campus, once a Nike missile base for the US army, was acquired by the local school district as an alternative school site. Although the buildings retain their institutional appearance, the carefully maintained lawn, shrubs and flowers remind observers more of a college campus than of a high school. Unlike most modern concrete school structures that compress large numbers of students into a single building for the entire day, 125 Croom students are scattered throughout a dozen buildings. The atmosphere, too, differs from the norm. No clanging bells mark the time for passing. Hall monitors and hall passes are non-existent. The walls and buildings are free of graffiti, and the manicured grounds are free of litter. School visitors are routinely cautioned by student guides that everyone keeps to the concrete walkways to avoid wearing paths across the lawn.

Auto Shop

Croom's auto shop was once an army motor pool facility. The concrete garage building and a temporary classroom are located on a hill. Nearby is the top of an abandoned silo that once contained a missile. Scattered around the auto shop grounds is an array of vehicles, some literally junk and others in various stages of restoration and repair. A few hundred yards to the west sits a cluster of buildings that house the horticulture and groundskeeping, and building trades shops.

The auto shop teachers, like those in the other vocational areas, seem adept at teaching their students the right things at the right times. The newest or least competent students are assigned the simplest tasks, while more accomplished students take on more difficult assignments.

One morning during an observer's visit, one student changed the oil on a car, a second student changed the fuel filter on a Volkswagen diesel, a third student was replacing a worn-out clutch on a pickup truck and another replaced the disc brakes on a Ford EXP. Yet another was in the process of dismantling an eight-cylinder engine pulled from an old Chrysler Imperial which was being restored by the school.

In the middle of all this activity the shop teacher and his aide made carefully timed moves from student to student to monitor each procedure. As each step of an operation was completed, one-on-one instruction on the next step was provided. This strategy emphasized what the student should expect to find and do; students also were urged to anticipate the unexpected. For example, disc brake calipers on a newer car ordinarily move freely, but what if they have become rusted and bind? Veteran students were challenged to think ahead to the next several steps in their work. One student, for example, was corrected for stopping to watch the oil run from the engine during an oil change. The teacher took the moment to instruct the student that in a real garage a mechanic would use the time to grease the car and gather the filter and oil needed to complete the job. In this way, students who have had few encounters with the requirements of the workplace are helped to acquire the skills and behaviors they will need to become employable.

On Becoming a Mother

The context shifts now from preparation for employment to preparation for motherhood. The setting is New Futures School in Albuquerque, which enrolls about 200 pregnant and mothering teens. The school, which has been in operation since 1970, is designed to meet the needs of young women who face the problems of bearing and raising a child, often without the support of a father.

Induction into Parenthood

'I didn't respect myself', said Jessie, looking down at her desk. 'I skipped school and partied all the time and did drugs.' When this Native American high school junior got pregnant, she, like most of her peers, felt that her 'life was ruined'. But New Futures School helped change her attitudes about herself and what her life could become.

'The teachers believe that we're smart, that we can be good parents, that we should be proud of ourselves for being in school', reports one student. At New Futures, students are taught that they are capable young women with responsibilities and future opportunities, not in spite of, but because of, their motherhood. The experience of their pregnancy and motherhood serves as a vehicle for motivating them to learn about their baby and their own health, as well as traditional academic skills and knowledge.

When Jessie enrolled at New Futures she was unsure of herself, still adjusting to the conflicting feelings that accompany pregnancy. She was excited about her baby but aware that society and many of her former friends castigated her as a teenage mother. Jessie said self-acceptance was difficult at her old high school. 'Trying to get used to the idea [of being pregnant] is not very comfortable when you're the only one in that predicament. At New Futures, everyone's the same; they understand how you feel.'

On Jessie's first day at New Futures, she joined eleven other girls in the sixth-hour child development class, one of three required parenting courses. At one class meeting, all of the girls wear typical teenage garb: blue jeans or corduroy pants. The tops they wear, however, are designed to accommodate their bulging bellies because the girls are obviously pregnant. Everyone in the class will deliver during the spring semester. Catherine, the instructor, is a mother of four, one of whom became a teenage mother. The course she teaches combines general knowledge with lab work in the school's infant nursery. Today she begins by reading aloud selected passages from a text about infant learning in the first, second and third months of life. This class work prepares the girls to work in the nursery with twenty-five children under three months of age who are cared for while their mothers attend classes.

Later in the hour, Catherine shepherds the girls across the carpeted hall into the double classroom, half of which is filled with rocking chairs, infant swings and aides holding babies. The other half contains wall-to-wall cribs, each of which has an attached clipboard for charting the child's care. Catherine demonstrates the routine that each girl will follow upon entering the nursery. A smock is worn over street clothes; hands are to be washed with soap and scrub brush. Each time a girl diapers a baby she must wash and scrub her hands. The girls are shown where to stow their purses, pick up clean smocks and deposit used ones. Catherine indicates that daily points toward completion of the child development course are awarded for washing their hands, wearing a smock and performing various caretaking tasks. The serious work of infant care has begun.

At this point, Gerry, an Hispanic woman in charge of the nursery, takes over the class. She greets the girls warmly and leads them through the laundry area to the diapering demonstration. Gerry has arranged to have an experienced girl demonstrate correct diapering and bathing procedures. The student removes the soiled diaper from a baby and places it in a basket. Gerry points out that she is careful to place the diaper pins out of the way so the baby cannot hurt himself with them. Gerry then describes how diapers are to be folded to create thickness in different places depending on the infant's sex. As the student performs each step, Gerry comments on the reasons for doing it 'just so'. As she speaks, she makes eye contact with each girl. Her tone and words are positive. Her frequent smiles, soft voice and personal style convey the loving, caring manner that the school tries to emphasize in its approach to its students. Gerry speaks to each girl with the concern and patience of a loving mother.

After the diapering demonstration the girls learn to mark a child's care chart that indicates when and by whom the baby was changed. Gerry stresses that the girls who leave their babies in the nursery expect expert care. 'Little things mean a lot to a mother', Gerry explains. 'They say, "I want to know everything about my baby".' A girl was upset one day because she found her baby had a scratch from a diaper pin, and no one had told her about it. To a mother, Gerry reiterates, such details are important.

The immersion of the girls into the work of the infant nursery can be viewed as an initiation rite into motherhood in which practical, serious and precise knowledge is passed from one generation to the next. That the girls at New Futures come to take their parenting, nursery and child-care work seriously stems in part from this ritualized initiation into the art of motherhood.

The girls appreciate the attention and preparation they receive in these classes. Kay, the mother of a 3-month-old said, 'The staff make you feel that you're special. They go the extra mile to make you feel like somebody.' Susan testified to the thoroughness of the classes: 'When I went into labor, I knew everything that was going to happen to me. You learn the name of every part of you and what's happening. You know *so much*.'

Overcoming Isolation and Resistance

From ritualized intitiation the scene shifts to a different type of educational induction. The School-Within-a-School in Madison, Wisconsin offers an example of how unusual efforts are made to break down the defensiveness of students who have learned over the years that school can be a hostile place. Here, the social barriers that students erect to block themselves off from teachers and other students are seen as barriers to learning that must be dismantled if individuals are to succeed academically.

David and the Ropes Course

Sixteen juniors are scattered among the thirty desks in Judy Luschen's math class. It is the second week of September and they are reviewing familiar work. Mrs Luschen reviews the procedure for figuring interest on time payments. She cites as an example the various promotional deals currently being advertised to stimulate end-of-the-year car sales. 'What will your monthly payments be if you buy a $10,000 car at 2 per cent interest and have to pay it off in three years?' Jeremy, a boy with shoulder-length hair and a miniature metal sword dangling from one ear, pulls out his calculator and computes the answer. Not all of the students are as involved in the lesson. Christine, seated behind Jeremy, inspects her nails and twirls her blonde hair.

Against the wall, David and Rob, the only black students in the class, ignore the question and converse quietly. David is a handsome young man of 18. Rob seems to hide behind a pair of very dark glasses. Their unengaged demeanor is emphasized by the fact that they are the only students in the last row of desks. Their conversation is disturbed when Mrs Luschen catches their eyes and stares at them in silence for what seems like a long time, expressing her displeasure with their interruption of the lesson. They quickly cease talking, but when she resumes teaching they go back to their hushed conversation.

With the five or six students who are willing to answer her questions, Mrs Luschen works through an initial set of problems, instructing them in the use of the percentage key on their calculators. Noticing that David and Rob are still engrossed in conversation, Mrs Luschen redirects her attention to them. 'David, your book is still not open. Will you please turn to page twenty?' David's once-animated face becomes set and impassive. Rob has turned around and stares past his open book. David pulls his book to the center of his desk and flips pages until he comes to the appropriate place, then looks straight ahead. Both boys now appear completely detached and isolated.

Two weeks later, the thirty-three students who comprise the junior class of the School-Within-a-School have been transported by bus to an old farm now used by the County Juvenile Department as a site for a stress-challenge or 'ropes' course. The morning is clear but brisk, and the students cluster around a small fire just past a set of out-buildings. As the students huddle around the fire, nearly all of them light cigarettes. Dr Jim, a burly man from the Juvenile Department, steps to the center of the circle and announces that the only place smoking is allowed is right here and that butts must be deposited in the coffee can he sets next to the fire grate. 'We don't want to see any butts on the grounds. Smoke here, nowhere else. Do you guys understand?' The students are impassive and give no indication of having understood anything. After a few minutes, Peter, a powerfully built man in his 30s steps forward, introduces himself, and begins to explain the day's events. 'I've been told by your teacher, Mrs Kinder, that you will be a cooperative group. It's important that you listen to us and follow our instructions carefully in order not to get hurt', he says. Peter raises his voice and repeats himself. Most of the students turn from their own conversations to pay attention.

'The stress course will give you a chance to get to know yourselves and one another in a way you might not be able to in your classrooms', Peter continues. 'If you allow yourselves to get involved and drop some of your notions of what's cool and not cool, you'll have a good experience and get something out of it. It's up to you.'

Throughout this introduction, David and Rob stand with their backs to the group, still engrossed in their own conversation. Peter nods to Dr Jim, who goes over to the two boys and turns them toward his partner. The boys are silent. 'We hope that you'll learn something about trust and reliability and the importance of group effort', Peter concludes before describing the first event in the course.

The morning's activities are directed towards eroding some of the walls of defensiveness and detachment erected by young people accustomed to failure or criticism. Activities culminate in a trust fall where everyone is expected to fall backwards from a four-foot high platform into the arms of peers and teachers. By lunch break, the students have played blob tag, taken blind walks, and held one another in a variety of exercises. Their attempts to maintain psychological distance have been challenged by the activities' requirements that they be physically close.

That afternoon the students are led to a grove of maple trees, still cool in the mid-day shade, where they find a log suspended ten feet off the ground between the forks of two trees. The dirt beneath the log is bare and packed. The students, guessing that difficult work lies ahead, laugh and joke about the impending scene. Shanae, vivacious but overweight, asks Dr Jim, 'You don't mean we're going to climb over that?'

'You got it', he replies with a big grin.

'No way am I getting up on that log', Shanae responds, and several students agree with her. But they all are quietly attentive as they listen to Dr Jim explain the exercise:

> As a group you have got to figure out how to get everyone over this log. No one can do it alone. The only way to succeed is by all working together. That's as much as I'm going to tell you. We'll spot you to make sure no one gets hurt, but it's up to you to figure out how to get everyone from here to the other side of the log. OK, let's see how long it takes you to do it.

From the outset, David and Rob take charge. Rob volunteers to be the first up. David and another boy grab Rob's legs and lift him high enough so that he can link his arms around the log and pull himself up. Straddling the log, he smiles triumphantly down on his classmates. Because the class has been divided in two, there are sixteen bodies yet to be raised over the log. Four or five of the more adventurous girls come forward and, one by one, step into the platform that David and his friend have made with their hands. Each grabs Rob's hand and he helps them onto the log and lets them down the other side.

This strategy, however, requires a degree of upper-body strength that not everyone possesses. David calls for a recess to develop a new strategy. During the break he huddles with four boys and they arrive at a new procedure. David and another boy bend forward and hold their knees while two other boys assist the remaining girls up the boys' backs and onto their shoulders. From there, people going over the log can grasp it closer to chest height and do not have to rely on the strength of their extended arms to pull themselves up. This strategy works well, though Shanae, short as well as heavy, requires additional verbal as well as physical assistance to complete the manoeuvre. She flashes a victory smile as she safely reaches the ground and her classmates cheer with approval at her success. 'I didn't think I was going to live through that one', she laughs. Finally, David is the only one who has not crossed the barrier. Two boys straddle the log ten feet in the air. One of them doubles himself over the log and lowers his legs for David to use as a human rope. David clutches the boy's legs and shimmies upward.

Finally, he is able to grasp the log and pull himself to a sitting position. All three boys lower themselves down the other side.

During the final event, which involves getting the group over a sheer fourteen-foot wall, David again takes a leadership role. The second person up the wall, he remains on top, hanging head down to extend his arms to those being lifted from below. After helping several of his classmates, he announces he can't continue working like this because of his fear of heights. He climbs down to join the others at the bottom of the wall.

During the debriefing at the close of the day, David speaks about the significance of his acknowledging that he is afraid of heights. 'I would have never grown to trust people in school like I have here. Letting you know about my fear of heights is really something. I feel like I can trust you all with that.'

Interviewed four months after the ropes course, David observed:

> I think that they should have that every year at the beginning because getting to know everybody right off and having trust in everybody is an important thing. It makes it a lot easier to study in school because it's more comfortable. If you make a mistake or something, I mean all these people know you anyway, and everyone's entitled to mistakes.

By the second semester, David had earned enough credits to join the senior class at the School-Within-a-School, though doing so meant leaving the junior class he had grown close to throughout the fall. He noted that '... when I got moved up, it's like everybody was happy for me, but they were kind of sad that I wasn't in their class anymore. And that kind of made me feel good, too, just knowing that we are all together.'

Some Lessons for Educators

These vignettes suggest a number of important implications for the education of at-risk youth. In Mrs G we see a Principal who is also a counselor. She is willing and able to extend her role beyond the official definition of her job. She becomes the prototype of the stern but caring counselor who confronts Terry honestly, even shocking him at several points, regarding his problems. Additional counseling for at-risk students is often among the recommendations made when people discuss strategies for helping these youth stay in school. The counseling provided by Mrs G is quite different from the approach common in public schools. Many school counselors would have neither the skills nor the inclination to probe Terry and his mother the way Mrs G does. In addition, educators and other observers talk often about parent involvement in schools, but what many at-risk students truly need is greater school involvement in the problems of their parents. Mrs G routinely helps families contact professional counselors and such self-help groups as Alcoholics Anonymous in response to their problems.

All too often school counselors have neither the time nor training to become advocates for young people, nor to help students recognize their problems and avail themselves of community resources in response. At Alcott the staff is willing and able to match young people with the variety of services in and out of the school system that can be helpful. This strategy springs primarily from a recognition that for many at-risk students, the problem of achieving school success requires more than receiving some remedial instruction, or more than simply trying harder and 'tending to business'. Personal and social contingencies often seem beyond the control of these young people. For many the only sympathetic adults in their lives who are in a position to help are principals, counselors and teachers in an alternative school like Alcott.

The Media Academy and Croom provide particularly good examples of the diversity of students to whom the at-risk label is applied. Some students at the Media Academy are quite able academically, despite sharing characteristics such as poverty and minority background often used to identify other at-risk youth. Media Academy students benefit from contact with successful adults who can encourage their development. The curriculum provides a rich set of experiences that is likely to stimulate students' aspirations and interests. Experiences in the adult world can provide guidance and a perspective that may be lacking in their own personal circumstances. Good schools must provide the stimulus of a personal vision that motivates the effort and commitment to achieve.

Croom students, too, typically are in need of stimulating experiences that will provide a setting for aspirations and opportunities for achievement. Generally, Croom students are willing to work but lack the experience that would make them ready for employment. For example, many of them have never painted a house, changed spark plugs in a car, or operated mechanical equipment such as electric drills or chain saws. Since Croom students have relatively poor academic achievement records, the goal is to immerse them in a broad set of basic experiences that prepare them for employment and further vocational education. Croom's instructional strategy involves providing closely supervised individual attention of the kind depicted in the scenario from the auto shop. Croom, like the Media Academy, demonstrates a varied curriculum that is often labeled 'experiential learning'. Such learning involves closely supervised experiences related to the adult world of work.

The child development class at New Futures is a working microcosm of strategies designed to develop 'mature' teenage mothers. The class also provides some general insights into those activities and approaches that successfully engage at-risk students. First, course content focuses on serious, important knowledge pertinent to the experiences and interests of the students. In the first hour, the girls were impressed with the importance of precise practices for handling children. The seriousness of child care is imparted through careful, detailed procedures presented by a loving, personal staff and experienced peers. The messages were clear: babies are precious; taking expert care of one's own baby is very important work; mothers are important, special people who need to learn the skills of expert care; the school will help the girls learn and practise these so that they are able to provide their own babies with the best care. Second, there is a variation of 'experiential learning' occurring in this class. Abstract information from books and teachers about human growth and development are blended with child-care activities that require the application of that knowledge. Student engagement in this course is extraordinarily high. The hands-on experience of child care, as well as the fundamental fact that they are about to become new mothers, provides a meaningful context for the knowledge that these young women are being asked to acquire. Like the Media Academy and Croom Vocational, New Futures offers a combination of abstract and concrete experiences. In fact, the curriculum at New Futures embodies a traditional set of courses like those offered in high schools across the country. Unique to New Futures, however, is that the theme of 'parenting' provides many opportunities to interject that crucial element of experiential learning.

Finally, the School-Within-a-School's challenge course event emphasizes what we consider to be one of the most important aspects of successful efforts with at-risk students. Most of them are in danger of dropping out of school because they have experienced a series of failures and received a host of messages from adults and peers that they are not worthy. The inevitable consequence is disengagement and alienation from school. In the face of an institution that communicates failure, inadequacy and rejection, the bonds of trust and affection that sustain people in social settings for a common purpose are broken or diminished. The institution itself loses legitimacy in the eyes of these students. Engagement in the work of being a student is rejected because to try and fail again is further confirmation of one's inadequacies. To refuse engagement and to deny the legitimacy of school activities may be an attempt on the part of students to assert their control and superiority over the institution that would make them feel worthless.

The challenge course is an initial step along the road to rebuilding the social bonds that tie students to the adults and norms of the school. David, who is obviously detached and unengaged at the beginning of the school year, is brought into participation, in part, through the challenge course. He is able to assert his talent for leadership and to display his physical agility. Even his Achilles' heel, a fear of heights, does not lessen the positive impact of the challenge experience on him; David is able to address his own limitation in an objective manner, and he feels more comfortable with his peers, even after his problem has been exposed. He recognizes the benefits of a cohesive group in which people are valued, their group membership an important factor in achieving individual success. In this context, an individual's success is welcomed and any departure from the group is recognized as a loss to all of its members. David experienced what we call 'social bonding' to the teachers, to the program and to his peer group. As a result, he was willing to engage sufficiently in academic work to acquire the credits he needed to continue in his quest for a high school diploma.

Diversity and Commonality: Themes Foreshadowed

The labels 'at-risk student' or 'dropout' mask the diversity of those youth who are described by these terms, and there is a resulting tendency in many schools to underestimate the range and complexity of students and their problems. There are three general causes or, more accurately, correlates of dropping out identified in the literature. One concerns social and family background factors. Virtually all studies correlate low socioeconomic status with higher dropout rates. And because minorities and children from single-parent homes tend to be poor, students with these backgrounds also drop out at a higher rate. Similarly, children from homes in which parents have a low educational attainment or where English is not the primary language are more likely to drop out.

A second general cause or set of correlates involves personal problems that tend to be independent of social class and family background. Included in this list are health problems, both mental and physical; substance abuse; legal problems; trauma from divorce or death in the family; pregnancy; and learning disabilities. Some personal problems are less visible to educators and may make their presence known in sudden, unpredictable ways.

Finally, there are school factors. Retention in grade, course failure, truancy, suspension and other disciplinary problems are strongly associated with dropping out. The immediate causes of dropping out are most often linked to school problems. An analysis of national data on dropouts indicates 'the critical variables related to dropping out are school performance, as measured by grades, and extent of problem behavior. These variables are most important in explaining dropout behavior than sophomore ability, as measured by test scores' (Ekstrom *et al*, 1986). From an educator's perspective, an attack on the dropout problem should begin with those factors over which the system has direct influence — those within the school.

Of course, these three sets of factors are interrelated and interact in ways that are not yet well understood. Moreover, we assume these factors affect students differentially, that is, situations or influences that affect one student's decision to drop out seem to have little effect on another's. The complexity of these causal factors suggests that students drop out for different reasons at different times. Early intervention, for example, may not be an appropriate dropout prevention measure for all students. An intersection of specific causal factors may place some students at risk of dropping out early (elementary or middle school), while others suddenly find they are in trouble at a much later stage in the educational process (eleventh or twelfth grade). The success of a particular intervention strategy often is due in part to its timeliness and its match with particular types of students with particular types of problems. Some programs target pregnant girls while others intervene with junior high youth who have become school phobic. Some schools offer vocational opportunities to older high school students, and still others seek out highly alienated groups such as 'punkers' or certain Native Americans, two groups that emerged in our study as viewing public schools as unacceptably hostile environments.

Such diversity among at-risk students demands a corresponding diversity in intervention if schools are to increase their holding power. School programs must develop inventive ways to meet the needs and problems of their students. In general, the educators we studied recognized that a continued diet of more of the same curriculum and teaching was unlikely to engage at-risk students who had a history of failure.

Having emphasized the critical issue of diversity, we must concurrently recognize that all adolescents share some common needs and goals that schools can help them meet. All youth — at risk or not — need to acquire a personal sense of competence and success, to develop a sense of identity and social integration, and to acquire the socially useful knowledge and skills that make an individual a good worker, parent and citizen. It is presumed that these are well-established goals, and that schools traditionally have made efforts to help young people achieve them. Efforts to retain at-risk students and to provide them with a valuable education must recognize the fundamental importance of these common goals, as well as respond to these students' more particular needs.

In general, our findings suggest the need for substantial changes in the structure of schools if they are to respond to the diversity of students and to help them achieve these common goals about which there is consensus. Reforms in teaching, curriculum and social relations between adults and students are needed before at-risk students are likely to be retained to graduation and to succeed in their quest for achievement. These changes, if broadly implemented, would require substantial restructuring of schools and a redefinition of teaching roles. The remaining chapters describe some examples of what has already been done towards this end.

Chapter 2:
Dropping Out: Can Schools Be Expected to Prevent It?

Chapter 1 presented examples of at-risk students and described several ways in which educators are responding to them. Some of these examples suggested a degree of success in preventing students from dropping out. However, there is a skeptical audience that doubts the general effectiveness of such school efforts. Historically, American educators, as well as the public, have been ambivalent about what, if anything, the *school* can do to retain the 'early school leaver'. This ambivalence has been articulated in competing arguments, one which claims that schools can introduce reforms to increase their holding power, while the other claims that schools cannot do much because the dropout is either willfully deviant or socially deficient due to home and cultural background.

In this chapter, we explore evidence as to whether schools can be expected to reduce substantially the number of students now dropping out. Is there evidence to suggest that it is possible for schools to respond effectively to students who come from homes and neighborhoods where poverty and various forms of social distress are common? Can schools hope to be successful with students who come from single-parent homes or from families that lack involvement with their childrens' education? Do children from lower-class backgrounds present such insurmountable difficulties for educators that dropout prevention efforts are unlikely to succeed?

Finn (1987), Assistant Secretary of Education, argued that schools should avoid reforms directed at students who are at risk of dropping out. In his view, such efforts are ill-conceived because they are likely to endanger what he sees as an 'excellence movement' now underway in public schools. The nation's educational agenda, according to Finn, should focus on raising standards, which will increase the value of the diploma. Students then will need to engage in a decision-making process in which they calculate the costs and benefits of leaving school without a diploma. In this world of rational choices, schools can '... leave it primarily to individuals to gauge whether the reward is worth the effort required to obtain it'. Finn argues that '... it is not unreasonable to assign the chief responsibility for making these calculations to the persons affected by them ...'

Apart from their supposed threat to the excellence movement, Finn also argues that school-based strategies for retaining potential dropouts are unlikely to achieve their intended effect because at-risk students come disporportionately from the 'underclass' of our society. Finn points out that nearly every study shows that dropping out is correlated with low socioeconomic class, minority status, low test scores and grades, and dissatisfaction with school. 'Along with hapless demographics and lagging educational achievement,' he argues, 'dropouts have a third set of characteristics: misbehavior of various sorts.'

Finn's thesis is that students drop out because of factors related to their social and family background situations over which the school has no control. 'The symptom is not likely to be eradicated by school-based remedies. Insofar as it [dropping out] is a manifestation of linked social pathologies and inherited characteristics, it is more like "going on welfare" or "committing a crime" than like the commonplace problems of school effectiveness that are susceptible to alteration within the framework of education policy and practice ...' Finn's is the quintessential argument against holding schools responsible for their dropouts or for offering interventions designed to retain them. As the argument goes, the problem exists not because of deficiencies in the schools but rather of deficiencies in individuals and families.

Finn does raise an important question: Can school efforts be effective in preventing students from dropping out? Unless there is evidence and theory indicating that schools can, in fact, act to retain and educate students in the at-risk group, the dropout problem cannot be defined as an educational one. In short, it would be senseless to advocate school reforms on behalf of the at-risk student if, in fact, the problem resides in the students and not in the schools.

In consideration of this issue, this chapter presents a brief historical sketch of the research on the dropout problem. The historical evidence suggests that schools have at various times succeeded in finding ways to increase their holding power with students who may have left before graduation. What are the possibilities today of continuing this trend by making schools effective with the remaining portion of youth who are still at risk of dropping out?

Historical and contemporary data hold out the promise of reducing the flow of dropouts. These data also suggest the need for a better theoretical and factual understanding of how schools can prevent students from dropping out. Our research takes a step toward this improved understanding.

Dropout Research: An Historical Sketch

Concern over the 'early school leaver', 'non-completer' or 'dropout' has waxed and waned over the years, often accompanied by controversy over the causes and consequences of this phenomenon. Recent attention to this issue is part of a recurring cycle that occurs when historical and social conditions are ripe. The conditions usually spring from some perceived national crisis or problem, such as immigration, a perceived threat to our technological superiority, as in the case of Sputnik, or economic productivity.

Today, it is generally accepted that about a quarter of all youth leave school before graduation. This 75 per cent completion rate is very high when viewed from an historical perspective. In 1900, about 90 per cent of all males did not receive a high school diploma; in 1920, the non-completion rate remained at about 80 per cent. It was not until the 1950s that the non-completion rate fell below 50 per cent. By the mid-1960s, the graduation rate reached its peak, where it has remained relatively stable at its current 75 per cent. Despite this impressive gain in school completion, the current dropout rate signifies a serious social problem because of the scarcity of good-paying jobs open to a high school dropout. Economic indicators predict a continuing decrease in jobs that rely on muscle rather brain power. It is the changing structure of our economic system that defines the serious consequences of dropping out today.

The first two decades of the twentieth century saw the rise of a wide variety of reform movements, and the nation's schools did not escape scrutiny. The need for school reform seemed evident; many were undesirable and unsafe if we can rely on the anecdotal evidence of the day. In 1913, for example, Helen Todd, a factory inspector in Chicago, systematically questioned 500 children in these factories about working and going to school. Would they choose to continue working in the dreary sweatshops or would they go to school, if their families were reasonably well-off and they did not have to work? 'Of the 500, 412 told her, sometimes in graphic terms, that they preferred factory labor to the monotony, humiliation and even sheer cruelty that they experienced in school' (Kliebard, 1986).

It is not an exaggeration that schools at this time often were joyless places that subjected children to various forms of corporal punishment and ridicule. School practices literally drove children into the factories at an early age. In 1910, there was a 50 per cent dropout rate from the *elementary* schools (Gulick, 1910).

One of the major arguments in favor of increasing school holding power was the 'social inefficiency' of non-promotion and dropout rates. Gulick saw the dropout rate as a great educational problem that 'transcends the importance of all questions . . .' He charged that the schools' academic standards were too high for many youth and claimed that the teaching was 'too dull' to retain students through the eighth grade.

In 1909, Ayres had published one of the classic educational studies of the period, *Laggards In Our Schools*, an investigation of the problem of non-promotion and dropouts in the elementary schools. In what has become a time-honored tradition, Ayres secured a foundation grant to study such questions as: 'When do students drop out of school and for what reasons? Are there any schools that succeed in educating an appreciably larger percentage of these children than do others? If so, how is it done?'

Using enrollment and achievement numbers from a wide range of school districts, Ayres' study documented the extent to which students fell behind in grade promotion and eventually dropped out of elementary school. It was shocking news to educators and citizens alike that in many cities not more than a third to two-fifths of the entering students graduated from the eighth grade. Based on his study, Ayres drew some conclusions about the inadequacies of the curriculum:

The facts which have been reviewed and the conditions disclosed reveal with startling clearness at least two disquieting characteristics of the course of study in vogue in our city school systems. The first is that our courses are not fitted for the average child. They are so devised that they may be followed by the unusually bright pupil ... but the average child cannot keep up with the work as planned and the slow child has an even smaller chance of doing so.

Ayres thought it was unconscionable to allow greater numbers of youth to leave school without the basic skills and knowledge needed for a productive life. Schools taught the 'habit of failure', which was bad for the individual and the society, he said. 'Success is necessary to every human being. To live in an atmosphere of failure is tragedy to many. It is not a matter of intellectual attainment; not an intellectual matter at all but a moral matter.' Ayres argued that it was indefensible for the schools to continue with those practices that produced dropouts because all of the students were capable of learning.

The public, especially in urban areas, became concerned about 'idle' and 'wayward' youth. Those interested in the 'efficiency' of social institutions saw the need to compel youth to attend school longer. 'Early leavers' were of concern because they were likely to be involved in delinquency and otherwise become a burden on society. Increasingly, during the first three decades of the twentieth century, schools sought to broaden their appeal to students. Vocational education and various extra-curricular activities were included to interest students otherwise not attracted by the traditional academic fare. In addition, child labor and compulsory attendance laws were enforced. The rise of professional educators, social workers and the new science of psychological testing promoted more schooling for all children. Gradually the rate of early leaving declined as the general norm of attendance spread and the schools found ways to accommodate a broader spectrum of youth.

In the 1930s, the issue of our schools' holding power reemerged. In *When Youth Leave School*, Eckert and Marshall (1938) restated the recurring theme of national concern: How can schools retain and educate a greater percentage of youth? Like Ayres thirty years before, they characterized the problem as one of school reform. The challenge was to make school more inclusive by extending education to those students who were now leaving. 'The characteristic American belief in the efficacy of education, reinforced by the limited opportunity which industry holds today for immature workers, has resulted in a steady lengthening of the period of training. As a result, the secondary school is increasingly being committed to the task of educating all adolescents.'

From their research Eckert and Marshall concluded that schools could do a better job of retaining those who left before graduation. Their discussions with dropouts suggested that the non-completer was not receiving the education needed to become a successful citizen, in part because the curriculum was too narrow.

'... an unsuccessful attempt has been made to extend to all pupils the traditional academic pattern, originally developed for students intending to go to college,' wrote. In so doing, Eckert and Marshall raised the issue of broadening or diversifying the curriculum to retain more students, particularly those who were not college bound.

They also pointed to evidence that secondary schools were biased in favor of middle-class youth. Schools were found to be selective in their retention, with a steady increase from grade to grade in the financial and cultural status of students. Of those who left school before graduation, 65 per cent were classified by the school as 'poor' or 'indigent'. In short, 'a marked correlation exists between privilege and opportunity, with the result that the economic disadvantage of withdrawing pupils is intensified by notably ineffective school preparation,' they wrote. The author's claim that students were poorly educated was supported by evidence that only one in six dropouts was minimally competent as judged by eighth-grade standards for reading comprehension and mathematics. In addition, these students possessed inadequate and inaccurate information about situations they would soon encounter as citizens and workers.

The schools in which these students had been enrolled seemed particularly unresponsive to lower class and less academically talented students. According to Eckert and Marshall, counselors were unacquainted with the students' home backgrounds, and where knowledge of the student existed, it was primarily concerned with 'deficiencies and liabilities': students' or parents' strengths were rarely noted. The authors observed that some students possess 'exceptional personal traits', but since these do not reveal themselves easily within the structures of the academic setting, they are rarely recognized by teachers. 'Teachers not only credit these withdrawing students with far fewer special abilities or talents than graduates possess, but are often unable to state whether or not the pupil has any unusual characteristics.'

Eckert and Marshall concluded that those youth's 'least able to acquire socially useful habits, information and points of view without formal instruction are those who are released first from any type of school supervision'. The ease with which students were able to leave suggested to Eckert and Marshall that the institution was remiss. No serious attention was paid to the problems of practical living that young people would face when they left school; they were ill-prepared for the transition into work and the school seemed little interested in preparing students for anything other than continued schooling. The curriculum, according to Eckert and Marshall, had been 'unwittingly extended to all students, so that almost everywhere a kind of academic stereotype appears .... In a benevolent but misdirected effort to promote social cohesion, the secondary school has extended to all a plan of education originally designed for and suited to the few.'

They also decried educators' lack of knowledge and understanding of the strengths and weaknesses of individual students. 'Fundamentally, this lack of knowledge is the most serious indictment, since under-standing is basic to any kind of individualized treatment,' they wrote. There was a marked separation between the school's adults and those young people who exhibited limited academic talent. Their interviews and questionnaires revealed that the 'outlooks' of certain groups of students escaped the adults who were responsible for their instruction and guidance. 'Lack of knowledge carries the almost inescapable corollary of absence of genuine concern,' they concluded.

Many of the questions, observations and conclusions offered by Ayres and Eckert and Marshall have a contemporary ring to them. Many students today view the school as failing to show concern for their problems and having little knowledge about the needs and talents of individuals. A persistent charge holds that some professionals are insensitive to the backgrounds of lower-class and minority students.

Whatever the historic or current criticisms of public schools, it is clear that over the years they have expanded the range of students that they serve; in general, public schools have become committed to educating most youth. Over time, schools began to offer a broader curriculum that included fewer academic courses, as well as different levels of many courses. By the 1950s, the national graduation rate passed the 50 per cent mark. A graduation rate of 75 per cent was reached some time in the 1960s and has remained there up to the present.

The question remains as to the extent to which schools should be expected to educate at-risk students. Since the 1960s, dropouts com-monly have been characterized as deviants. Because schools had achieved success with most students, it became relatively easy to argue that it was the dropout, and not the school practices, that were at fault; collective reasoning held that if the majority of youth can succeed in school to the point of graduation, the school must be an effective institution. Thus, dropouts are aberrant individuals who are deviant, dysfunctional or deficient due to personal, family or community characteristics.

Much of the research on dropouts since the 1960s parallels this common-sense construction. Researchers typically examined a sample of dropouts in terms of the personal and social characteristics they had in common. This strategy of searching for quantifiable central tendencies, while not without its legitimacy or merits, has the effect of suggesting that it was the social characteristics that were causing students to drop out. The causes lie within the victim. By focusing exclusively on their common personal and social characteristics, dropouts appear deviant, deficient or negligent with regard to school. This focus contributes to the pathological view of these youth articulated by Secretary Finn's analysis. The description of some youth as deviant and the products of pathological circumstances serves to deflect attention away from problems in the school itself.

Cervantes (1965) offers the most dramatic example of research labeling dropouts in this way. His book appeared at the very time graduation rates reached their zenith. Through a series of case studies, Cervantes developed a social-psychological portrait of the dropout. He claimed to have discovered a 'variant breed of teenagers'. They were a social problem who were 'clumsily dysfunctional in the computer-precise, machine-oriented, communication-saturated society'. He predicted dropouts would become an 'outlaw pack' who could not be absorbed into society.

From his case study data, Cervantes arrived at a list of bipolar characteristics that distinguish the dropout from the graduate. His list of characteristics, pairing dropout against graduate, include:

Instinctoid/Holistic
Radical/Conservative
Class-bound/Upwardly mobile
Proletarian/Capitalistic
Affectless/Affectionate
Hyperactive/Alert
Leisure and thrill-oriented/Occupation and goal-oriented
Sexually exploiting/Monogamous
Double standard/Single Standard
Pawn of environment/Master of environment

Viewed from a contemporary perspective, Cervantes' value-laden and fanciful characteristics appear to be a form of unwarranted negative labeling. Some of his categories would seem humorous except that they reflect a persistent definition of the problem that continues even to the present. As then, we see today a construction of the problem that identifies the dropout, his personal deficiencies or his home background as the sole or primary cause for his failure to complete school.

Subsequent dropout studies were more subtle in their descriptions and categorical selections than was Cervantes. Nevertheless, a chain of studies posits the view that basic research on this issue should measure the personal, family and social-class characteristics of those who drop out. This chain was maintained when Combs and Cooley (1969) used Project TALENT data on 440,000 ninth graders. In 1971, Bachman, Green and Wirtanen used the Youth in Transition data on 2000 boys. More recently, Rumberger (1983) analyzed the National Longitudinal Survey of Youth Labor Market Experience. Finally, the most recent national data base is High School and Beyond, a longitudinal study of a national sample of 1980 sophomores. Early analyses of these data produced a number of descriptions of the contemporary dropout (for example, see Peng, 1983). Consistent with earlier conceptions, these studies focus primarily on the student characteristics associated with dropping out.

While the several data bases and analyses have differed in certain respects, mainstream research has tended to create a rather one-sided view of dropouts. It is the characteristic of *students*, along with their families and cultural backgrounds, that are responsible for their dropping out. Whatever the differences in their findings, the major studies do *not* question the policies and practices of schools. These studies have not been open to questions about whether some schools are more effective in retaining the potential dropout. Thus, research has not encouraged enquiry into the possibility that schools themselves may be part of the problem. Instead, the research would suggest that school as an institution is healthy, rational and performing appropriately for students, except for a few deviants who are incapable of succeeding.

More recent analyses of the High School and Beyond data and other enquiries into dropping out have begun to produce a more complex and balanced picture of the problem. There is strong evidence that course failure and school disciplinary problems, in combination with chaotic personal, social and family background conditions contribute to dropping out (Ekstrom *et al.*, 1986; Wehlage and Rutter, 1986; Fine, 1986).

Combining school factors with family background and personal problems, one arrives at the following hypothesis to explain dropping out: If one comes from a low socioeconomic background, which may signify various forms of family stress and personal difficulties, and if one is consistently discouraged by the school because of signals about academic inadequacies and failures, and if one perceives little interest or caring on the part of teachers, and if one sees the institution's discipline system as ineffective and unfair, but one has serious encounters with that discipline system, then it is not unreasonable to expect that one will become alienated and lose one's commitment to the goals of graduating from high school and pursuing more education.

In contrast to studies devoted primarily to identifying social background correlates, a recent counter line of research following the tradition of Ayres and Eckert and Marshall describes the way schools contribute to the problems of at-risk youth. Two studies that describe how policies and practices of school systems exacerbate the dropout problem are presented as examples of the shift in concern toward school effectiveness rather than an exclusive focus on student characteristics. The first example is a study of the Boston middle schools and the second focuses on Milwaukee high schools.

Boston Middle Schools

The Boston school system recently reported a drop-out rate approaching 50 per cent. To help explain this phenomenon, Wheelock (1986) used Boston district data to provide evidence of the way in which middle school policies and practices contribute to students' decisions to drop out, either in middle school or in high school. Wheelock's study addresses policies and practices concerning attendance, non-promotion, failure and suspension. Student's experiences in these areas, it is argued, contribute to the perception that school is no longer an option. In some of the schools, truancy appears to be tolerated; one of five middle school students is absent more than 15 per cent of the school year, and this rate is on the rise. Moreover, 5 per cent of the students are absent more than half of the time, suggesting that as middle school students they are virtual dropouts now despite being carried on enrollment rosters. Poor academic performance is a virtual certainty from students with high rates of absenteeism. Poor academic preparation and performance leads to failing courses and grades, both of which are strong predictors of dropping out.

According to Wheelock, the student retention policy in Boston appears to exacerbate the dropout problem. The official policy tends to encourage retention under the assumption that 'social promotion' is even more harmful. The result, however, is that one of six, or 1786, students were not promoted to the next grade during the 1985/86 school year. This represents an increase in non-promotion over the previous two school years, with black and Hispanic students disproportionately held back. As a result of this practice, large numbers of over-age students clog the middle schools. By 1985 1137 students had been held back two or more years. Such students can contribute to serious discipline problems as well as exacerbate social conflict among students. In the absence of improved academic achievement, a reduction in the drop-out rate, and sufficient remediation programs, the wisdom of grade retention for so many students is doubtful. Maintaining high academic standards is an essential task for schools, but failing and retaining large numbers may not be the best way to meet this objective.

Wheelock views the policy of suspension as yet another contributory factor to the eventual 'pushout' of students. School suspension is a message that a student is not welcome. At the middle school level it can contribute substantially to the future attitudes and general disengagement of students. More than 1000 students, or about one in ten, were suspended from the middle schools in each of the last several years in Boston, and the rate is increasing. Moreover, school district data indicate that black and Hispanic students are suspended at higher rates than are whites. Seven of twenty-two middle schools in Boston were responsible for half of all students suspended in recent years, while five schools suspended fewer than 5 per cent of their students.

The study of Boston middle school policies and practices involving attendance, retention in grade and suspension is used as an indicator of the system's health. The data reveal how the institution of school responds to students. Attendance, and particularly truancy, tell us something about the ability of schools to engage students. An inability to attract and hold middle-school students on a day-to-day basis portends a much weakened holding power in terms of high school graduation, as the nearly 50 per cent dropout rate in Boston attests.

Milwaukee Public Schools

Course failure is one of the best predictors of dropping out among high school students (Ekstrom *et al.*, 1986). As with the practice of retention in grade in the elementary and middle schools, failing students centers on the issue of maintaining academic standards. Passing courses should indicate some level of student proficiency and acquisition of skills and knowledge. Certainly one cannot advocate passing students through courses in disregard of reasonable standards of success and competence. But many school systems are plagued with massive course failure at the high school level. At some point, the number of students failing courses becomes so great that one must question whether the institution's conceptions of learning, curriculum and standards for passing and failing are functional.

A case in point is the failure rate for students in the Milwaukee high school system (Witte and Walsh, 1985). For the 1982/83 academic year, the Milwaukee school system calculated the failure rates for one or more core courses (math, science, English, social studies) among ninth-grade students. The percentages of students failing a given course were calculated for blacks, whites, and others. With the exception of King, the special college preparation magnet school, no school had less than a 21 per cent failure rate among black students, and most schools had 30 to 50 per cent failure rates for blacks. For whites (and others), the typical high school's failure rates fell in the 20 to 30 per cent range. These data emphasize the fact that many ninth-graders end their first year in high school with credit deficiencies; the prospect of graduation is already beginning to dim. It is not surprising that the dropout rate in Milwaukee is at least 40 per cent.

The inability of the conventional school system to function effectively with urban youth is underscored by other data from Milwaukee. In a school system of 24,857 students, 18,812 suspensions were issued during the 1984/85 school year, a 0.76 ratio, equal to three-quarters of the student enrollment. The suspension rate at four high schools exceeded 100 per cent of their populations; obviously, some students were suspended more than once. Attendance rates, another indicator of school holding power, averaged about 87 per cent in the fifteen Milwaukee high schools. However, several schools reported attendance figures of 82 to 83 per cent. It is not surprising that all of the schools with high dropout rates reported relatively weak attendance rates.

This cursory examination of data from the Boston and Milwaukee school systems suggests several hypotheses to be pursued. District policies and practices that result in massive suspensions, failures and grade retentions are very likely to be associated with high dropout rates. Whatever justification there may be for applying such policies and practices to individual students in particular schools in order to maintain order and academic standards, they are probably counter-productive when used routinely with many students over the course of a school year. The likely outcome is that students disengage from the institution of school and from learning in general, that they question the legitimacy of school, and that, for many, the ultimate alternative is dropping out.

In addition to school level practices that discourage at-risk students, some systems operate magnet or specialty schools with strict admission requirements, thereby concentrating less academically able students in a limited number of buildings. Hess and Lauber (1985) report that a policy of 'educational triage' operates in the Chicago public schools. The lowest achieving students attend inner-city and less attractive schools while the highest achieving group is siphoned into schools where they have the benefit of special facilities and motivated teachers. Moore and Davenport (1988) report this pattern is widespread in other urban systems, including Philadelphia, Boston and New York. They found principals and teachers in the non-selective programs frequently perceive themselves as caretakers for essentially uneducable students. The policy of creating selective schools for those with particular interests and talents means that those most in need of high quality, innovative educational programs are least likely to have access to them. Not surprisingly, the dropout rates from the least selective and attractive schools are considered alarmingly high — over 60 per cent in some cities.

In summary, our brief sketch of research from the turn of the century to the present indicates periodic public and professional concern over the dropout problem. Schools have been challenged from time to time to accommodate more students, and they have succeeded in doing so in a variety of ways. Tempering this movement to accommodate more students has been a tendency to label dropouts as incompetent in school because they possess characteristics identified as the products of deficient homes and cultural backgrounds. Such students are defined as unmotivated, lacking ability, slow and disruptive. Historically, the percentage of students who were judged incompetent because of their personal, social and family background characteristics declined gradually. Educators and the public came to believe that the majority of young people were indeed capable of graduating from the eighth grade, when this was the norm, and eventually from high school as this became the accepted standard.

At issue now is the extension of effective schooling to include the group of youth who remain at risk of dropping out. Can the schools extend the benefits of a quality education to this final group of students who are leaving school without a diploma? Is it possible for schools to alter their policies and practices in ways that make them effective with these youth in the face of their personal, family and social characteristics?

Catholic Schools: An Empirical Case of Effectiveness

A partial answer to this last question is found in the work of Coleman and Hoffer (1987). Their analysis of High School and Beyond data, a national study of over 25,000 students in 1000 schools, reveals that Catholic schools are more effective than public schools with at-risk students. This important study opens the door to an understanding of the relationship between school practices and dropping out. Their analysis of Catholic and public schools, while limited in several key aspects, lends support to the general view that schools are capable of responding effectively to those at risk of dropping out.

First, we acknowledge that a question can be raised regarding family background differences that exist when a conscious choice is made to send children to a Catholic school. Regardless of class, income, race and other variables, choosing to send one's child to a Catholic school may indicate a commitment to education otherwise absent in families of similar backgrounds. This elusive factor of family choice and the likelihood that there are real differences existing among schools of choice have not been studied, and one can only speculate as to their impact on achievement and graduation.

Despite this gap in our knowledge, Coleman and Hoffer's findings are provocative. Their work suggests that Catholic schools were markedly more effective than public, or other private schools, in retaining to graduation not only poor and minority youth, but also other students who came from what they define as 'families with deficiencies', and students who had academic and disciplinary problems that typically make them at risk of dropping out. Coleman and Hoffer found that Catholic schools were substantially more successful with black and Hispanic students than either the public or other private schools. For blacks, the dropout rate was 17.2 per cent in public schools, 14.4 per cent in other private schools and 4.6 per cent in

Catholic schools. Hispanic rates were 19.1 per cent in public schools, 22.9 per cent in other private schools and 9.3 per cent in Catholic schools. Data on socioeconomic status, which is one of the traditionally strong correlates of dropping out, showed that Catholic schools did much better with low SES students than did the public schools.

In addition, the Coleman and Hoffer study examines a number of important family background factors that have been correlated with high dropout rates. An important question concerns the relative success exhibited by Catholic schools with students from these disadvantaged family situations. For example, are Catholic schools successful in retaining children from homes in which there has been a divorce? It might be claimed, of course, that the favorable differences shown by Catholic schools with respect to dropout rates are due to the advantage of greater stability in students' homes regardless of race, ethnicity or income.

Coleman and Hoffer devised two indicators for what they term 'family deficiency'. 'Structural deficiency', refers to single-parent households and homes in which the mother is employed in the paid labor market. Their assumption that such homes are deficient is certainly open to question; nevertheless, they categorize as disadvantaged those homes in which the mother is head of the house or works outside the home. The second indicator, 'functional deficiency', refers to homes in which parents are not involved in the activities or education of their children. According to Coleman and Hoffer, this deficiency is evidenced by a lack of shared activities and an absence of verbal communication between parents and children; this categorization assumes that in such families the knowledge, experience and value orientations associated with middle-class status are not transferred to the children. Characteristics that distinguish middle-class homes and that are thought to have a powerful effect on school performance and expectations toward obtaining higher education may be missed in these families. According to Coleman and Hoffer, 'functionally deficient' families fail to transfer to the children the 'social capital' the parents have acquired.

Their analysis of the High School and Beyond data suggests that Catholic schools are especially effective with families exhibiting these functional and structural deficiencies. Their interpretation of their results merits quotation:

The Catholic sector benefits are especially great for students

Table 1: Dropout Percentages for Students from Families with Varying Degrees of Functional/Structural Deficiencies

	Public	Catholic	Other private
None	6.8	2.7	9.5
1	11.8	3.1	5.1
2	18.5	4.6	13.4
3 or 4	24.3	4.1	40.2

from families with deficiencies, whether structural, functional or combined. The relation of dropout to deficient families is small or absent in Catholic Schools, which show very low dropout rates for students from all types of families. In contrast, the public sector and the other private sector show strong relationships of dropout to family deficiencies, whether structural, functional, or combined.

Coleman and Hoffer also determined that Catholic schools were markedly more effective in retaining to graduation those students who had experienced school problems (i.e., academic or disciplinary difficulties). In fact, their findings indicate dropout rates for students with academic and behavior problems were very similar in the public and other private schools. The Catholic schools, on the other hand, experienced significantly lower dropout rates than either. This key finding supports our fundamental assumption that schools often exacerbate the dropout problem by discouraging many students who have academic and disciplinary problems.

The evidence is clear and dramatic. Coleman and Hoffer designated four categories to elaborate the concept of at-risk student — minority, poor, 'deficient families' and school problems. Their analysis produces a clear empirical case for the effectiveness of Catholic schools; in their words, the Catholic school 'rescues students at risk of failure'.

Table 2: Dropout Rates by Sector for Students with Scholastic or Disciplinary Problems

School problem	Public	Catholic	Other private
Grades below C	37.0	22.6	35.3
Discipline problems	28.0	13.1	27.1
Probation	32.7	13.3	34.8
5 or more absences	33.2	13.3	40.3

The data also argue directly against the commonly heard claim that Catholic schools can eliminate their problem students by shuffling them off to public schools. In fact, it appears that the reality is quite the opposite. Catholic schools retain their at-risk students to a greater degree than do public schools. If there is a 'push out' phenomenon, it is occurring in the public sector, where schools continue to receive financial support regardless of their ineffectiveness with at-risk youth. Catholic schools, whether for moral or economic reasons, or both, work to retain students who are in danger of dropping out.

Apparently there is something markedly different about the way Catholic schools interact with at-risk youth. The operational characteristics of this difference and why they exist are yet to be fully explained. Still, it is our assumption that many of the qualities that make Catholic schools relatively more effective in retaining at-risk students can be reproduced in the public sector.

The Need to Look 'Inside' Schools

Coleman and Hoffer theorize that the difference between Catholic and other schools arises **outside** the school as a product of what they call 'functional communities'. First, there is a value consistency among the parents of the children who attend Catholic schools. Second, and crucial to their argument, value consistency in such communities is generated and sustained through a degree of functional social interaction. This interaction occurs among parents of children in the school system, and it is cross-generational in that it also occurs between parents and students. Such interaction reinforces values about schooling for children, parents, teachers and the school itself. Face-to-face interaction among adults and children is the key to generating and sustaining functional communities.

While their functional community theory may have some validity, at best it offers only a partial explanation for Catholic school effectiveness. Its fundamental inadequacy is that it is based on a methodology that treats the school as a 'black box'. We contend that researchers failed to look inside the school to determine what, if anything, is unique about the characteristics and practices of Catholic schools.

Instead, Coleman and Hoffer present an input-output model that treats communities, students and families as the input, dropouts and achievement data as the output. Between the two is the school building where the daily activities of students and teachers occur, but almost nothing is revealed about the day-to-day events there. Based on an extensive body of ethnographic data that now exists on the importance of the culture of schools, it would seem any explanation for the differential success of schools that ignores the internal workings of the institution must almost certainly be inadequate. A theory of school effects ought to include factors arising outside of the institution, as well as those resulting from the culture and social relations inside it.

Evidence exists that Catholic schools are organized differently, respond to students differently, and therefore produce different effects on students (Chubb and Moe, 1986). This difference is due in part to the fact that Catholic schools tend to be small, less bureaucratic and more client oriented, as well as to the influence of the doctrines and ideology of Catholicism. Evidence also suggests that the Catholic school culture is broadly supportive of all who attend. The overriding philosophy of these schools is that one should love God, oneself, and that it is important to care about others. Studies of Catholic schools confirm that such principles are more than mere doctrine, but exert direct influence on the actions and attitudes of the entire school population (Lesko, 1988). They are communicated to students in religion classes, masses, school bulletins and various school events, and they have an impact on peer group relations. Teachers assume a responsibility to monitor student behavior closely; the differences in Catholic school culture are exhibited, in part, by the extra effort extended by faculty in support of the success of young people. Faculty views its role as broader and more fundamental than providing instruction in a subject-matter area. Teachers also are concerned with the character and moral integrity of each student. A number of Catholic school teachers have reported that they consider their work a ministry and their role as one of shaping the character of young adults (Bryk *et al.*, 1984). In one sense, a Catholic school can be viewed as a 'safety net' that protects all of its members — even those who are not ideal students. This commitment, it is suspected, wields an important impact on Catholic school students who are at risk of dropping out.

Our research in the fourteen schools identified a parallel commitment to at-risk students. We have labeled this as the process by which students achieve 'school membership'. Our study revealed that this membership is generated intentionally by adults through certain social relations that contrast with those in most conventional public schools. The difference in social relations is due primarily to educators' concern for students who have failed academically or who have particular personal problems that have resulted in their alienation from school. These educators help students overcome impediments to school membership. In the process, the school becomes a community of support. In subsequent chapters we will present an empirical and theoretical foundation for our view that the school culture generated by day-to-day practices has a significant impact on effectiveness with at-risk students.

Summary and Conclusions

This chapter began with a question: Can schools prevent students from dropping out? In answering this question, we have explored the issue of school holding power from several different perspectives. Historically, there has been ambivalence about the ability of schools to increase the portion of youth held to graduation, initially from the elementary schools and then from the high schools. Some of this ambivalence springs from doubts about the competence of poor and minority youth to benefit from more education. Despite this doubt, public schools have over the years found ways of retaining more youth to graduation. The current graduation rate of 75 per cent is a plateau that is now being challenged by critics who advocate that schools can and should increase their effectiveness with that portion of the population that still drops out.

It was also argued that much of the research on the high school dropout problem has focused on the personal and demographic characteristics of dropouts themselves. The assumption fostered by much of this research is that dropouts are deviants or the products of deficient homes; the problem then must be viewed not as an educational issue, but as one of fixing up deviant and defective students. In the light of its focus on students as the problem, there is little in this research that suggests implications for action by educators. This means there is also little in this research suggesting schools contribute to the dropout problem. From this perspective, there is no indication that the policies and practices of schools are problematic; in fact, it appears that they are healthy and rational institutions. Proponents of this view of the dropout issue are naturally doubtful that schools can effectively retain this residue of students.

Of course, it must be acknowledged that students' home and personal problems contribute to their failure in school. The case has also been made, however, that schools contribute in important ways to the problems of students. Evidence supporting this argument was drawn from studies of Boston middle schools and Milwaukee high schools, as well as High School and Beyond studies. This evidence called into question policies and practices that cause many students to be suspended, to receive failing marks, and to be retained in grade. The wisdom of these practices is questionable if schools are concerned about their dropout rates, since research indicates a strong correlation between such policies and the incidence of dropping out.

Finally, the success of Catholic high schools in retaining dropouts was discussed. The heartening message here is that this success includes children from a broad range of backgrounds, including those who are poor, minority and from families described as 'deficient'. It appears that Catholic schools have succeeded in establishing a 'safety net' of support for these students.

Our findings suggest that careful attention by adults to social relations produces school membership for at-risk students, and that this membership depends upon specific commitments and practices by adults. School membership becomes a fundamental concept in the theory explaining how schools can prevent students from dropping out.

Chapter 3:
At-Risk Youth: Uncovering Their Diversity

Many discussions of dropouts begin with a set of assumptions about who they are and why they leave school. Stories in the mass media, as well as research findings, have supported the stereotype that dropouts are urban, poor, minority and of low ability. While these labels may apply to many, such perceptions depict only one facet of the actual problem. While it is the case, for example, that nearly all studies using large statistical data bases show that dropouts tend to score lower on standardized tests or have lower grades than do graduates, this does not mean they are necessarily low in ability. A case in point is Chicago where nearly a third of all students who dropped out of the Chicago public schools in 1984 were reading at or above grade level (Hess and Lauber, 1985).

The label 'low ability' is a gross and rather meaningless judgment, and too often it implies that students are uneducable when in fact they may have many abilities not readily apparent in school. Moreover, the fact that minorities have a higher *rate* of dropping out than do whites obscures the fact that, holding socioeconomic status equal, blacks are slightly less likely to drop out than are whites (Rumberger, 1987). It also obscures the fact the total number of white dropouts is substantially greater than the total of blacks and Hispanics combined. In 1985, for example, census data revealed that approximately 61 per cent[1] of all dropouts were non-Hispanic whites. This means the problem of dropping out is not only the problem of identifiable special groups — minorities, urban poor — it is a problem which involves all groups, and one which demands ownership by all citizens of this country.

Two strains of research have contributed significantly to the public's perception of dropouts. One of those strains, represented by Hodgkinson (1985), has focused attention on the increasing proportion of minority and disadvantaged youth who will attend our public schools in the near future. The other, represented by Peng (1983), Rumberger (1987) and others, shows dropout rates vary significantly by race, ethnicity, gender and class, and that these rates are highest among black and Hispanic youth, two groups that are concentrated in major cities. Together, these observations have led to the perception that dropping out is largely a minority and urban problem.

Based on an analysis of US population pyramids, Hodgkinson projects that by 1999 one-third of US schoolchildren will be of minority backgrounds. Using the 1980 sophomore data and the 1982 follow-up from High School and Beyond, Peng (1983) reports an overall dropout rate (sophomore to senior year only) of 13.6 per cent. Stratified by ethnicity, these rates varied from a low of 3.1 per cent for Asian-Americans and 12.2 per cent for whites to 17 per cent for blacks, 18 per cent for Hispanics, and 29.2 per cent for American Indians.

This research also shows dropout rates vary by gender: 14.1 per cent of black females in the High School and Beyond sophomore sample dropped out while 20.3 per cent of black males dropped out before high school graduation. Overall, 12.6 per cent of females in the High School and Beyond sophomore sample dropped out, while 14.7 per cent of the sophomore males dropped out without a high school diploma. Census cohort data for 18- to 19-year-olds reflect similar variance by race and gender: 14 per cent of white females, 19.7 per cent of black males and about 26 per cent each of male and female Hispanics were classified as dropouts (Rumberger, 1987). Finally, Kolstad and Owings (1986) show that dropping out also varies by socioeconomic status. They report that 8.9 per cent of students from the highest socioeconomic class dropped out, while 22.3 per cent of students from the lowest socioeconomic class left school before graduation.

These data demonstrate the diverse racial, ethnic, gender and class characteristics of this country's at-risk population. Significant numbers of whites, blacks and Hispanics succeed in school, and significant numbers of each group also drop out. We offer three caveats regarding the use of national statistics as the basis for conceptualizing the dropout problem. First, by focusing on dropout rates rather than proportions, most studies using national data have inaccurately led us to believe that dropping out is a problem linked to particular populations, primarily inner-city minority groups. Attention to proportions rather than rates, however, reveals that the problem is much more widespread.

Second, the use of correlational studies tends to overlook the complex reasons that underlie school failure. Simply correlating race and home status with dropping out, for example, does not mean that all such individuals will be at risk of dropping out, yet a student with such characteristics often will be tagged as at risk by educators relying upon checklists of common identifiers. Similarly, children who do not possess these common identifiers may be ignored, although they are at risk for other reasons.

Third, reliance on national data disregards the important contribution of the school to the dropout problem by identifying the issue as one of student characteristics. As discussed in chapter 2, this orientation often blames school failure on students and their home backgrounds rather than recognizing that the school also must be held accountable for the educational progress of all students.

This chapter describes the diverse characteristics of students we studied who were at risk of dropping out. Though students in the fourteen schools involved in our research cannot be construed as a statistically random sample of the total at-risk population, they certainly represent a broad cross-section of American youth. Interviews revealed complex and frequently idiosyncratic conditions contributing to their educational disaffection and failure. These multifarious factors are summarized in table 3. It is this complexity and idiosyncracy that educators and policy-makers must acknowledge in addressing the dropout problem.

As discussed in chapter 1, students drop out of school for many different, often interrelated, reasons. Course failure, the most accurate predictor of dropping out, is often the result of a complex web of student characteristics that interact with the characteristics of the school. Students do not fail simply because they are black or poor or

Table 3: General Characteristics of At-risk Youth

Family and social background	Personal problems	School problems
Low socioeconomic status	Substance abuse	Course failure
Minority race/ethnicity	Pregnancy/parent	Truancy
Single-parent home	Learning problems	Passive/bored
Low parental support	Legal problems	Disciplinary problems
Family crisis	Low aspirations	
Community stress/conflict	Low self-esteem	Credit deficient
Family mobility	Alienation	
Limited experience of dominant culture	Rejects authority	
	Mental/physical health problems	Retained in grade

pregnant or from a single-parent home. They fail, in part, because schools are not responsive to the conditions and problems accompanying these personal and socioeconomic characteristics. Tammy is a case in point.

Tammy is a pretty, white, 15-year-old with a 9-month-old son. She loves her child very much and seems to talk about him constantly. Tammy and her son live with her father, who provides food and shelter. Although she is supported financially by her father, it is clearly Tammy's responsibility to care for her child. She admits that being a teenage parent is difficult, but she says it is never more than she can handle.

After experiencing some difficulty finding a daytime sitter, Tammy returned to school a few months after giving birth. She is bright and well-liked. She enjoys school and wants to graduate. Her attendance, however, became sporadic. Some days the sitter had other plans and Tammy had to stay home and care for her child. Other days the child was sick (he had frequent ear infections) and/or needed to be taken to the doctor. As with all students, Tammy's absences were monitored by the office. As her unexcused absences accumulated, Tammy was suspended and given failure marks for each of the days she did not attend classes. In addition, her teachers were required by district policy to fail her after she had missed ten days. When it became clear that Tammy had no chance of maintaining normal school progress, she dropped out of junior high.

Tammy's case is noteworthy because, like many dropouts, she fits the dropout stereotype only in part. She is not black or Hispanic, does not reside in the inner city, and is not on welfare. She is not of low ability or irresponsible. She does not appear to lack parental support. She does not dislike school or have low aspirations. She is, however, a teenage parent who resides in a single-parent home. Though Tammy shares these two characteristics with many dropouts, it would be inaccurate and misleading to say she dropped out because of them. Her membership in a single-parent family contributed to Tammy's dropping out only in that there was one fewer adult to care for her child when the regular babysitter had other plans.

Tammy failed courses and eventually dropped out because the demands of being a responsible parent conflicted with the attendance requirements of her school. Locked into bureaucratic procedures that punished absences with suspensions, the school was unable to respond to the unique demands placed on this young mother.

A more flexible attendance policy that would have taken into account her extenuating circumstances could have prevented Tammy's dropping out. The provision of a school-supported day-care program might also have enabled her to fulfil both sets of responsibilities — those to her child and those to the school. The school's failure to accommodate Tammy's needs resulted in her dropping out. It is this focus on the interaction between students and school practices that is often missing when stereotypes and modal characteristics are applied.

As states and school districts continue to devise and implement plans to reduce high school dropout rates, it is essential that policy-makers take a more critical look at the diverse factors that may lead young people to become at risk of not graduating. They must then devise programs that respond in appropriate ways to that diversity. When programs fail to take into account the actual characteristics and needs of at-risk youth, inappropriate interventions are likely to result.

This was the case with a junior high dropout prevention program not included in this study but visited by one of our research staff. This program was designed to respond to local educators' perceptions that the increasing cultural diversity of the school would lead to higher dropout rates. While the school was, in fact, enrolling larger numbers of Hispanics and Cambodians, by far the highest percentage of at-risk students was white. (At-risk students were defined as those having twenty-one or more absences in the previous year.) Nonetheless, by design, the program's student population was one-third Hispanic, one-third Asian and one-third white, and its curriculum emphasized multi-cultural understanding. When students' attendance rates in their regular classes were broken down by race/ethnicity, it was found that attendance improved markedly for Asian and Hispanic youth but actually declined for white students enrolled in the program. By failing to match its offerings to the characteristics of the students who, in fact, constituted the majority of the school's at-risk youth, the program was unable to alter the overall dropout rate for the school in any significant way.

Responsiveness to the actual characteristics and educational needs of specific children and groups of children who are at risk is essential in designing effective programs. Assumptions about students must be tested before programs are constructed. Success in creating generic programs responsive to all potential dropouts is very unlikely. In the next section, we explore some of the primary factors that produced diversity among the students in our study.

Student Demographics[2]

Race and Ethnicity

Half of the fourteen programs we selected for intensive study enrolled significant numbers of minority students. At Lincoln High School (Atlanta) and the Urban League Street Academy (Minneapolis), for example, 100 per cent of the students were black. At Orr Community Academy (Chicago), 81 per cent were black and 17 per cent were Hispanic. At the Center School (Minneapolis), 100 per cent of students enrolled were Native American. In addition, New Futures School (Albuquerque) and the Media Academy (Oakland) enrolled significant numbers of Hispanic students (60 per cent and 44 per cent respectively) and the Media Academy, Croom (Upper Marlboro, Maryland), and Plymouth Christian Youth Center (Minneapolis) had black enrollments of 48-60 per cent. Some programs enrolled large numbers of white students. At Alcott Alternative Learning Center (Wichita), for example, 72 per cent of the students were white. At Wayne Enrichment Center (Indianapolis), 96 per cent of the students enrolled at pre-test were white. At the School-Within-a-School (Madison, Wisconsin) and Sierra Mountain (Grass Valley, California) about 81 per cent of the students were white; and at Loring-Nicollet (Minneapolis) 89 per cent were white. Table 4 summarizes race and ethnicity in each of the fourteen programs.

Socioeconomic Status

The distribution of students in three socioeconomic classes (lower, lower-middle and middle) varied considerably by program in our sample.[3] The per cent of students characterized as lower socioeconomic status (SES) varied from a high of 63 per cent to a low of 26 per cent. In eight of the fourteen programs, over 40 per cent of those for whom SES data were available were classified as lower SES. The free-lunch data support this, with eight of eleven programs reporting 50 per cent or more of their students qualifying for free lunch.

Nevertheless, these programs also enroll significant numbers of lower-middle and middle SES students. In one program, 65 per cent of students were classified lower-middle SES. The mean per cent of students classified lower-middle SES across fourteen programs was 35 per cent. In one program, 43 per cent of students could be classified

Table 4: Demographic Characteristics of Students Enrolled in 14 Programs for At-Risk Youth at Pretest

Student Profile	Mean age at Pretest	% Age Distribution					% Sex		% Race/Ethnicity					% Socioeconomic Status			% Eligible for Free or Reduce Lunch
		14 or younger	15	16	17	18 or older	Male	Female	Black	Hispanic	White	American Indian	Asian	Lower	Lower Middle	Middle	
Alcott Alternative Learning Center (n¹ = 128)	14.33	70	23	7	0	0	56	44	11.2	8.4	72.0	5.6	2.8	32	42	26	23
Croom Vocational High School (n = 126)	16.9	0	0	28.3	53.3	18.3	60	40	60.7	1.6	32.8	3.3	1.6	39	32	29	55
Lincoln High School (n¹ = 47)	15.47	13.3	57.8	26.7	2.2	0	40	60	100	0	0	0	0	50	33	17	77
Loring-Nicollet School (n = 66)	16.41	4.3	8.7	37.0	41.3	8.7	39.1	60.9	6.7	0	88.9	4.4	0	32	25	43	NA
Media Academy (n = 51)	15.09	16.7	61.9	19.0	0	2.4	29.3	70.7	51.2	43.9	2.4	0	2.4	26	65	9	ND
Minneapolis Education & Recycling Center (n = 56)	16.88	0	0	40.0	32.0	28.0	68	32	25.5	4.1	61.2	6.1	2.0	63	32	5	NA
NA-WAY-EE, The Center School (n = 79)	16.04	16.3	14.0	30.2	27.9	11.6	62.8	37.2	0	0	0	100	0	46	38	15	66
New Futures School (n = 222)	16.32	8.5	17.9	25.5	29.2	18.9	0	100	5.7	60.4	23.6	10.4	0	58	35	7	95
Orr Community Academy (n = 579)	14.92	30.3	50.2	16.1	3.3	0	52.4	47.6	80.8	17.3	.2	1.7	0	42	41	16	66
Plymouth Christian Youth Center (n = 191)	16.77	1.4	9.9	30.3	26.8	31.7	52.5	47.5	48.6	2.8	43.0	5.6	0	59	22	19	27
School-Within-A-School at Madison Memorial High School (n = 81)	16.72	0	8.3	25.0	53.3	13.3	46.7	53.3	15.3	3.4	81.4	0	0	38	32	29	50
Sierra Mountain High School (n = 148)	15.25	14.1	52.9	28.2	3.5	1.2	60	40	2.3	2.3	81.4	12.8	1.2	47	35	18	64
Urban League Street Academy (n = 28)	ND	ND	ND	ND	ND	ND	ND	ND	100	0	0	0	0	ND	ND	ND	100
Wayne Enrichment Center (n₁ = 132)	16.42	6.8	9.6	27.4	46.6	9.6	29.4	70.6	2.7	0	95.9	1.4	0	62	29	9	15

School (n)	% Whom Do You Live With?					% Hours Worked Per Week in a Part-time Job					% Number of Schools Attended Prior to Program Entry				% of Students Credit Deficient Upon Entering Program	Pretest Reading Score (DRP)	% of students At or Above 50th Percentile on a Nationally Normed Test of Math Ability
	Father Only	Mother Only	Father & Mother	Other Relative	On My Own	0	1-5	6-15	16-25	26 or more	1	2	3-5	6 or more			
Alcott Alternative Learning Center (n¹ = 128)	4.6	40.7	43.5	8.3	2.8	67.5	14.1	10.1	5.2	3.1	9.3	34.3	52.8	3.7	NA	39.70	22
Croom Vocational High School (n = 126)	1.6	44.3	45.9	6.6	1.6	44.6	16.1	14.3	7.1	17.9	6.5	65.6	26.2	1.6	99	34.34	10
Lincoln High School (n¹ = 47)	0.0	60.0	26.7	13.3	0	76.7	9.3	9.3	2.3	2.3	78	22	0	0	0	63.22	54
Loring-Nicollet School (n = 66)	2.2	52.2	23.9	4.3	17.4	43.2	11.4	13.6	18.2	13.6	0	39.1	58.7	2.2	79	70.63	71.5
Media Academy (n = 51)	2.4	34.1	58.5	4.9	0	78.0	17.1	4.9	0	0	33.3	50.0	16.7	0	NA	55.17	50
Minneapolis Education & Recycling Center (n = 56)	4.0	42.0	22.0	16.0	16.0	31.9	23.4	6.4	23.4	12.5	10.0	26.0	52.0	12.0	93	53.49	51.5
NA-WAY-EE, The Center School (n = 79)	4.7	53.5	25.6	14.0	2.3	71.4	11.9	2.4	4.8	9.5	11.6	34.9	51.2	2.3	87	53.8	48.5
New Futures School (n = 222)	5.7	24.5	35.8	17.0	17.0	79.2	6.3	4.2	5.2	.9	18.7	44.9	35.5	.9	82	49.17	46
Orr Community Academy (n = 579)	2.8	48.9	38.1	7.8	2.4	75.0	14.6	7.1	1.5	1.8	30.9	45.8	21.2	2.1	22	37.23	3.5
Plymouth Christian Youth Center (n = 191)	4.9	45.8	26.8	12.7	9.9	50.4	11.5	9.2	9.2	19.8	21.3	45.4	29.8	3.5	96	51.02	46.5
School-Within-A-School at Madison Memorial High School (n = 81)	8.3	36.3	33.3	13.3	6.7	50.8	1.7	16.9	20.3	10.2	33.3	50.0	15.0	1.7	100	51.39	35 (juniors only)
Sierra Mountain High School (n = 148)	3.5	32.9	47.1	11.8	4.7	39.8	24.1	24.1	9.6	2.4	8.1	25.6	61.6	4.7	55	49.77	ND
Urban League Street Academy (n = 28)	ND	ND	ND	ND	ND	ND	ND	ND	ND	ND	ND	ND	ND	ND	91	44.82	35.5
Wayne Enrichment Center (n = 132)	4.1	26.0	41.0	15.1	13.7	41.1	6.8	5.5	17.8	28.8	13.7	60.3	24.7	1.4	40	62.64	45.5

¹N reflects total students completing Wisconsin Youth Survey at pretest. NA = not applicable, ND = no data.

as middle SES, and in four of the fourteen programs, 25 per cent or more of students were middle SES. Taken together, the mean per cent of students in all fourteen programs classified as either lower-middle or middle SES was 53 per cent. In other words, slightly less than half of all students came from families in which parental occupation (or the lack thereof) placed them in the lowest socioeconomic status category.

Academic Performance

Two measures of students in these programs challenge the perception that at-risk youth lack academic ability. In one notable case, the students at Loring-Nicollet correctly answered, on average, 70.5 out of a possible seventy-seven questions on the Degrees of Reading Power Form PB-4, a test that requires students to fill in appropriate words in progressively more difficult reading passages. Overall, students in eight of thirteen programs answered two-thirds or more of the questions correctly.

Programs also were examined to determine how many students ranked at or above the 50th percentile on some nationally normed test of math ability. In eight of the thirteen programs for which these data could be obtained, 40 per cent or more of the students ranked at or above the 50 percentile. Thus, contrary to expectations, many students demonstrated competency and even high achievement on tests, and this occurred despite the fact most students entered these programs with credit deficiencies. It would appear that their recurrent course failures were linked to other factors. At Loring-Nicollet, for example, students scored highest on the DRP and ranked highest overall on a nationally normed test of math ability. Yet 79 per cent of these students were credit deficient at the time of enrollment. In eight of twelve programs for which data are available, about 80 per cent of the students who entered were credit deficient at enrollment.

Home Status

The data collected for students in these programs underscore a number of other important characteristics of at-risk youth. The per cent of students who live with both parents ranged from 22 per cent at the Minneapolis Education and Recycling Center to 58.5 per cent at the Media Academy. Less than 27 per cent of students in five of thirteen programs live in a two-parent family. A relatively small per cent live with their fathers, from 0 per cent at Lincoln to 8.3 per cent at the School-Within-a-School. Significant numbers of students live with their mothers; percentages range from 24.5 per cent at New Futures, where many students manage their own households, to 60 per cent at Lincoln High School.

The percentages of students living with another relative or on their own are sometimes striking. More than 10 per cent of students in eight of thirteen programs live with relatives other than their parents. In five of thirteen programs, 10 per cent or more of the students live on their own; in three programs about 17 per cent of students report living independently. In six of thirteen programs, 20 per cent or more of the students report living either with another relative or on their own; in three programs, the total is 29 per cent or higher.

Somewhat related to home status is mobility, or the number of schools these students have attended prior to entering a special program. Approximately half the students in five of thirteen programs reported they had attended three to five schools prior to program entry. In one school (MERC), 12 per cent reported they had attended six or more schools prior to their enrollment.

Work

Contrary to the expectations of certain programs, and to some extent in spite of their work emphasis, large numbers of students enrolled in these programs were unemployed. More than half reported working zero hours in eight of the thirteen programs. Most students who reported working devoted between one and fifteen hours per week to a part-time job. Significant numbers of students at the Wayne Enrichment Center, the School-Within-a-School, Croom, Loring-Nicollet, the Minneapolis Education and Recycling Center, and the Plymouth Christian Youth Center reported working sixteen hours or more a week. Of these, four of the five schools had jobs coordinators and/or stressed work-related experience as part of their intervention strategy.

Demographic Summary

In summary, demographic characteristics of students in the fourteen schools indicate that a broad group of adolescents are at risk of dropping out. Our data provide concrete examples of the diverse range of academic abilities and social characteristics exhibited by students at risk of school failure. This diversity is often buried in the quantitative data and stereotypes typically used to describe this population.

An important implication of these data is that educators need to understand the diversity of the at-risk population they are serving. Demographics is a starting point for dropout prevention, but it is necessary to go beyond demographics to understand qualitatively the complex interrelationship between the personal circumstances and the school experiences of at-risk youth. It is the counterproductive nature of this interrelationship that leads many youth to drop out.

Sociocultural Characteristics

Interviews with students, their teachers and their counselors provided an opportunity to understand more thoroughly the sociocultural characteristics and experiences related to dropping out. The interviews, supplemented by document analysis, allowed us to construct personal histories of students that revealed patterns of behavior and unique experiences that resulted in disengagement, school failure and dropping out.

Academic success appears to be tied to the way in which family, community *and* school collectively contribute to the support of students during their crucial adolescent years. When schools fail to take into account the social, economic and cultural contexts in which students live, the ability of many children to remain motivated and perform well in class is jeopardized. Children from any background, regardless of academic talent, are not immune to the confusion or loss that can arise when different aspects of their lives become chaotic and are no longer able to provide the physical, emotional or intellectual support that is the foundation upon which learning is constructed.

Limited Experience in Mainstream Culture

It is the children of the poor who often experience the least congruence between their homes and neighborhoods, and their school experiences. This incongruence is particularly visible in a stark lack of familiarity with the skills and knowledge often taken for granted by people who have grown up in more affluent surroundings.

One teacher at Orr Community Academy observed that her students 'don't know to try'. She felt her students were unaware of how to take a bus downtown, let alone apply for a job or admission to college. As a result, many youths from disadvantaged backgrounds make no attempt to act in ways that might improve their situation.

Students at Croom Vocational High School exhibit a similar lack of experience. Most reside in older suburbs that now appear over-crowded. Many stores have been abandoned, streets are littered, and much of the housing is in disrepair. At Croom, students have an opportunity to learn the skills that their more advantaged peers would acquire in middle-class suburban homes — skills such as using a paint brush, cutting a lawn, planting flowers and shrubs, tinkering with a car or preparing a nutritious meal. Because most adolescents who attend Croom dwell in apartments maintained by landlords, they have little chance to learn how to paint a building or maintain a yard, nor are there safe places where they can work on a car for any length of time.

This lack of experiences, which seem so simply and readily obtainable, puts Croom students at a serious disadvantage when they try to enter the local job market where groundskeeping and horticul-ture, auto repair and racing, office and apartment maintenance, and construction are major sources of employment. This fundamental lack of work experience makes Croom students doubly disadvantaged: Young people with poor academic records might be hired regardless of their school performance if they were able to demonstrate some expertise in the entry-level job they were seeking. Without special instruction, Croom students would be unable to demonstrate even this most basic kind of compensatory experience. Such limitations also affect students' sense of competency, and their knowledge and aware-ness of the world beyond their home communities.

These students experience a discontinuity between experiences they have encountered in their own neighborhoods and the expec-tations of the school or workplace. Unless recognized and then bridged, this discontinuity can lead to protracted academic failure or minimal achievement. The alternative schools we studied accepted the task of helping students become familiar with the demands and assumptions they will encounter in the economic and political institutions dominat-ing much of the terrain of contemporary life.

Despite this stance by the schools, it should be recognized that many students continue to find school experiences out of tune with their home and community. The social relations and knowledge they encounter in school are difficult to absorb when they seem to create two incongruent, disparate worlds. For minority students in particular, this disjuncture can be painful and frightening. Success in school often means rejecting family and peers, and for the majority, this choice is unacceptable (Connell *et al.*, 1982; Rodriguez, 1982; Weis, 1985).

Family Crisis

Erosion of the strength of any of the mediating institutions upon which children rely for support and social continuity can have an adverse impact on their school performance. Family instability or crisis is the most common precursor of the erosion of this support. Gary, who attends Alcott Learning Center, lives in a single-parent home. Gary does not lack experience in the dominant culture and is regarded as academically able. In elementary school he was placed in a gifted and talented program. His mother, however, recognized that he was a behavior problem in the classroom and unsuccessfully attempted to find counseling help for him within the school.

Gary's mother arranged for him to attend junior high at Alcott where she hoped that his teachers would deal with, in Gary's words, 'my temper and my big mouth'. By his own admission, Gary is hard to live with and 'stuff I pulled here [at Alcott] would have gotten me thrown out of any other school in town'. According to a teacher who is close to Gary, he has a problem with his father, who has remarried since he and Gary's mother were divorced. His father reportedly beat Gary as a child and 'put a lot of anger into him'.

Despite these problems, Gary has been sustained by his success as an all-star baseball player on a local team, and he plans to attend college on an athletic scholarship. By attending a school where teachers address his anger with counseling rather than avoidance or expulsion, Gary may be more likely to realize his goal.

Like Gary, Jessica was adversely affected by family problems. When she was in the fourth grade, her father, an accountant, left home for a month with no warning. A divorce followed, and the experience remains a traumatic memory. An excellent student in elementary school, Jessica continued to earn high grades until the eighth grade, when her father remarried. Then, as she says, 'everything started to go downhill'. She and a friend, whose mother had left her father at the same time, began cutting classes. This behavior continued through the tenth grade, although Jessica was often in trouble for truancy. As a sophomore, Jessica attended only those two classes in which teachers made a special effort to communicate with her. As a junior she enrolled in the School-Within-a-School, where teachers were willing to provide the kind of personal attention and counseling she needed at this time in her life. Her attendance stabilized and she maintained a B average during the year.

David, described in the account of the ropes course in chapter 1, became understandably disengaged from the educational process during the final months of his mother's bout with cancer. During her illness, he attended Madison Memorial High School where he had maintained a C average. As she became more seriously ill, however, he gave less and less attention to his studies. After her death, he moved to Milwaukee to live with relatives and enrolled in a new high school. It wasn't long before he stopped attending classes. Predictably, he failed courses and fell behind in the number of credits he needed to graduate. The following fall, David returned to Madison and entered the School-Within-a-School, hoping the program would enable him to earn the credits he had lost. Eventually David graduated with his class.

Mobility

Mobility can foster another kind of instability only rarely discussed in the at-risk literature. Even with a supportive family, students can experience serious disorientation after moving away from a community of peers who provided social identity. Beth, for example, had been an A and B student in her small home town in northern Wisconsin. Her family's move to Madison required her to enroll in a comprehensive high school of 1800 students. The isolation she experienced there was devastating.

> It was like sitting in a room full of faceless people because I didn't know any of them. None of them wanted to know me because they all had their own little cliques, little groups. So I found I was doing really bad in school because I was scared to talk to people. I was scared to ask the teachers questions. I started skipping school because I didn't want to go to class. I was with people who didn't care about me, and that I didn't care about, so it was really hard.

Before long, Beth had turned a strong academic record into a collection of Fs.

Christine had had a comparable experience after moving away

from her school friends in Chicago. Throughout the elementary grades and junior high she had been a strong student who at one point was chosen to attend special courses for gifted youngsters at the University of Chicago. An interest in broadcasting had prompted her to develop her own radio show on a local station during which she read children's stories over the air. Her family's move to Madison changed all this. Like Beth, Christine stopped attending school.

Both girls were able to overcome their sense of isolation only after enrolling in the smaller, more personal educational environment provided by the School-Within-a-School. There they were able to establish relationships with new peers and teachers and to overcome the sense of isolation that had paralyzed them both after their respective moves.

Teenage Pregnancy or Parenthood

Like family problems and mobility, teenage pregnancy knows no class boundaries. It is estimated that approximately one-third of the girls who drop out of high school do so because of reasons related to pregnancy (Earle, Roach and Fraser, 1987). While attendance policies regarding teenage mothers have changed dramatically over the past two decades (Title IX prevents districts from expelling students with children from school), remaining in class pregnant or as a teenage parent is too difficult for many girls. Despite their common condition, teenagers who become pregnant also face unique demands from family relationships, their social and economic situation, and the degree of involvement of the child's father. It is important that educators involved with pregnant teens recognize that young people can respond to pregnancy and/or impending parenthood in a variety of ways.

Evelyn, a student at New Futures School, is 13 an eighth-grader. She is bright and ambitious, even a bit dissatisfied with a workload she considers too easy. Her family is affluent and her mother was prominent in the PTA at her previous middle school. Evelyn was mortified by her pregnancy, though with the support and encouragement of her parents she decided to keep the child. Like most girls, when Evelyn discovered her pregnancy she thought her 'life had ended'.

> At first when I found I was pregnant, I didn't want to go anywhere. I thought my life was ruined. But here [at New Futures], they help and say, 'Your life isn't ruined'. You just go on.

Evelyn *is* going on. In seventh grade she took the entrance exam to attend a local Catholic high school and planned to begin there as a freshman. 'I always wanted to be a lawyer', she said. She still intends to complete college and attend law school. When asked whether she would consider having another baby and, if so, when, Evelyn replied, 'Maybe when I'm out of college and I don't have to depend on anyone, and I can take care of myself'. At New Futures, teachers were able to provide support for Evelyn by helping her adapt to her new identity and responsibilities. They convinced her that she was, in fact, capable of continuing on with her life.

Evelyn's ambitious, middle-class life goals set her apart from many of her peers at New Futures, as does the close relationship she enjoys with her mother. What is common in Evelyn's story, however, is the pressure from her boyfriend and parents to have neither an abortion nor to release the baby for adoption. The consequence of such pressure is that school completion becomes more difficult unless a girl's parents or boyfriend are willing to support her in her decision to keep her child.

Like Evelyn, Frances was fortunate in receiving such support, in this case from her boyfriend. Frances, 17, began attending New Futures in the fall of her senior year; she delivered her son two weeks after school started and graduated in the spring. Before attending New Futures, Frances lived with her parents on one of the many Native American reservations in the area. She had expected to drop out of high school when she discovered she was pregnant because she had no one to care for the baby. Her gynecologist recommended New Futures and she and her boyfriend, the father of the baby, moved into town so she could enroll. There, a school-based child-care program made it possible for her to complete her education.

> We didn't *plan* for me to get pregnant. I wasn't on any kind of birth control. I *should* have been, but I wasn't ... At first there was a lot of pressure to get married. Our parents wanted us to get married *right away*. They left it up to us and we decided to wait until I was 18 and I didn't have to have my parents' signature and we could have a wedding in a church. We're thinking maybe next year in the summer [we'll get married].

The father of Frances' child also graduated from high school and is completing a two-year course at the local technical school to become a machinist. He often took care of their baby so Frances could study and maintain the good grades that won her a four-year scholarship to the state university where she planned to study engineering.

Marilyn, a black 18-year-old mother at the School-Within-a-School, did not have the benefit of such support. She has lived on her own since she was 16 and receives funding from AFDC. Daycare for her daughter while she is at school and work is paid for by Title XX and the local Single Parent Program. Marilyn's mother had opposed her keeping the child and insisted she find her own apartment when Marilyn refused to give the baby up for adoption. Now that they are living separately, their relationship is amicable, though Marilyn says she can't depend on her family for anything.

After becoming pregnant, Marilyn attended classes at the local district's School Age Maternity program, and then entered the School-Within-a-School the following fall. She chose to enroll there because she knew its program allowed students with few credits to make up deficiencies more quickly than was possible in a conventional school.

After she dropped out, Marilyn's mother nagged her and told her she would never become anything.

> And I just wanted to prove to them that I was [something]. That's what really made me go on back to school because everybody thought that because I had a baby at such a young age I was never going to be anything. I was going to be on AFDC all my life, and I just wanted to prove to them that they were wrong.

Not all teenage mothers, however, demonstrate the determination of a Marilyn, Evelyn or Frances. The counselor at New Futures estimates he is able to 'make a difference' with only half of the 450 girls with whom he has contact each year. While those who do stay in high school through graduation often display a level of maturity and self-confidence unusual for girls their age, many others drop out of the program for various reasons. Nevertheless, schools such as New Futures have a positive impact on the lives of a large number of young women every year. Without such interventions, the negative consequences for individual and for society would be significant.

Substance Abuse

Students with a history of drug dependency may present the greatest challenge to today's educators. It is difficult to know how many students are at risk as a result of drug abuse, but the experiences of those who are struggling to regain their footing in the straight world offer some indication of the devastating impact that marijuana, alcohol, cocaine or LSD can have on school performance. Reconnecting such students to schools is one of the most difficult tasks faced by teachers in programs for at-risk youth.

Marty, a ninth-grader at Alcott, is a 16-year-old on his way back from dependency. Repeatedly truant, he was retained in grade as a result of his drug use. 'I was into drugs and alcohol real bad', he says, and his daily drug use exacerbated his epilepsy, resulting in some 'real bizarre behavior'. Marty's mother worked and his father was in prison, so there was little supervision or direction at home. Marty began using drugs at the age of 9, when his brother gave him marijuana and alcohol. His brother has remained very involved in the use and sale of drugs.

After his enrollment at Alcott, Marty was placed in a treatment center for forty-five days; he subsequently joined a support group with which he continues to meet each week. Treatment and involvement with a support group, both the result of his decision to attend Alcott, had a major impact on Marty. Today, some of his best friends are members of his support group; he stays away from former friends, all of whom are drug users.

Marty has now been drug free for more than a year, and he sees his progress as a 'one-day-at-a-time thing'. He participates in a cross-age drug education program sponsored by Alcott that takes former drug-using students into local elementary schools. His grades have improved such that he passed all of his courses and will be able to enter high school next year.

Eric, a junior at the School-Within-a-School, has a history similar to Marty's. A loner through most of elementary school, Eric finally made friends in the fifth grade with an older boy who introduced him to marijuana. When Eric entered high school, the older boy drew him into his circle of acquaintances. 'The only way to be cool with all of them was to get high and cut classes. And that's what I did the whole time, but not the *whole* time. I actually did pass some of my classes.' In the ninth grade Eric managed to earn six credits, although he attended many of his classes high. His grades, however, steadily declined from Bs and Cs to Ds and Fs, a pattern that persisted through the beginning of the eleventh grade.

Finally, Eric came home 'real messed up one time' and slept on the couch for a couple of days. 'I guess it was a blackout because I got up a couple times', he remembers. When he came to, his mother informed him that he was going to a drug rehabilitation center. Although Eric initially denied he had a problem, by the end of treatment he recognized he wasn't acting in his own best interests. Drug-free for a year, Eric has come to rely on friends he has made in Alcoholics Anonymous. 'It was real tough when I started', he says, but making friends who are no longer into the drug scene has made his task easier. Eric, however, is by no means immune from relapses into his former dependency. 'I'm straight because it gets me to function better, and I have a good time with friends who are straight. It's like if I didn't have a good time being straight, I wouldn't stay straight', he admits. Two months after this interview, Eric was caught smoking marijuana in the school parking lot and was suspended from classes until the beginning of the next quarter.

Students who have been drawn into the drug culture are not uncommon in programs for potential dropouts. Approximately 13 per cent of students across the fourteen programs had been or were involved in drug/alcohol rehabilitation programs during the year of the study. Even more common is the regular use of intoxicants. When, like Eric and Marty, students have recognized their dependency and are attempting to grapple with it, they often become more willing classroom participants. Regular users can be virtually unapproachable.

The most difficult students at Sierra Mountain High School often share this characteristic. Jeff Rogers, 15, newly-grown into a man's body, felt 'bored' at a school for younger students and wished instead to transfer to the local continuation high school where he could be with his older friends. In an apparent attempt to precipitate a confrontation and force Sierra Mountain staff to expel him from school, Jeff had been 'surly' and used profanity in the classroom. When his teacher asked him to step outside the door and wait until she could speak with him individually, he had refused. When she then instructed him to go to the counselor's office, Jeff left the classroom and the school grounds.

At a parent conference the next day, Jeff sat impassively as his father and teachers discussed his behavior. Drugs had been a problem the previous spring and, when asked whether they might still be interfering with his work at school, Jeff responded equivocally, 'Not really'. Throughout the meeting he gave no indication of his feelings, although for a few seconds he stared incredulously at his father who had suggested that his son's growth had occurred in his body but nowhere else. Jeff quickly resumed his demeanor of calm detachment, however, unintentionally illustrating his father's comment that 'Talking to him is like talking to a stone wall'.

Sierra Mountain teachers comment on the 'self-absorption' of some of their students, a self-absorption that is common in adolescence but which can be exacerbated in young people who are regularly using drugs. Students like Jeff keep themselves beyond the reach of adult influence, refusing to acknowledge the consequences of their behaviors or to entertain the possibility of change. In schools that depend upon the formation of personal relationships, such a refusal effectively blocks most formal educational efforts. The system's failure to reach youth like Jeff underlines the importance of drawing students into membership in the school community. When regular drug use interferes with this process, it becomes very difficult to help a student overcome patterns of behavior that lead to academic failure.

Legal Problems

A varying proportion of the students in the fourteen different programs we studied have had dealings with the law. At schools like New Futures or the Media Academy, virtually none of the students have been involved with the local juvenile court system. At others, like the Minneapolis Urban League Street Academy or the Center School, 40-50 per cent of the student populations have been apprehended as a result of their participation in illegal activities. Criminal activity runs the gamut from vandalism to car theft or burglary. As in the case of substance abuse, altering behaviors that lend a sense of excitement and intensity to lives circumscribed by poverty, adult rejection or school failure is a formidable challenge.

Though teachers at the Minneapolis Street Academy attempt to redirect their students' energy to learning and behaviors less likely to result in trouble with the law, the lessons they convey do not translate well into the neighborhoods in which their students live. Several male students who had been referred to the Street Academy as an alternative to incarceration were arrested during the Christmas recess for a variety of offences. Outside of school, many students, both male and female, participate early in life in such adult activities as smoking, drinking alcoholic beverages and sex. Many also use drugs or are involved in crime. Even though schools enforce prohibitions against most of these activities (smoking is allowed in certain areas), there appear to be few constructive ways to rechannel this youthful energy. Neighborhood gangs are common, and it is likely that some of the Street Academy's students are being courted for membership.

Such behaviors pose serious problems for those who teach at-risk youth. Even when only a handful of students are involved in illegal activities, this behavior is often generalized to the student population as

67

a whole and may jeopardize public and administrative support for the program. Like students who are heavily involved with drugs, those engaged in other criminal behavior also tend to refuse to enter into the personal relationships at the heart of what makes many of these interventions successful.

Alienation

Other forms of alienation and opposition — those that are not chemically or criminally reinforced — can be more easily addressed by teachers. The Center School in Minneapolis deals with Native American students who often have experienced alienation as a result of their racial and cultural backgrounds. Many students at the school report that former teachers generally had low expectations of them and anticipated their dropping out after reaching the age of 16. Two students currently at the Center School felt that they were discriminated against in special school activities. Both were accomplished musicians and were interested in playing in the school stage or pop bands. Neither, however, was invited to do so, and each assumed he was passed over because of his ethnic heritage. They imagined that band personnel viewed Native Americans as undependable and unlikely to follow through on commitments. Though this assumption may have been incorrect, it speaks to the lack of responsiveness these students encountered in their previous school.

At the Center School, staff members make a concerted effort to overcome students' perceptions of incongruence or exclusion. Native American traditions and issues are incorporated throughout the curriculum, and significant emphasis is placed on drawing students into school membership through activities drawn from their own cultural background.

Loring-Nicollet, another of the five Minneapolis Federation of Alternative Schools, serves alienated youngsters, the majority of whom have adopted the style of punk rockers. For the most part, these students wear black clothing. Leather vests and long skirts are popular, as are black boots and wildly colored tennis shoes. Their hair is jet black — or blue, orange, yellow, purple, or all of the above. Their hair styles range from mohawks to spikes to ratstails; a few have shaved heads. They embellish themselves with ear and nose rings or paint their faces with rouge and mascara; several wear white face make-up.

As indicated earlier, the students at Loring-Nicollet achieved an average score on the Degrees of Reading Power of 70.5 out of a possible seventy-seven. Many are socially aware, but decidedly pessimistic. In general, they project a sense of skepticism and alienation. Some are beyond being angry at society's injustices; many have taken to self-destructive behavior. Most are polite but not friendly. Their skepticism pervades much of their talk and their reactions toward school.

These students are taught by teachers who share their skepticism and their language, and this may be a key to understanding why this school is functional for these youth. Not only do staff members validate student attitudes, they tolerate student eccentricities, helping bridge the gap that 'punkers' often encounter between their own world and the social environment that pervades most conventional schools. Perhaps most importantly, teachers at Loring-Nicollet are willing to give students the individual attention that is often the desired goal of youth who adopt unusual styles or behavior. Thus, oppositional behavior is deflected and students who would otherwise refuse to attend class are willing to tolerate at Loring-Nicollet what they would reject in conventional classrooms. Regardless of their tolerance and improved attendance, however, few students exhibit much clarity about their own goals or the purpose of the educational process they are willing to endure.

Lew, a 16-year-old, had earned only three credits prior to enrolling at Loring-Nicollet. His lack of credits, however, had nothing to do with academic potential. Lew had obtained perfect scores on the three Minneapolis 'benchmark tests', one of only three students in the district who had accomplished this. Nor could his failure to succeed in a regular comprehensive school be attributed to any lack of social skills, since he had just completed a successful experience as a counselor at a summer camp in northern Minnesota. Teachers at Loring-Nicollet suggested his lack of school success arose from a sense of aimlessness about school. He was returning to school because his father wanted him to do something with his life — and 'school counts'. 'I need to find something worthwhile to do between summers', Lew said. 'I need some skills to survive in the real world; camp is not the real world' — phrases which may have been his father's rather than his own. His real goal, he said, was to go to Los Angeles to become a comedian.

Jocelyn shares Lew's academic potential and aimlessness. She had earned a 3.7 grade point average at her previous school in northern Minnesota, but she had missed seventeen days. When asked to explain her absences, she said that she hated school and was always tired on

Mondays. Pressed further, she said she found life 'up-North' boring. In her words, it was 'too cold and dead up-North'. Jocelyn thought Minneapolis would be exciting and would expose her to different cultures. To escape her boredom, she had moved in with her 32-year-old sister.

Though Loring-Nicollet may not help all of its students achieve a sense of personal direction, it appears to be keeping them in school so that their options do not become narrowed or foreclosed.

Chronic Truancy

Another group of students exhibit neither the nihilistic attitudes of young people at Loring-Nicollet, nor patterns of drug dependency, nor direct institutional opposition. They instead have become estranged from school and are passive, bored and chronically truant.

A tenth grader at Sierra Mountain High School, Bob's history of school failure began in second grade:

> I had this teacher, Mrs. Nathan. She was a mean teacher. I never really knew my math problems. [When] I couldn't do it, she would take me over her knee and spank me. And I was the only one that she did that [to] because I could never get it. I wasn't good at math.

By the sixth grade Bob hated school and was earning Ds and Fs. His experience in junior high reinforced his earlier disenchantment. He recalled a class in Baton Rouge:

> I was usually asleep, but I was interested in what we were doing [that day] and I raised my hand, and [the teacher] goes, 'No, I don't help people, I don't acknowledge people that don't bring their stuff to work'. So I said, 'Screw it', and I just kicked back and slept after that. ... I made a B in PE; the rest of the classes I made all Fs. I just didn't feel like doing it.

Bob was a chronic truant in high school until his mother, who had moved with him to California, read about Sierra Mountain in the local paper. Bob enrolled, and with the support of teachers who 'give you a chance', he maintained a satisfactory average and missed only four days in the entire school year.

Jason is a junior at the School-Within-a-School in Madison. Like Bob, he became disenchanted with formal education in elementary school. Academically able, it wasn't long before he learned to write absence excuses for himself and started taking two days off each week. At home, he read novels like *Huckleberry Finn*. It was a pattern that persisted into high school. Despite his refusal to participate in class, Jason remained intellectually active, teaching himself geometry and continuing to read avidly. One of his friends remarked that although Jason had never completed an advanced math class he could help friends enrolled in Algebra II with their homework.

Though curious and very able academically, Jason disliked doing what others told him to do; he also found classroom routines totally uninteresting. As a result, he withdrew from the academic process. The year before entering the School-Within-a-School, Jason had been in class only 58 per cent of the time and had earned a D average. Though still largely disengaged in this special program, Jason conceded that its accountability system, one that precludes forged excuses, enabled him to miss no more than 14 per cent of his classes and to raise his GPA to 3.10.

Earle, like Jason, chose to focus his attention somewhere other than his academic classes, though his interest in music led him to school relatively more frequently. A singer and instrumentalist, he was active in the school band and chorus, and the local drum and bugle corps. Earle also worked twenty-five to twenty-eight hours each week at a restaurant a few blocks from school. When he came to the School-Within-a-School, he had earned credits only for band, chorus and science. To graduate, Earle knew he would have to alter his previous pattern of truancy. As with Jason, a clear accountability system for attendance was a major factor in geting him into class. 'I never had any [academic] problems with school; I just didn't feel like going, so I didn't. If I didn't show up, it got to the point where teachers didn't even know if I was [assigned to] the class.' At the School-Within-a-School, where persistent non-attendance results in expulsion from the program, Earle has become more cautious about cutting classes, raising his attendance rate to 95 per cent compared to 74 per cent the year before.

Jason and Earle are extreme examples of students who choose to remain uninvolved in a school's agenda. While other students like them may be equally disengaged, they comply with the expectations of the school to the extent that they come to class and complete the minimum amount of work required to pass their courses. Until entering the School-Within-a-School, neither Jason nor Earle were willing to involve themselves in even a limited relationship with the school. They had chosen to disregard the rewards granted those who apply themselves academically. Both had turned their allegiance elsewhere. Formal education had failed to capture either their imagination or their will.

Despite their apparent conformity, it would be incorrect to assume that the School-Within-a-School has elicited Jason's or Earle's active intellectual engagement. Both boys continue to resist volunteering more than the minimal amount of participation required to remain in the program. Though educators could wish for more, Jason's and Earle's improved attendance and academic records have meant that high school graduation, previously an impossibility, has once more become an option for them.

Social Outcasts

While Jason and Earle chose to remove themselves from the world of school, the idiosyncracies of some students in effect deny them entrance into that world. These students, too, can become at risk of dropping out as a result of their inability to become personally connected to their peers or teachers.

Melody, described in chapter 1, is one such student. Derided by peers because of her weight, she dropped out. Janeen, a student at Croom Vocational High School, had faced similar, though more violent, pressure as a result of her small stature. At her previous high school, she encountered ongoing taunts because of her shortness. To protect herself, she formed an alliance with some other small girls who came to be called 'The Littles'. Walking in the halls remained a frightening experience, however, particularly because people would strike or touch her. Finally, after one incident in which a large youth grabbed her umbrella and hit her over the head with it, Janeen dropped out; school had simply become too threatening. Although she is academically capable and, in this sense, atypical of the majority of Croom's students, this alternative school provides a setting in which she can feel safe while she completes her education.

Mike Jacobsen is frequently recognized by both students and teachers as one of Sierra Mountain's outstanding students. As a pre-schooler, Mike was seriously burned in a car accident. His face and hands were disfigured, but his appearance today makes little difference to his peers. Sierra Mountain provides an intimate and caring environment in which Mike can pursue his education without encountering the rejection inevitable in larger educational settings, where most students would respond to his appearance rather than his personality.

Summary

Most striking about students in programs for potential drop-outs is that they fail to conform to stereotypes. Complex reasons and experiences trigger their disengagement from the process of schooling. It is essential that educators realize that a wide range of students can become at risk of school failure, that students at risk of dropping out are not necessarily those with the least intellectual ability, and that standard labels for student characteristics do not capture the nature of the interaction between at-risk students and the school. It is this interaction between student and school that plays a crucial role in an individual's decision to drop out.

We suggest that schools set aside some of the labels and categorizations that too easily classify student's symptoms and problems. Careful examination of the data about those who drop out of particular schools may reveal that many are students who have academic or other talents, but who do not conform to certain school expectations and therefore do not succeed. This type of self-examination by schools is an essential first step in the formation of educational interventions to improve achievement and retention. To do otherwise is to create stereotypes that blind educators and policy-makers alike to the circumstances and conditions they must address. More importantly from our point of view, such stereotypes direct attention away from ways schools themselves contribute to the academic failure of at-risk youth.

Virtually all of the fourteen schools we studied sought to establish programs matched to the characteristics of particular groups of at-risk youth. By carefully assessing their students, most were able to develop innovations that spoke to the needs and circumstances of specific young people. Chapter 4 will explore the ways in which perceptive teachers and school administrators have been able to shape diverse educational responses to match the unique problems and needs of individual students.

Notes

1 Based on October 1985 Census Data reported in Waggoner (1987: p. 28). Of 4,773,000 dropouts aged 20–24, 3,716,000 (or 78 per cent) were white. This figure, however, includes Hispanics who are distributed among the tallies for white or black dropouts. Kominski (1988) reports that as measured in the SIPP and Current Population Survey (CPS) 95 per cent of Hispanics report themselves to be of white race. To arrive at an estimate of

the dropout proportion for non–Hispanic whites, one can take 95 per cent of the total number of Hispanic dropouts, 825,000 and subtract it from the total number of white dropouts (3,716,000 white dropouts minus 783,750 white Hispanic dropouts). With this calculation, the non–Hispanic white dropout rate is 61 per cent.

2   The data described those students who were enrolled in fourteen programs for at-risk youth during our first visit to each of these programs in late summer 1986. These data are not intended to represent a random sample of these characteristics in the dropout population at large. Rather, they are presented to illustrate how the characteristics of at-risk students in particular schools and communities can differ from those commonly associated with youth who drop out. Our data support the conclusion that definitions of at-risk students based primarily on low SES, minority status and low achievement is inappropriately narrow.

3   We sought to measure socioeconomic status in two ways. First, we asked students to indicate with whom they lived and the occupation of their father and/or mother. Second, we determined through school district data the percentage of enrolled students who were eligible for free lunch. The data on whom the students live with and parent occupation were used to calculate SES in the following way. If the student lived with his/her father only or his/her mother only, the occupation of that parent was used to determine SES. If the student lived with both parents, the determination varied depending on the occupation of both parents. If only one parent worked, the occupation of that parent determined family SES. If both worked and both occupations were associated with lower SES or with middle SES, it was assumed family SES was also lower SES or middle SES. When both parents worked and both occupations were indicative of lower-middle SES, family SES was assumed to be middle SES. If the student lived on his/her own, SES was assumed to be lower. If the student lived with another relative, SES could not be determined. For some schools, our SES data are based on relatively modest percentages of total students enrolled because of incomplete data (see table 4).

Chapter 4:
Diverse Programs for Diverse Students

Chapter 3 argued that at-risk students arrive at their disengagement, failure and decision to dropout via many different routes. These different routes must be taken into account if schools are to be helpful to at-risk youths. Generic programs intended to serve all who might be in danger of dropping out are unlikely to be as effective as programs designed with specific students, situations and aims in mind. For example, pregnant teenage girls need a different intervention than inner-city black male youths over 16-years-of-age who have experienced problems with the law. Strategies for each group would be likely to have different aims, curriculum, staffing decisions and daily program routines. Similarly, a school serving junior high age students will necessarily emphasize different educational goals, curriculum and school climate than a school for older youth about to enter the labor market. It is likely a program for younger students would emphasize high school graduation as one goal, while the program for older youth might target passing the GED tests and employment training.

This chapter describes how components in seven of the fourteen programs were developed in relation to a particular group of students. Thus, one program was designed for teenage mothers; another worked with low-achieving inner city white and black youths; another served high school juniors and seniors of widely varying levels of achievement, but who were all seriously credit deficient.

In the sections that follow, we examine the ways schools tailored their educational responses to the specific situations of students. We describe this as 'matching' interventions with students. We found this matching of program and students to be fundamental to their mutual success and provides a foundation upon which to build more adequate secondary schooling for at-risk students. In the next chapter we describe ways in which schools go beyond this match and meet the common educational needs at-risk students share with other students.

Sierra Mountain High School

The majority of students at Sierra Mountain are 'involuntary' transfers from one of the two comprehensive high schools in this rural California district, Nevada Union or Bear River. As a result of course failure, poor attendance and behavior problems, a number of ninth and tenth graders are recommended for an alternative, Sierra Mountain High School. Students are frequently those who did not 'fit in'. One of the deans at Nevada Union attributed their difficulties to an individualistic orientation and an unwillingness to conform to expectations most students accept.

Many students at Sierra Mountain have adopted or been socialized into unconventional cultural orientations. Punkers, students into heavy metal rock music, children whose families remain loyal to the '60s and '70s counter-culture, as well as kids who are simply poor and in trouble find their way to its classrooms. In the district's comprehensive high schools they often experienced alienation and disaffection. Not infrequently, they viewed the rules and requirements of their teachers as unnecessary or unfair. As a result of their idiosyncratic appearance and interests, or in the case of some, extreme shyness, relations with other students were also generally poor. School was a difficult place for most Sierra Mountain students, a place that challenged rather than nurtured the development of their positive sense of self. Their response was to avoid or resist what they encountered in their former schools.

Some students at Sierra Mountain also exhibit more serious problems related to substance abuse and juvenile delinquency. Staff at the school estimate that approximately a fifth of their students are in this category. Called the 'hard core' by the school's Principal, Earle Conway, they are the students who occupy a majority of his time. In the minds of many local district patrons, they also constitute the majority of the school's students. One of Sierra Mountain's most difficult tasks is to dispel this mistaken impression.

The primary means by which staff at Sierra Mountain attempt to overcome the persistent academic and social failure of their students is through a school environment that encourages attendance and participation. Perhaps the most important element of this environment is the school's emphasis on 'placing people before subject matter'. The

Table 5: Sierra Mountain High School—Match Between Student Characteristics and Program

Commonalities		Differences	
Student characteristics	*Program response*	*Student characteristics*	*Program response*
COURSE FAILURE	Variable credit. Appealing classes	CREDIT DEFICIENCY	Students can take optional independent study classes and earn extra credit for regular coursework
POOR ATTENDANCE	Calls to home when student absent. Saturday detention for truancy	ACADEMIC ACHIEVEMENT	Independent study classes. Option to earn extra credit
ISOLATION	Focus on 4 As: acceptance, appreciation, affection, attention	SUBSTANCE ABUSE	Work with district drug counselor
BEHAVIOR PROBLEMS	Personalized discipline, Saturday detention	LEGAL PROBLEMS	Close interaction with local juvenile justice system
LOW SELF-ESTEEM	Regular awards assemblies. Much positive feedback from staff to students		
PASSIVITY/BOREDOM	Hands-on courses. Active learning. '5-1-5' calendar		
AGE (14–16)	Greater focus on social integration than on fulfillment of graduation requirements		
DISTRUST OF AUTHORITY	Informal relations between teachers and students		

school's motto is the 'Four As': acceptance, appreciation, affection and attention.

It was the absence of the care and respect embodied in these terms that often led students into withdrawal or oppositional behavior in their previous school. By presenting themselves as friends and counselors, teachers at Sierra Mountain attempt to draw students into an experience of membership in a school community. Teachers and students alike speak of the school as a family. Within the context of its formality there is much joking, laughter and playfulness. The division between youth and adults that led to distrust of authority in the district's conventional schools is softened here. Consequently, it is not unusual for students to become supporters of the school's ethos and rules.

Not all students are immediately, or even over time, amenable to this approach, so staff at Sierra Mountain have adopted additional measures to encourage attendance and appropriate behavior. In each instance, the approach remains personal and avoids a punitive tone. Students who continue patterns of truancy are called by an attendance secretary and must meet with the Principal on their return to school. Similarly, students who fail to treat either their peers or teachers with the respect seen as essential for the smooth operation of the school are referred to the counselor or Principal. In such situations, discipline is based on the establishment of a respectful and supportive relationship. The response to truancy or misbehavior also includes spending a few hours at Saturday detention doing janitorial or yard work around the school, something Conway says allows students to give back to the program what was taken away as a result of not abiding by school rules. Staff also work closely with the local juvenile justice system and the district's drug counselor in order to assist students with more serious personal problems.

Another important means for encouraging school attendance and participation involves the way in which learning is presented at Sierra Mountain. Teacher–student ratios, the school calendar, evaluation and rewards, curriculum and pedagogy all display characteristics aimed at 'hooking' formerly resistant students into the process of education. Classes at Sierra Mountain generally have no more than fifteen to twenty students; a few may have only four or five. This low ratio allows teachers to cultivate the personal relationships upon which much of the school's program is based.

Recognizing the problems many at-risk students have sustaining concentration over the course of a normal academic term, teachers have also divided the school's calendar into five-week units followed by a week-long vacation, even though this has meant extending the length of the school year. In an attempt to avoid the negative consequences of failure, the procedure for awarding course credit at Sierra Mountain has also been transformed. Students earn credit for work completed; failures occur only when students refuse to complete any assignments. Students also have the option of earning extra credit, or they can take independent study courses as a means for overcoming credit deficiencies if they choose to do so.

Positive school performance is encouraged through regular awards assemblies where students who have demonstrated the most improvement or excellence are recognized. Class-related trips are also offered as an incentive to students who become actively involved in their coursework. The biology class, for example, made trips into the Sierra Nevada mountains and to the Pacific coast, and the drama class regularly attends plays at the Oregon Shakespearean Theater. These activities are earmarked for those students who become responsible and committed participants in class activities.

Also significant is the orientation of staff to the presentation of coursework. In addition to a traditional core curriculum containing English, science, history and mathematics, a wide variety of classes likely to engender student interest is also offered. Such courses include guitar-making, drama, music composition (on a sophisticated synthesizer), photography, computers, weight-lifting, peer counseling, log cabin building, woodworking, gardening and school maintenance. Teachers at Sierra Mountain strive to develop classes that demand active participation.

Active engagement of students is particularly vivid in the following description of a drama class taught by one of the school's visiting artists-in-residence.

Thirteen students sauntered by pairs and threesomes into Mike Menzie's classroom. Identical to the other Sierra Mountain classrooms in its square shape, dark blue carpet and window panes with blue trim, the room appeared more spare with bookshelves on one side and risers on the other. The tables were pushed to the back, and students brought chairs into a circle around John Deaderick, an actor and instructor at a local community college. John is a large man, wearing jeans and a red tropical print shirt. Once a week he passes on some of his formal theater training by taking over Mike's drama lesson, changing the class atmosphere with the fact of his being a 'real' actor from the world outside the school.

John narrated the stretching exercises that he led the students through. As they slowly stretched arms, legs, back, chest and neck muscles, he reiterated the necessity of a relaxed body for good acting. When an actress is in tune with her body, she will respond naturally to a situation, there will be no *acting*, just human beings responding to real situations. The class continued its relaxation exercises with facial massages, working on the points where tension is held: forehead, eyes, jaw. John reminded students of the importance of breathing from the diaphragm and led them through voice stretches — making noises with the range of body parts from throat to belly, which John called the 'flute to bass fiddle' range of sounds.

John moved directly into the lesson for the day — interpreting body language. 'What does a posture "mean"?' John spoke briefly about how bodies established territories and what happened when another person invaded one's territory. He asked students to consider the range of physical responses when their personal territories were invaded. Then he asked two students to read a scene from a play and to apply their understandings of human bodies and their interactions.

John asked for a female volunteer, someone who could read well because the scene was difficult. He chose Pamela, a knowledgeable choice for she was a self-assured actress with mental quickness. John recruited Tom, a new student, for the part as a lawyer. The passage was from a play set in 1736 and depicted the interrogation of a Quaker woman who was six months pregnant and a former high-priced London prostitute. Implicated in the murder of a nobleman, she was questioned by a ruthless attorney, devoted to discovering the truth. John explained that Pamela must demonstrate the strength of faith and the zeal of a new convert. Tom's attorney was suspicious, mistrustful, intolerant of religious believers and women. John verbally sketched a misogynist for the students. The point of the exercise, John emphasized, was to experience the way these characters would move.

The two students began reading the play, with Tom initially affecting an accent. John told him to speak naturally. After a few minutes, the lawyer circled the seated witness, and John directed Tom to invade the woman's physical space when he had an important point to pursue. Tom did this for a minute or so, and then John asked the two to improvise the scene without the text. He wanted the two students to get beyond the words, which he said, '... don't matter. You can't say a wrong word if you become the person and go for your objectives.'

After a few more minutes of working on the scene, Tom stood with head bent, drooped shoulders, yet said with some defiance, 'I can't do this'.

'How can you say you can't do this when you are doing it?' responded John. 'I will let you off the hook when you have done well. I won't allow you to give up before that.'

Tom started his interrogation again, but he stumbled. John handed him a book and told him to begin again. With that simple prop the scene came alive: at one point Tom moved in on Pamela with an aggressive, pointed accusation and she backed away naturally and expressively. John stopped them. 'You've peaked here', he praised with a big smile for each of them.

This drama scene portrays the demands placed upon students at Sierra Mountain, the way the teacher guides them toward a successful experience, and the overarching approach to actively involve students. Teachers strive to develop stimulating, inviting classes to reconnect their alienated students to teachers and to learning. For many students who are disaffected, who have failed classes due to absence or behavior problems, the active classes coupled to a revised school calendar and flexible options for accumulating credit reestablish possibilities for school based learning.

School-Within-A-School

Students in the School-Within-a-School have in common a record of course failure, poor attendance and credit deficiency. They also have in common their average or above-average academic abilities and their age: all are juniors and seniors. They must as well demonstrate a desire to graduate during admission interviews. This characteristic, more than any other, is seen as most crucial in admissions decisions by teachers in the program. Given these fundamental commonalities, the School-Within-a-School provides a supportive structure aimed at enabling students to alter former attendance and behavior problems, pass courses, and accumulate missing credits more rapidly than they would be able to in the conventional school.

As eleventh and twelfth graders, the students are aware of the need to abide by the school's strict requirements regarding attendance and behavior in order to graduate. Inevitably, however, some students continue to be tardy, cut classes or act inappropriately, and they are given 'points' for their misbehavior. If they accumulate more than five points during a quarter, they will be dropped from the program. Students can earn a positive point for each 'perfect' week. This disciplinary process forces students to always know exactly where they stand in relation to success or failure in the school. In the comprehen-

Table 6: School-Within-A-School—Match Between Student Characteristics and Program

Commonalities		Differences	
Student characteristics	*Program response*	*Student characteristics*	*Program response*
AGE (16–18)	Career exploration, experiential curriculum, focus on school-to-work transition	MOBILITY	Small school community
		BEHAVIOR PROBLEMS	Point system: behavior modification program
POOR ATTENDANCE	Point system: explicit behavior modification program. Calls to home when student absent	HEALTH PROBLEMS: MENTAL/PHYSICAL	Personal Development class, informal and formal counseling, close work with school social workers
CREDIT DEFICIENCY	Rapid credit accumulation through double credit for some classes (English/Social Studies, PE/Personal Development); credit for work experience	SUBSTANCE ABUSE	Mandatory drug evaluation for students suspected of abuse
		LOW SELF-ESTEEM	Structured and informal student recognition, success in experiential education
		DISTRUST OF AUTHORITY	Accessible and caring adults
		FAMILY CRISIS	Counseling
		POVERTY	Coordination of JTPA placements and other social service support

sive high school, on the other hand, many had found they could cut classes for weeks with impunity. Ironically, students often indicate that the School-Within-a-School's point system is one of its most valuable features, since it gives them a clear signal as to their status and the support they need to complete high school.

Despite realizing the importance of earning a diploma, many students in this program remain beset by diverse problems that interfere with achieving this goal. These problems include substance abuse, family crisis, isolation that has accompanied a family move, pregnancy/parenthood, mental problems and legal difficulties. A class in personal development is required of juniors and seniors and is aimed at raising issues related to these problems in a group context. Staff members also assist students individually with more serious problems by providing counseling and working closely with social workers, counselors and psychologists in the parent high school. The staff consciously creates a caring social environment on the premise most of the students come from homes in which there is a lack of support.

Given the proximity of high school graduation and possible entry into the workforce, teachers in the program emphasize the importance of helping these youths acquire the skills necessary to find and retain jobs. As juniors, all students are required to participate in four vocational internships, three of which are at sites outside the school. These internships include work in building rehabilitation, day-care, health services and office procedures. Seniors take courses in either food services or marketing and must supplement coursework with paid employment in these areas.

These courses are obviously vocational, but this curriculum is intended to be 'experiential' in the sense it provides a range of experiences to help young people develop and mature. Most of the experiences are carefully arranged to help students establish positive relationships with adults. Furthermore, there is an emphasis on cooperation and responsibility to others at job sites. This is done to promote more mature behavior, pre-empt behavior problems, such as emotional outbursts or anger, and helps students recognize their interdependence with others. The experiential component of the School-Within-a-School was designed with its students' common characteristics in mind and their need to begin the school-to-work transition. The variety of work experiences increases the likelihood of engagement by students. The following account portrays the kinds of experiences students encounter during the building rehabilitation component of the SWS curriculum.

Students arrived via bus or car for their shifts on a warm September afternoon. The work-site was a well-built, but old two-storey home in a lower middle-class neighborhood. At this point, new exterior siding was already in place and the outside of the house evidenced a professional level of work. Five girls and three boys comprised the crew for that afternoon. The supervisor, Bruce, was an economics and math student at the state university. He was employed by Operation Fresh Start, a social service program that hires disadvantaged youths to rehabilitate old buildings owned by a non-profit corporation. In addition to his carpentry skills, Bruce had also performed informal counseling in the course of his work with this crew from the SWS. He had established a comfortable relationship with these students, engaging in friendly banter but also making sure his word was taken seriously when it came to matters about rebuilding the house.

Bruce assigned Karen, Margo and Serena the job of setting nails in the woodwork in the living room and dining room on the first floor of the house. Once set, they were to putty over the nails and then stain the putty. Bruce carefully demonstrated the task for the girls, emphasizing the importance of not marring the wood and removing all excess putty. When the three girls were under way, he sent Ken and David, who had been observing, to the downstairs bathroom with painting equipment. Bruce then took the remaining three students to the attic to install insulation. Once again, Bruce showed the students what to do: Nate filled in places where there were gaps in the first layer of insulation. Another student placed a second layer of insulation in the ceiling, and Bruce and Lauren placed two-by-fours over the second layer to hold the insulation in place on the walls and lower ceiling. Bruce worked in the attic most of the time, patiently answering the recurrent question, 'What do I do next?'

Even when Bruce was checking with other students on their work, the attic crew continued skillfully with its tasks. Vera explained how to install styrofoam vents to a co-worker. Meanwhile, Lauren and Nate had moved on to a more skilled carpentry task: measuring and marking the two-by-fours to which the plywood walls would be attached. Nate adeptly used an electric drill to place holes and set screws and Lauren practiced her ability to toe in nails. They made mistakes and occasionally had to redrill holes; Bruce responded with patience and encouragement to do it again. When the finishing surface was largely in place, Lauren remarked, 'This place looks a lot nicer'.

Mid-afternoon brought a soda break. Afterward everyone went

back to their tasks or found a new one. The attic crew had moved on to insulating the stairway ceiling. Whenever students finished their part of a task, they moved on to another part of the house. Two people moved down to the second floor to fill in depressions and holes in the drywall. Once again, Bruce demonstrated how to perform the job, making sure the students understood his directions, and then moved away to other work. About thirty minutes before quitting time, students began cleaning up: putting tools away, finishing a particular portion of a job and cleaning up the work site.

This scenario demonstrates several features of effective work experience programs and the thrust of the School-Within-a-School program. First, students worked cooperatively and with sustained attention. Second, they appeared proud of what they accomplished. For example, Karen and Serena were pleased and proud they were able to complete the living and dining room woodwork during their shift. At another point in the afternoon, Vera and Lauren commented on their growing ability to hit nails with precision. Nate was delighted with his mastering of the power screwdriver. Third, they could see actual accomplishments that had involved the use of mental and manual skills. Fourth, students developed a positive relationship with Bruce, a skilled craftsman who provided a strong role model for these youths.

The focus of this experiential aspect of the School-Within-a-School program is on the development of general work attitudes, behaviors and skills. The sampling of diverse work settings is intended to promote a belief in a student's capacity to learn different kinds of abilities and knowledge. It is not anticipated students will seek jobs in child care or in the building trades, but that students' knowledge about different kinds of work and belief in themselves as capable persons will be enhanced. The emphasis is on successful experiences which integrate different kinds of skills, cooperative work, motivation enhancement and the accumulation of credits toward a high school diploma.

The coordinator of the School-Within-a-School work experience program, emphasizes how important it is for students that the work be meaningful; students must feel they are doing something necessary for them to develop a commitment and motivation to the work. Child care, health services and building rehabilitation are all important and worth-while activities to which students regularly become committed. Developing such commitment is essential if these students are to complete their high school education and then have successful occupational experiences.

Media Academy

Unlike the predominantly white student populations at Sierra Mountain and the School-Within-a-School, students at the Media Academy are black and Hispanic. As such, they often share a lower social class background and lower occupational and educational aspirations. They are diverse in terms of levels of academic achievement. Few students at the Media Academy have entered into the forms of institutional opposition — expressed through non-attendance, course failure or behavioral problems — that often characterize other at-risk youth, and some might challenge their inclusion in a study such as our own. Such students, however, are also in danger of dropping out and of failing to fulfill their own potential.

Before entering the Media Academy, most of its students discounted the possibility of college or other post-secondary training because of their backgrounds. On standardized tests of reading and mathematics, half scored above the mean and half below on each test. As a result of these skills, many performed adequately as students, but few were genuinely engaged in academics. Behind low aspirations and lack of engagement were factors related to inner-city urban life. In our interviews with these students, few could point to strong support from either peers or family for pursuing academic success. There was a scarcity of knowledge about the resources and effort it takes to pursue higher education. Few had encountered representatives from their own racial or ethnic groups who have actually succeeded in society's economic mainstream.

The Media Academy attempts to address these issues through a program using a variation on experiential education. Coursework is designed to improve students' writing and thinking abilities and overcome their low educational and occupational aspirations through involvement in the cooperative production of stories for print, radio and television. As a means for encouraging involvement in the program, teachers emphasize issues related to the local community and minorities in particular. Students are also exposed to previously unimagined vocational possibilities via guest speakers and field trips. The curriculum is designed to link experiences outside the classroom with academic learning. The intent of experiential learning is to spur minority students with low educational and occupational aspirations toward higher goals and achievement.

The curriculum of the Media Academy continues over three years, beginning with students in their sophomore year. It is designed to

Table 7: Media Academy—Match Between Student Characteristics and Program

Commonalities		Differences	
Student characteristic	Program response	Student characteristic	Program response
RACE/ETHNICITY (Black – 51% Hispanic – 44%)	Focus on issues related to local community and minority students. Exposure to successful minority media professionals. Spanish-language newspaper	AGE (14–18)	Use of older students as role models
		ACADEMIC ACHIEVEMENT	Production tasks for people with different skills. One-on-one coaching and tutoring
LOW ASPIRATIONS	Public dissemination of student work. Exposure to tasks of media production. School tasks are directly connected to real media work	GENDER (Male – 29%, Female – 71%)	Leadership opportunities and models for boys and girls. Girls attracted to program where attention to detail and willingness to work hard are rewarded
COMMUNITY STRESS/CONFLICT	Create alternative peer environment		
LIMITED EXPERIENCE	Off-campus field trips to media work settings, conferences, national parks		
SOCIOECONOMIC STATUS (Working class)	Learning tasks based upon cooperation among students		

provide students with increasingly complex knowledge and skills about media and communications preparing them for direct entry into an occupation or enrollment in higher education. In addition to a regular fare of courses from the main high school, students take journalism, a course which becomes their 'major' during the three years. Initially, the journalism course teaches the basics in writing and speaking. Students begin writing not only for course assignments but also for the school newspaper. There are also opportunities to write small pieces for radio and television programs. In the first year of the program, an Academy student had two stories broadcast through the Youth News Service on an Oakland radio station.

Students are also exposed to professionals in the field of journalism who describe their work and the skills they need to do it. By the end of the first year, students had visited businesses concerned with all of the major aspects of the media, including newspapers, telecommunications, advertising and television newscasting. Eventually, during the second and third years, they have more sustained involvement with media professionals in the fields of radio, television, newspapers and advertising.

Journalism classes developed skills and knowledge directly applicable to media work. For example, early in the fall semester, students in Steve O'Donoghue's class were assigned to do an interview with a classmate and to write a short biographical sketch about that person. The students responded eagerly to the interview, but writing the account was more difficult. Many struggled over how to write in the third person. Others pulled out dictionaries to correct their spelling. O'Donoghue circulated from student to student checking on their progress and offering a few subtle suggestions about how to proceed, or how to improve what they had written. He collected the writings to make comments on them, using shorthand editing symbols that he kept on the board for their reference.

Another journalism class in mid-year reflected the way O'Donoghue integrated students' experiences with writing. He and the students reviewed the previous day's visit to the Harbor Bay teleport (described in chapter 1), a business and communications facility. After recounting a few of the topics discussed, he asked the students to use their notes from the session to write a news account of the visit. As students began to write, he, as usual, moved around the room reading their narratives and making short suggestions. The stories were handed in at the end of the hour for more careful scrutiny. The best story would be included in the next issue of the student newspaper.

O'Donoghue consciously assigned concrete activities and experiences requiring students to produce a written product to which he could respond with pointed comments. Often he had students work in pairs or small groups. Each student had a standard textbook on journalism from which some assignments were drawn. However, the emphasis in classroom lessons was not on recalling the content of this book, but rather on applying the content to produce written articles. This was a course in writing.

The journalism class was situated in the ongoing excitement and action of producing a bi-weekly, award-winning student newspaper. The journalism classroom was adjacent to the newspaper production room where cameras were checked out, plans for the next issue of the paper discussed, stories typed and staff members met for socializing. Not only is the Fremont High School newspaper, *The Green and Gold*, produced there, but also a Spanish/English newspaper, *El Tigre*, that targets the Hispanic community near the school. A young Mexican-American woman took an intensive three-week journalism course from O'Donoghue during the summer and became the founding editor of the new paper.

The production room attracted students all day long, many of whom were on the newspaper staff, but also students who worked with O'Donoghue on independent study. These students performed various tasks including clerical work, word processing, typesetting and other production steps. Production room work started before school in the morning and continued until 4.30 or 5.00 p.m. almost every day.

Many of the newspaper staff were self-directed in their work, occasionally consulting with O'Donoghue. Sometimes students sought him out for an answer or solution to a problem; other times a student approached with a story that was incomplete or poorly written. O'Donoghue was sympathetic, but he refused to rescue a student by writing the story. As in the classroom, his usual response was to question them. What options do you see? What are you trying to say? What point do you want to make? His role was to remain in the background and give ownership and direction of the paper to the students.

Involvement in the production of these newspapers provided students with a number of important opportunities. The variety of tasks associated with the paper gave students with mixed academic abilities an opportunity to contribute their own talents to this collective effort. Students who could not write well, for example, could work as photographers, advertisement sales people, or be responsible for layout and design. The work of all students could therefore be valued and recognized.

Work on production also allowed students of different ages and experience to interact with one another as teachers and learners in a situation where they labored as members of a team. Younger students could see their more experienced peers accomplishing tasks they would be expected to perform in the next year or two. Such modeling underlined teachers' attempts to convince black and Hispanic youth they can perform sophisticated and socially valued work that is also personally rewarding.

Involvement with the school and community newspapers provided significant leadership opportunities for boys and girls who had often become lost in a large urban high school. Newspaper production offered significant opportunities for girls, in particular, making use of their attention to detail and willingness to work hard on tasks involving writing and thinking. Finally, the Media Academy offered an alternative peer network for students inclined to imagine different futures for themselves than the ones most readily visible in their own communities where poverty and crime rates were high. Such support is often essential if children from difficult backgrounds are to risk school achievement, something that can often attract the derision of their peers.

Student testimony and observations of the Media Academy point to a number of elements that contribute to the success of at-risk students in an experiential education program. First, students are actively involved in writing stories and interviewing, which provide relief from the usual passive schoolwork that is disconnected from work and life beyond the classroom. Second, their written products have a wider audience than just a classroom teacher; the fact that they write for a newspaper, or other medium, contributes additional motivation to perform well. Third, students see a connection between learning to write well and future career and economic prospects. Thus, media experiences appear 'relevant' to students' lives. Fourth, at-risk students tend to thrive in cooperative settings where they work in collaboration with peers (Levin, 1987). Finally, the Media Academy utilizes the attraction of younger students to older to help foster a student culture that supports norms for achievement and engagement.

The Media Academy, after its first year of existence, had achieved high status in many students' eyes. Despite their misgivings about having to work harder than peers in other schools, students saw it as a program that had helped them improve in writing and public-speaking.

Student comments suggest the Media Academy makes Fremont High School a special place, a cut above other schools. Thus, there is a complexity to the Media Academy approach to education that makes it more than simple training in basic skills (writing), training in newspaper production, or training in work habits, though all of those elements are present. The Media Academy staff push students toward internalizing norms for high achievement, which they see as essential to these minority youths' occupational success.

Croom Vocational High School

Like the Media Academy, Croom Vocational High School has chosen to work with a group of students who often come from communities where economic hardship is common and aspirations for a better life are low. In contrast to the Media Academy, however, among the central criteria for admission to Croom are course failure, credit deficiency and low academic ability. Croom is clearly a 'vocational' program for students unlikely to attend college. Like the School-Within-a-School, it works with 16- to 18-year-olds, and its primary purpose is to help students make a more successful transition from school to the labor market.

Part of smoothing that transition entails reversing the psychological impact of years of school failure. Students frequently come to Croom with damaged self-esteem and little hope for the future. In the main office building, they are greeted with a sign, 'Welcome to Success'. In their interaction with students, staff members underline their belief that the young people they teach are capable of mastering vocational skills and acquiring the positive work habits that will allow them to find and keep jobs in the local economy. Just the simple location of Croom — situated on an abandoned Nike missile base in the lush Maryland countryside — serves to indicate that the world is broader than the economically depressed neighborhoods from which many of its students come.

Much of Croom's program is directed towards helping students overcome some of the limitations that have been imposed upon them as a result of being economically disadvantaged. One of these limitations, as mentioned in chapter 3, is simply the difficulty these students have in acquiring skills in possible vocational areas such as auto repair, building maintenance, and yard care that many children growing up in more affluent surroundings acquire as a matter of course. Another limitation

Table 8: Croom Vocational High School—Match Between Student Characteristics and Program

Commonalities		Differences	
Student characteristic	*Program response*	*Student characteristic*	*Program response*
AGE (16–18)	Vocational training and remedial classes	ALIENATION	Small class. Supportive teachers
		LACK OF PARENTAL SUPPORT	Home visits
LOW ACADEMIC ACHIEVEMENT	'Coaching' pedagogy	PASSIVITY/BOREDOM	Variety of vocational offerings. Experiential learning
LOW SELF-ESTEEM	'Welcome to Success' orientation		
LOW ASPIRATION	Development of knowledge and skills in seven vocational areas	SUBSTANCE ABUSE	Close surveillance of students at school. Removal of students from urban environment
LIMITED EXPERIENCE OF DOMINANT CULTURE	Training in basic vocational skills and work attitudes; field trips to Washington, DC		

is their lack of knowledge about the extended urban environment in which they live. Many students who attend Croom had never visited the sights of Washington, DC, even though the city is easily accessible by train from their homes. Teachers at the school attempt to expose them to the cultural and economic opportunities that exist there.

A third limitation involves the lack of support parents of many Croom students can give their children regarding how to successfully complete their education and find satisfactory work. To address this situation, staff members at the school make home visits and attempt to establish closer ties with students' families. Finally, the distractions and potential dangers of growing up in an economically depressed neighborhood can often make it difficult for minority youth to attend to school and orient themselves to the future requirements of the workplace. Lifting them out of that environment can provide some insulation from the attractions of drug abuse, gang membership or early pregnancy.

When students enroll in Croom, they agree to participate in a structured two-year program aimed at acquainting them with automotive repair, food preparation and service, building maintenance and painting, business occupations, groundskeeping, child care and geriatrics, and building trades. As juniors, students rotate through six of the seven shops. During their senior year, they will 'major' in the vocational area which seemed most appealing and approachable to them. They will also be placed in a regular, paid job. In addition to the three-hour shop class, students work on basic academic skills during the morning (juniors) or afternoon (seniors) in preparation for the Maryland competency tests.

All students completing two years at Croom receive a vocational certificate. Some years, as many as 40 per cent of these students receive a high school diploma, while others receive a GED. For students who are seriously credit deficient and unlikely to graduate from high school, the incentives of a vocational certificate and GED are important to committed participation in the program.

Part of the strategy to help students either graduate or complete the requirements for the vocational certificate is the rotation through the different shops, boosting the likelihood of students experiencing work that they enjoy. In addition to structured rotations, teachers are skilled at slowly introducing ideas and attitudes to students through a teaching process that relies on close, interpersonal 'coaching' between teachers and students. Garland Proctor, the building maintenance teacher, demonstrates this strategy in his deliberate, steady induction of a new student into his specialty.

As the class makes its way through the different buildings on the campus, Mr Proctor, a black man in his mid–30s, offers instruction about the specific problems encountered in each space. For example, in the math room he showed two boys how to combat old wax that had yellowed and stained the floor tiles. In addition to performing invaluable cleaning services, Mr Proctor fosters an understanding of some complexities of the job through visits to janitorial service companies throughout the Washington, DC area. Students gain the thanks of the school community, personal satisfaction of studying math in a classroom they just cleaned and an appreciation for the knowledge that is necessary to be a top maintenance person.

Proctor's interactions with a shy boy from Appalachia demonstrate the dominant strategy of the Croom teachers to help develop habits, skills and attitudes in their students that foster their employability. Darryl actively opposed doing any of the tasks with his fellow building maintenance students. This lanky young man with wispy blond hair sat on a window ledge watching his classmates wash walls and clean floors in various classroom buildings. Mr Proctor never forced him to work; rather, he chipped away at Darryl's resistance in short conversations:

Proctor: What kind of work do you want to do?

Darryl: I dunno.

Proctor: What do you like to do?

Darryl: I like to play around with cars, maybe do some building. I don't like to clean toilets.

Proctor: What don't you like about washing floors and the other things we do in here?

Darryl: (mumbling with head down): Anybody can do this work; it don't take no brains.

Proctor: Don't you take some pride in how this room looks when we're finished?

These conversations got Darryl to talk about work in general, and how he felt about building maintenance as a specific kind of work. Mr Proctor, like all of the Croom instructors, talked about work satisfaction, pride in doing tasks well. This soft, incremental, understanding approach worked with Darryl. A few months later, during building maintenance shop, Darryl proudly enumerated all of the new things he could do and added that his favorite thing was running the power floor cleaner. He smiled when he announced that he was planning to choose building maintenance for his major shop as a senior.

Croom's students have poor academic skills and frequently have had few experiences in which to develop manual skills. Croom teachers introduce them to different kinds of work, guarantee positive experiences in the shops for all students, and help them get an initial job. These are ambitious goals and the Croom staff does admirable work, especially in their slow, skilled 'coaching' of students through unfamiliar tasks. Since they are committed to students achieving through positive, satisfying work experiences, staff do not coerce students whom they know have difficulty adjusting to unfamiliar tasks, but slowly ease students toward a willingness to try something new. The staff are very talented and successful in their strategies that lead to student skill development, a positive attitude toward work, the ability to get and hold a job and a high school certificate. Once again, a match exists between salient student characteristics and program goals and strategies.

New Futures School

By choosing to work with pregnant or mothering teenagers, New Futures targets a clearly identified student population. By acknowledging the unique characteristics of this group the school has developed an educational intervention appropriate for the specific needs of the young women who enroll. This population shares a number of important common characteristics: they are all young women who are pregnant or the mothers of infants, most have problems with attendance and credit accumulation and a large share are from working-class backgrounds. The staff at New Futures have built upon these commonalities and created a program focused on issues related to childbirth and parenting and the demands of pregnancy and child care.

Student differences are also accommodated. Because New Futures students range in age from 12 to 21, represent diverse racial and ethnic backgrounds, demonstrate very different levels of academic achievement and often encounter physical or mental health problems related to pregnancy, the school is flexible in the provision of academic, counseling and medical programs tailored to individual student needs. Since teenage pregnancy can be a traumatic event, the school provides counseling and support that may not exist in a young woman's home. This support is intended to help the girls see that, given their pregnancy, they should not view the situation as a tragedy, but rather an opportunity to develop maturity and competence.

New Futures School addresses all dimensions of pregnancy and

Table 9: New Futures School—Match Between Student Characteristics and Program

Commonalities		Differences	
Student characteristic	Program response	Student characteristic	Program response
PREGNANCY/MOTHERHOOD	Child care. Curriculum includes courses related to child-bearing and child-rearing	AGE (12–21)/ACADEMIC ACHIEVEMENT	Individualized instruction
POOR ATTENDANCE/CREDIT DEFICIENCY	Homebound tutoring program, lenient absence policy, and individualized instruction to prevent credit loss during pregnancy and motherhood	HEALTH	Regular check-ups at school-based clinic
		LOW SELF-ESTEEM	Formal and informal counseling. Supportive teachers help girls succeed academically. Parenting classes help them become competent mothers
		SOCIOECONOMIC STATUS (Working class)	School assistance in finding employment and financial aid for further education
		FAMILY CRISIS	Counseling
		LACK OF FAMILY SUPPORT	Teachers, counselors and nurses provide support and attention

motherhood, a fact that sets it apart from programs that just enroll pregnant girls or programs without day care for school-aged mothers. The school's strategy is to offer a comprehensive program: instruction about pregnancy and mothering, counseling, medical care, child care services, a job program and an individualized academic curriculum, including a homebound teacher.

Most New Futures students enroll when they are between three and five months pregnant. These girls are placed in courses required for a high school diploma, as well as in two special parenting classes, the curriculum for these having been developed by New Futures staff. The program is designed for one-year: in two semesters, a girl takes three parenting classes, has her baby, and makes progress in her graduation requirements. Girls who subsequently cannot arrange their own day care, or who desire the nurturing atmosphere of the school, may continue beyond the two semesters. Selection of students to continue is based on staff assessment of the young woman's progress and her need to remain at New Futures.

New Futures staff aim to help their students become good decision-makers, good mothers and successful high school graduates. The school is a separate facility designed to help girls adjust to their pregnancy in a supportive environment. While carrying a child, girls help tend babies and toddlers in one of the three nurseries. In classes they learn about their own developing foetus as well as about the stages of development in infants. The knowledge about exercise, nutrition, labor and delivery is transmitted within an environment of love of children and concern for their well-being. Nurses, teachers, nursery aides and counselors each concern themselves with the development of the mother, the foetus and later the baby. Medical care is provided by nurses who also teach the first parenting course and by the staff of the weekly health clinics provided by the University of New Mexico Medical School.

Counseling plays an integral role in maintaining the mother's mental and physical health. Five counselors meet regularly with students and also lead a group session once a week in each of the parenting classes. One counselor portrayed these group counseling sessions as handling the emotional dimension of pregnancy and motherhood, the emotions about accepting a pregnancy, being a new mother and living with parents or in-laws as a new mother.

In one child development class a counselor initiated the topic of difficulties encountered in living with parents or in-laws. Dianna commented that she found different discipline standards to be a problem in living in her mother's home. 'My mother is too lenient when she babysits my son', Dianna said. Stephen was then a terror when she returned after a weekend away. Other girls contributed similar or different experiences. As girls made suggestions for alternative courses of action in dealing with problems, the counselor wrote them on the board.

Teachers and counselors at New Futures were experienced with the common problems of school-aged mothers and had a repertoire of topics that generated discussions and collective thinking about solutions. In addition to these group counseling sessions, individual visits to counselors and nurses often took precedence over class attendance because it was believed learning could only occur when psychological or physical problems were removed.

A supportive environment is crucial but not sufficient for girls' progress toward education and employment goals. On-site child care was essential for the seventy-five girls who had no other access to child care. The school's three nurseries also provided child care 'labs' for the parenting courses and peace of mind for young mothers whose children were close and in good hands.

New Futures also provided opportunities for girls who needed a paying job or were interested in work experience. Girls who enrolled in a work experience class were eventually placed in jobs that gave them entry level experience and income. Job placements included traditional secretarial and clerk positions as well as sales. The employment component was controversial at New Futures because academic teachers complained jobs made academic classes an even lower priority after mothering and work, but other staff members understood that many girls needed to earn some money to support themselves. Even when living at home, most students needed to pay for expenses such as diapers and clothing.

Individualized instruction is a standard characteristic of alternative educational programs. At New Futures this developed because pregnant girls were often absent with illness and as mothers often tended a sick child at home. Teachers individualized in several ways. Some prepared lessons and units of instruction that could be completed by students on their own. Carol Nuzum, an English teacher, devised her own writing units. She initiated a masterful series of lessons, all of which could be completed at home if a girl or her child were ill. Nuzum said, 'I learned to teach all over again when I came to New Futures because I had to devise lessons that students could successfully complete on their own'.

Another example of individualized instruction was the homebound teacher position. Staff were acutely aware of the academic problems that absences caused, yet they also knew these absences were often necessary and legitimate. In order to keep the girls working on their classes, the school obtained private foundation monies to hire a teacher to regularly visit students at home. The incidence of failure due to absence has been greatly reduced at New Futures.

New Futures exemplifies a comprehensive approach to meeting the needs of school-aged mothers. The program includes education for pregnancy and motherhood, counseling, medical care, on-site child care, work experience and individualized instruction. The integration of these elements allows teenage pregnancy to become, in many instances, a maturing experience for young women, not the first step of a tragic, inevitable slide into poverty.

Alcott Alternative Learning Center

Alcott is considered a 'school of last resort' for junior high students in the Wichita district. Seventy per cent of its students are below grade level in achievement and 75 per cent have been retained at least one year. On the Iowa Test of Basic Skills 75 to 80 per cent are below the 50th percentile in mathematics and reading. Almost every Alcott student has a history that makes him or her at risk of dropping out of school. In addition to academic difficulties, conversations with the Principal or counselor about individual students and their families elicit stories about poverty, child abuse, drug addiction, pregnancy, incarceration and various illegal acts such as shoplifting and drug selling.

Alcott thus serves young adolescents with the most serious personal, family or academic problems. Many of these students choose to attend Alcott after encountering failure and frustration in a conventional junior high. In some cases parents select the school after receiving advice from psychologists, psychiatrists, probation officers or other parents. Sometimes principals or counselors from other junior highs will make a referral after failing in their efforts to deal with a student.

In the words of Beverly Gutierrez, the school's Principal, Alcott's students are those 'no one else wants'. What these youths hold in common are extraordinarily difficult home and community environments that have interfered with their growth and social development. Alcott staff see previous interaction with adults as the key contributor to their students' condition of being at risk. 'Adults have been unwilling or unable to shield youngsters from their environments, whether those

Table 10: Alcott Alternative Learning Center—Match Between Student Characteristics and Program

Commonalities		Differences	
Student characteristic	*Program response*	*Student characteristic*	*Program response*
AGE (15 or younger)	Successful transition to high school seen as primary goal	SUBSTANCE ABUSE	Required drug evaluation and rehabilitation if deemed necessary
COURSE FAILURE/POOR ATTENDANCE	Remedial academic curriculum. Small staff allows for close monitoring of student attendance and academic performance	ACADEMIC ACHIEVEMENT	Small classes allow for flexibility and individualized approach
LOW SELF-ESTEEM	Focus on providing students with successful learning experiences	MENTAL/PHYSICAL HEALTH	Small program allows for greater personal attention
BEHAVIOR PROBLEMS/ALIENATION	Informal and formal counseling. Human development curriculum	ISOLATION	Small program allows for more attention and tolerance
DISTRUST OF AUTHORITY	Focus on developing close interpersonal relationships between students and staff		
LACK OF PARENTAL SUPPORT/FAMILY CRISIS	Intake interviews involve parents. School sponsors special programs related to parenting problems		
SOCIOECONOMIC STATUS (Working class, poor)	Part of intake process devoted to linking family to appropriate social services		

are family, neighborhood or school', said Mrs Gutierrez. 'Adults have abused them physically or have exploited them.' These background factors push the staff to emphasize helping students develop stronger self-concepts through close, supportive counseling relationships with trustworthy adults, as well as fostering their successful progress in academic subjects.

Mrs Gutierrez sees the students as having fragile egos despite their swagger and street-wise facade. She reads much of their behavior as a defense against the negativism they have experienced in and out of school. She finds them defeated in school by failure and negative labeling from peers and teachers. In response, Alcott staff seek to nurture students in the following ways: building up their self-confidence, helping them confront dysfunctional behavior, such as hostility toward adults, by communicating in many ways that adults care about them. The educational goal is to help students learn to act in productive rather than negative and hostile ways.

A school document describes the program as follows:

> Alcott provides a safe, nurturing environment for both students and parents where it is acceptable ... to discuss family problems, personal problems, and anything that has bearing on the student's health, personality, and well-being.

In line with this purpose, most Alcott teachers judge their success by the amount of progress students experience with personal and social problems rather than primarily by academic achievement.

Mrs G clearly sets the tone of the school through her warmth, insight, compassion and brutal honesty. The vignette in chapter 1 describing Mrs G's interview with a new boy and his mother portrayed her substantial skill and knowledge as a counselor, as well as the beginning of the typical close relationship between staff and students at Alcott. Small talk between staff and students was the norm in classrooms and in the halls. Much of this small talk focused on serious topics, but there was also kidding about boyfriends or the fall of some favored sports team. Several teachers ate lunch with the students each day as another way of maintaining personal contact. There was frequent hugging and friendly touching. Some students recoiled from the hugging, but Mrs G succeeded in giving even the most recalcitrant student a hug.

Georgia Deatrick was the official counselor at Alcott. She was skilled at dealing with the most distraught students. Some students relied on her almost daily for counselling — for reassurances or a shoulder to cry on. She conscientiously contacted some each day, to give them what she described as 'their warm fuzzies'.

Counseling, however, was not only the responsibility of Alcott's Principal or official counselor. All teachers performed counseling functions. For example, John McEachern, the shop teacher, often engaged students in conversations involving his analysis and recommendations about their personal situations. In one exchange with an eighth-grade girl, she talked about her boyfriend who was substantially older and a heavy drug user. John urged her to see beyond her romantic feelings for the boy. He counseled her that a drug addict would only exploit her to support his habit, and she should think about herself and end that relationship. Even though such advice was hard to hear, the girl's relationship with John was close enough that she was willing to discuss the situation. Her close attention to his words suggested she knew from experience his advice was likely to have merit and was not just an attempt to denigrate her decisions or control her actions.

Group counseling also occurred at Alcott in the form of a required course, 'Essentials of Living', focused on personal development and group discussion of problems. Much of the content of this course came from students' own problems with family dynamics, drugs, or abusive relationships.

One class on the topic of stress illustrated the general class format. The teacher began with a questionnaire to get students thinking about how they react to stressful situations, for example, being stuck in a traffic snarl or moving to a new residence or new city. The questionnaire provided the springboard for a discussion of reactions to stress in students' lives. Marty volunteered some thoughts about the connection between stress in his life and drug use. He claimed stress caused him to use phenobarbital, which, in turn, exacerbated his epilepsy. He recapitulated the problems he had while on drugs and acknowledged how much better he had felt since his three months in a drug treatment center and with the ongoing recovery work. 'Essentials of Living' provided a forum for students to talk about difficulties in their lives in an open and accepting environment.

The strong emphasis on counseling at Alcott is based on an understanding of students' need for ongoing support, attentiveness and support from adults. Because of the difficult behavior problems, including truancy, drug use, lying, stealing and physical violence, the Alcott staff created a program that is safe, affirmative and stresses self-reflection. The intent of this strategy was to help students confront the underlying problems that cause their self-destructive behaviors.

Students need a safe, comfortable place where they can be helped to see themselves without distortions and build trusting relationships with adults. Central to this aim is good communication between the adults and students; teachers must be honest with students and students must feel comfortable to talk to teachers and be able to listen to the responses. Given Alcott's students and its program aims, all teachers must be counselors because discussion of students' problems, good communication with caring, attentive adults and a feeling of being accepted are essential to positive growth for these young adolescents.

Plymouth Christian Youth Center

Plymouth Christian Youth Center Alternative School evolved out of a private social service agency's desire to improve the living conditions on the North-east side of Minneapolis. Once an enclave of upwardly mobile working-class immigrants, the neighborhood experienced significant economic decline in the past two or three decades. Although recent attention to the area's problems has manifested itself in some signs of renewal, the North-east remains a troubled area. The Plymouth Christian Youth Center is dedicated to serving the neighborhood originally by providing recreational opportunities for youths and, more recently, schooling.

Nearly all students who attend PCYC are dropouts from the Minneapolis public schools. Most have academic records marked by course failure and credit deficiency, though the academic achievement of students at the school is mixed. Many students also experienced alienation in the public schools and responded with behavior that resulted in suspensions and expulsions. Curricular and pedagogical innovations such as shorter academic units and an emphasis on cooperative learning are intended to help students overcome their academic difficulties. The school's small size and caring climate help reduce student alienation. Perhaps the most important commonality students bring to PCYC, however, is living in a neighborhood that is poor and riven with racial and gang-related conflicts.

With this in mind, PCYC has attempted to match its program to the experience of students in this particular neighborhood. At one level, PCYC serves the neighborhood by providing alternative schooling for youths who were unsuccessful in the typical large conventional public high schools of Minneapolis. But, more importantly, PCYC serves the neighborhood by using the school to model and instill pro-social

Table 11: Plymouth Christian Youth Center—Match Between Student Characteristics and Program

Commonalities

Student characteristic	Program response
COURSE FAILURE/CREDIT DEFICIENCY	Basic skills emphasis. Short units. GED preparation
SOCIOECONOMIC STATUS (poor) COMMUNITY STRESS/CONFLICT	Program emphasis on the development of pro-social attitudes, the break down of inter-racial suspicion, use of positive community role models, involvement of parents, and integration of school and social service agencies

Differences

Student characteristic	Program response
RACE/ETHNICITY	Model cooperative relations between white and black staff members
ALIENATION	Small school. Emphasis on building a caring community that reflects fundamental Christian values
BEHAVIOR PROBLEMS	Discipline handled within the context of close, interpersonal relationships
AGE (14–18+)	No distinctions in classrooms based on age or grade
ACADEMIC ABILITY	Identification of individual academic deficiencies. GED preparation. Skills block integrated into regular curriculum

attitudes likely to reduce the hostility which stands in the way of success for many neighborhood youths.

Tim Higuera is one of these youths. He has lived in the same house in North-east Minneapolis his entire life. He is bright, energetic and an accomplished rock musician. Although he would like to make his living by playing in a band, he is realistic about his chances. Consequently, he plans attending a technical school after graduation to learn auto mechanics or electronics.

Tim attended several Minneapolis schools before enrolling at PCYC. At Henry High School, he was expelled for being disruptive, or in his own words, 'beating too many people up'. Asked why he was always fighting, Tim said it was a necessary response. Students called him a 'white boy', 'nigger', 'mulatto', or 'zebra', taunting him about his mixed racial background. According to Tim, 'You had to force your way into the school — who you were and what you looked like made all the difference at a school like Henry'.

According to Tim, the animosity and competition fostered in the outside merely carried over into the school.

> In school you're known. There are so many dudes that just don't like you. So many times, it's the 'metallers' against the 'brothers' and we'd always try to win. We are ruthless. We'd do anything to win — we'd even bring guns to school. It's rough on the streets, and if it's rough on the streets, the dudes who are forced into the schools are bringing that with them. It gets rougher and rougher.

Tim argued that large public schools can't really control this. 'The school is too large, and the staff is too small to deal with these tensions.' He claimed his high school was obsessed with maintaining a daily routine and teaching irrelevant content. He also felt that most public schools make it hard for students to pass in order to push out those seen as undesirable by the staff.

At PCYC, however, he has encountered people able to deal effectively with youth who grow up on the streets. He credited much of PCYC's success to the emphasis teachers place on supportive relationships between staff and students. The help they have offered to him has led Tim to consider helping others as well.

> I want to do things to help other people. I never thought I would want to help people until people started helping me. It makes me feel good to be able to say I'm not that bad anymore. I used to treat people like they were cabbage and I was the king.

> I have more understanding. I took this handicapped class, and I have more respect for people who are visually impaired or mentally retarded. They are still people. I feel like more of a person. I see what real people ought to be acting like.

This kind of transformation was seen as the outgrowth of certain programmatic characteristics developed by staff members at PCYC. They consciously attempt to model personal interactions for young people whose community lives are often marred by fear, violence and intolerance. In response, staff offices are deliberately arranged to pair black and white or male and female staff members together. According to PCYC staff, their students are not accustomed to seeing men and women or blacks and whites sharing responsibility or working together. By deliberately pairing staff of different races and sexes, staff prevent students from seeking assistance from teachers or one race or sex. Eventually, students learn to work constructively with members of the opposite sex or of races other than their own.

PCYC's efforts to break down inter-racial suspicion and animosity is evident in classes as well. All PCYC staff have been trained in cooperative learning techniques and teachers must incorporate some cooperative learning activities into their curriculum. This process requires that students of different racial and ethnic backgrounds begin to work together and depend on one another. The goal is to reduce suspicion and break down stereotypes.

PCYC realizes the importance of positive role models for neighborhood youth. Community members who have established themselves in business or civic affairs are encouraged to visit the school and make presentations to the students. Others volunteer to teach units, thereby supplementing the PCYC curriculum. Perhaps most interesting of all is PCYC's effort to identify and train local residents as PCYC staff. Although this kind of in-house training requires tremendous time and patience, the benefits are enormous when students regularly see members of their neighborhood performing useful and positive social roles.

PCYC is not isolated from the neighborhood it serves. An unusual example of this was the recent purchase of a nearby pornographic theater and its transformation back to respectability. More representative of PCYC's commitment are its efforts to regularly involve parents in the school. Students are required to have their parents participate in the student's registration each trimester. This is seen as a good opportunity to keep parents apprised of the student's progress, to let parents comment about various aspects of the school, or to allow parents to raise concerns about a problem that their child is experiencing. Furthermore, the school social worker maintains regular contact with each student's parent(s) during the trimester. PCYC believes that the early, regular exchange of information between home and school increases the likelihood that problems will be identified early and an effective intervention designed.

Finally, PCYC integrates social service and school. As a teacher and participant in all staff meetings, the social worker is able to remind the staff that the student must be seen as a member of several, often dysfunctional, social systems and that school performance should not be viewed in isolation. For example, when a student at the school decided she couldn't live at home any longer, the entire staff recognized that her school performance would change. When she found it difficult to focus on school and began to attend irregularly, she was asked to wait until the next period to try again. In the meantime, the social worker maintained contact with her and worked to mediate and resolve the home situation. Although the student's education was interrupted, the interruption was relatively brief and her return to school took place within an atmosphere of support and encouragement.

By recognizing and responding to the larger social environment in which its students live, the Plymouth Christian Youth Center has developed a program aimed at counteracting behavioral patterns that often divide, distract and alienate economically disadvantaged youth and prevent them from acquiring a high school diploma and further training. Committed to making the neighborhood in which it is located a better place to live, PCYC demonstrates to its students productive forms of personal behavior and social interaction.

Program Match in Other Schools

Other Minneapolis Alternative Schools

Each of the other four schools in the Minneapolis Federation reflects a similar responsiveness to the characteristics of a particular group of at-risk students. NA-WAY-EE is located in a neighborhood with a high number of Native American families. Many children from this group find it difficult to achieve academic success in conventional high schools. At NA-WAY-EE, teachers strive to create a cultural environment which is more comfortable for the school's students, all of whom are Native Americans. The exterior and interior decoration of the building incorporates traditional Native American motifs, and rituals such as pipe ceremonies punctuate the school year. The curriculum, as well, reflects Native American concerns, particularly in the areas of art, social studies and earth science. In order to grapple more effectively with the problem of substance abuse that not infrequently troubles Native American communities, NA-WAY-EE provides as many counselors as teachers, hoping through support and guidance to steer its students into less personally damaging forms of behavior.

At NA-WAY-EE, schooling is set within the cultural milieu of its students. Rather than drawing students away from the tradition of their families, it seeks to ground them more fully in that heritage at the same time it helps them acquire the skills they will need to survive economically in the mainstream society.

Loring-Nicollet School, like NA-WAY-EE, works with another group of students who experience alienation from conventional schools. These students are often called 'punkers'. Like many Native American youth, white children who adopt the styles and belief systems of this sub-culture feel at odds with the dominant society. Their dress, attitudes, and beliefs often lead teachers and peers to reject them as well. This 'outsider' status can have a serious impact on the school success of such students, regardless of the strong academic abilities many of them can demonstrate. Loring-Nicollet attempts to overcome their isolation and alienation by drawing 'punkers' together in a single place and offering a curriculum that matches their concerns. Course work focuses on social action and personal growth, areas of significant interest to the school's students. Recognizing students' preoccupation with choice and individual expression, the school also avoids forcing students to do anything as a group and instead provides opportunities for much individualized instruction. Finally, teachers at Loring-Nicollet share many of their students' critique of American culture and political life, so students find in them a confirmation of their own vision. Staff at the school attempt to help its students transform that vision into action rather than despair.

The Minneapolis Urban League Street Academy serves a student population that is 100 per cent black. Its students, like those at NA-WAY-EE and Loring-Nicollet, find the Minneapolis public schools incompatible. The Street Academy offers a setting more in keeping with their own cultural background. As an arm of the Urban League, the school is seen as a legitimate black institution. Its predominantly black staff and its curricular concern with the black experience lend credence to that legitimacy. Many students at the Street Academy are also over-age for their grade level, have children, or may be married; most seem more like adults than high school teenagers. The Street Academy's open enrollment and relaxed attendance policies respond to its students age and conception of themselves as adults. The school treats its students as young adults capable of making their own decisions.

Their school intends to provide an opportunity for either a Minneapolis high school diploma or a GED. While a large proportion of students who initially enroll in the Street Academy fail to stay with the program or continue their education at other schools, the school does offer an important opportunity for those students who wish to complete their education in a culturally more congruent environment.

Students who attend the Minneapolis Education and Recycling Center generally do so for economic rather than cultural reasons. Youth who enroll in this program have failed in school and are either emancipated minors or from poverty-stricken homes. In either case they need some form of economic support. Most MERC students, however, lack skills, have never worked, and are described by their teachers as unemployable. One of the primary aims of MERC is to provide them with paid part-time labor and help them acquire behaviors important for job retention.

MERC, however, is more than just a job. Students must attend classes where they are helped to master fundamental academic skills. They are also drawn into the process of governing both the workplace and the school. Regular workers' meetings are held where students are given the opportunity to discuss their rights and responsibilities. Meetings regarding the operation of the school give them a chance to express themselves about school policies. Such meetings provide an important setting where the communication and thinking skills developed in academic classes can be applied to the occupational environment many of these students may find themselves in upon completing the program.

Wayne Enrichment Center (WEC)

Unlike the Minneapolis programs, the Wayne Enrichment Center near Indianapolis has not chosen to work with students who can be identified by race, ethnicity, socioeconomic status or cultural orientation. Instead, its students have become estranged from a large comprehensive high school. Some just do not fit into the competitive environment of sports and a college-bound academic orientation. Others have particular life circumstances that make it difficult to attend school on a regular schedule. For example, a number must work to support themselves or a family. Finally, a number of girls attend WEC irregularly because of their pregnancy.

The school program is three hours of class a day with a highly individualized curriculum based on learning packets. The curriculum is required to duplicate courses from the main high school, but the individualized mode allows students to accumulate credits more rapidly than a normal schedule allows. In fact, maintaining good standing at WEC requires students to earn at least six credits in a semester. This allows those who are credit deficient to make up lost ground. Frequently, students at WEC require this assistance for only brief periods, often for a semester or perhaps a year; permission, however, will be granted for additional semesters when this is judged appropriate.

Underlying this structure is a supportive environment created by teachers who practice a counseling role as well as an instructional one. This informal counseling and regular family meetings provide the settings in which students receive the care and support they need. Significantly, WEC teachers continue to remain in contact with many students once they have returned to the main high school. Group meetings for these students offer ongoing support in an attempt to prevent them from becoming lost or estranged again.

Conclusion

This chapter emphasized successful programs for at-risk youth matching their responses to a number of the salient characteristics of sub-groups of students. Descriptions of programs demonstrated a match of program components with low achieving students, alienated students, school-aged mothers, poor youth or those with low self-esteem and serious home and family disruptions. Matching emphasizes the need for schools to adapt programs to some common characteristics of students. Regular comprehensive schools contribute to their students' failure and becoming at risk of dropout when they refuse to adapt to students and expect students to do all the adapting. The case of a school-age mother such as Tammy in chapter 3 is a clear example of how a school's failure to take into consideration family responsibilities leads to her suspension for absences and her eventual dropout.

However, matching a program to particular students' needs is not an easy task. This calls for expert judgment, and in some instances educators may miscalculate their students or the effects of their programs. For example, at one site, 400 black and Hispanic students were placed in a program that stressed close attendance monitoring and a concentration on two academic subjects per semester in an attempt to reduce truancy and course failure. Quite correctly the dropout problem was diagnosed as students failing courses, becoming credit deficient toward graduation and eventually becoming discouraged and dropping out.

While the failure rate for academic classes diminished in this program, its narrow conception of concentrated remediation on two subjects received positive acclamation from neither students nor most teachers. This is in contrast to the strategies employed in most other schools we studied. We attribute this lower positive response to the assumption that only two common characteristics were crucial among the many students who were failing — truancy and a need for academic remediation. It ignored both other commonalities and differences. Some students were, in fact, academically skilled and clearly not in need of remediation, despite failing. Ignored were other factors contributing to failure, such as low aspirations and lack of experience in the mainstream culture. The limited positive response from students should be understood in terms of these other factors making them at-risk of dropping out. Obviously, staff interpretations of their students' characteristics must be thoughtful and analytical enough to determine why students are at risk in a particular context.

When we look at who fails in school we find social class, racial/ethnic, and gender backgrounds have a strong impact on students' ability to succeed in school (Ogbu, 1987; Erickson, 1987; McDermott, 1987; Moll and Diaz, 1987). These authors and others argue that perceptions of access or lack of access to economic opportunities affect students' willingness to care about school success. For example, if no parents or other adults in a community are employed, high school graduation is probably meaningless in the eyes of most adolescents.

Good programs must do more than just provide educational components integrated with students' immediate circumstances and needs. It is our belief that school programs must move students toward goals that involve the good of both individual students and the good of society. Thus, while schools must adapt to the particular needs of students, their interventions must also be grounded upon what all students have in common as social beings and as young learners. It is to these broader views of schools as social and intellectual organizations that our analysis and discussion now moves.

In order to be successful, in the final analysis, school programs must help students overcome isolation and alienation, help them succeed in school and, optimally, develop an interest in continued learning. Training beyond high school is increasingly necessary for people to obtain employment that pays a living wage. Reconnecting at-risk youth to school means that educators must reduce isolation, alienation and promote a desire to continue development of their intellectual and physical capacities.

In chapter 5, we argue that all youth need to develop competence in mental and manual tasks, feel valued and be part of a social group, and to have some link to adult roles and a positive future for themselves. Merely matching program components to student characteristics does not alone produce a sense of involvement with peers and teachers or a sense of congruence between one's background, school expectations and various occupational opportunities. Programs need to begin by assessing their students' characteristics as they affect their ability to learn and succeed in school at the present time, but successful programs also foster a sense of belonging to the school community. This sense of belonging to a school community is both an end in itself and a means to sustain school success. Chapter 5 discusses the importance of school membership as we found it in these programs and as discussed in literature on education in general.

Chapter 5:
School Membership

Chapter 3 described a range of circumstances and characteristics that place students at risk of dropping out of school. We illustrated the processes by which the conditions of young peoples' lives outside of school interact with school experiences to produce discouragement, failure and withdrawal. And we argued that schools should become more knowledgeable about the diversity of conditions that can make students at risk of dropping out. Moreover, we suggested that schools should devise ways of responding constructively to these students and their problems.

Chapter 4 described the responses of a number of schools to the problems faced by at-risk students. We attributed school effectiveness to success in matching programs to the characteristics of students. Our examples of matching indicated how particular schools reached particular populations of students that shared a number of common characteristics. From another perspective, these schools successfully selected students for whom their program was a good match.

In this chapter, we expand our argument to acknowledge that successful schools not only match interventions in response to differences and variations in student characteristics, they also respond to basic, common deep-seated needs. For at-risk students in particular, schools must take an active role in responding to fundamental needs that frequently are unmet by contemporary schools. One need shared by most students is for a sense of school membership. This chapter describes and defines school membership and indicates ways schools can promote it, thereby creating a supportive school community with the potential for holding students who might otherwise drop out.

The Importance of School Membership

At the beginning of chapter 1, several vignettes described various at-risk students. One of these students was Melody, an academically bright junior high girl who found school intolerable. Melody, who suffered problems with her size and weight, developed unproductive responses to the cruel taunts of her peers and the unkind comments of a few adults. At one point, Melody dropped out of school to avoid conflict and embarrassment. In a scene from the Media Academy, a shy student named Maria interviewed a news anchorman via satellite television. This scenario presented a picture of an immigrant girl struggling with the English language. Maria desperately wants to succeed in school, but she is often lost and confused in classes. She misses the subtle points made by teachers; she needs far more attention than most school staff can give her. Among her peers, she doesn't catch the comments, jokes and innuendos that seem so important in teenager banter. Despite the apparent goodwill of many of those around her, Maria often feels like an outsider.

These are examples of students in need of school membership. They want to belong and to be accepted as part of a peer group, but they also want the support and approval of adults. In our interviews with students, we repeatedly encountered expressions reflecting the importance of membership in the school. Asked about the strengths of their alternative school, students persistently described ways in which these were friendlier and more caring places than their previous schools had been. They talked about peers accepting them and teachers caring about them. They volunteered their observations about the importance of adults displaying a willingness to help them overcome academic and personal problems, and the value of being accepted as an individual.

These expressions were linked with students' own willingness, in turn, to reciprocate with participation in school activities and conformity to school norms. It is this reciprocity between students and teachers that distinguishes most of the schools we studied. And it is this reciprocity that provides the context for membership that appears lacking in the previous school experiences of at-risk students.

Bill, a student in School-Within-a-School, talked freely about his views of the school. He calls it a 'tough program with people who care', and he says the best thing about the program is the 'companionship' he experiences. 'It just seems like it was yesterday that I was a junior in the program, and now I'm a senior. It is a home away from home. If you like school, it goes by real fast.'

Mike, another student, talks about the difference between the School-Within-a-School and the regular school. 'It's got a lot different attitude than regular classes. It's a lot more open. You get to know everybody. I mean when I was in (regular) classes, I'd know one or two people, and the rest of the people I didn't really care to know. And at SWS I got to know everybody. And everybody was in every class.'

David credits the teachers at SWS for his success because 'they push you. They let you know you are doing bad. They may set you aside and tell you that you may be "pointing out" next week, and they let you know that they don't want you to point out. And you yourself don't want to do it anyway, but it's good that they have that concern.' David credits this concern by staff for the program's feeling of family. 'When I say family, I mean the whole School-Within-a-School... All of us and the teachers like going to class.' David says the relationship between teachers and students at the School-Within-a-School is different from other schools in two important ways: 'it is more relaxed', he says, 'and you can "joke around" with the teachers'; secondly, SWS teachers 'explain a little more' than other teachers do.

Much the same kind of social relations exist between students and teachers at Sierra Mountain. School staff very consciously attempt to extend their role to draw students into close relationships. One of the teachers described his approach as follows:

> I tend to treat the kids with respect, and come straight across with them. I have expectations of what their behavior should be and what their achievement should be in my classes, and I put that out without any conditions to my respect, other than respect be returned. I think that I put out affection for these kids. I feel real protective of them. They're my kids. I think that helps. Treating the kids with the feeling that they are your kids, the kids sense that. They sense that I care about them, what happens to them.

Teacher perceptions that students sense this extension of concern are well-founded. Jean, a student at Sierra Mountain, concurs: 'If you need to talk about [something] they'll take you aside and they'll help you, whatever it is, whether it's school problems, problems in that class, or family problems'.

Alex, another student at Sierra Mountain, indicates that the sense of caring displayed by teachers is reciprocated by students as concern for the school in general.

> When ... students see other students doing something wrong, they tell them. 'Say, hey, you know, knock it off, you really shouldn't be doing that.' Like I've seen people smoking pot in the bathroom, and I just tell them to not do that. That's how it is. The students are really pretty much responsible for things that happen at the school. ... And it's our responsibility to try to keep people from doing stuff. Because really they [teachers] can't keep 'em from doing it, but the students can.

This personal identification with the goals and welfare of the school is rare among students, particularly among those labeled at risk. Yet evidence of such affiliation was not uncommon at the schools we studied. At Croom, for example, school membership was clearly in evidence when a student guide reminded a visitor to use the walkways rather than cutting across the well-groomed lawns. All groundskeeping and building maintenance were done by students as part of their vocational training, and the students were proud of their accomplishments.

In all of the schools, we found young people willing to become school members, but many had been overwhelmed by experiences in large comprehensive high schools. Some were afraid for their physical safety, others found the impersonal adult relationships of a big school too alienating. Course failures and other school problems began to accumulate and these students were unable to develop the coping strategies that would produce survival and success. Other students had searched in vain for a niche in their traditional school where they could achieve, establish an identity and have hope for the future. Such experiences understandably led students to feel alienated from the school. With very few exceptions, the fourteen schools in the study recognized these conditions and responded by working actively to establish membership for students.

School Membership: Theory and Research

Earlier research on at-risk students and programs laid the groundwork for our findings about school membership (Wehlage, Stone and Kliebard, 1980; Wehlage, 1983; Wehlage, Rutter and Turnbaugh, 1987). These studies examined both comprehensive schools and alternatives in an effort to understand why students either dropped out or stayed in school. One finding of this research identified the importance of social bonds that connect the student to the school. During the course of the current study we have refined our understanding of this process and have come to recognize that social bonds to the school are an essential element of our definition of school membership for all students.

The term *social bonding* describes a social-psychological state or outcome in which a student is attached, committed, involved and has belief in the norms, activities and people of an institution (Hirschi, 1969). A student is socially bonded to the extent that he or she is attached to adults and peers, committed to the norms of the school, involved in school activities and has belief in the legitimacy and efficacy of the institution. School membership requires students to meet these four conditions of social bonding.

Attachment refers to social and emotional ties to others. It is best expressed when an individual cares about what other people think and expect. He or she feels a personal stake in meeting the expectations of others and conforming to the norms of 'good' and 'proper' behavior as defined in a particular social setting. If attachment to individuals is missing or weak, one can act without regard for the feelings and expectations of others. According to our theory, this attachment is reciprocal. When students have low attachment to teachers and administrators, they do not care what these people think about them, especially as students. In reciprocation, dropouts perceive that these adults do not care about them. Under these conditions, it is easy to feel rejected by the school and, in turn, to justify rejecting the school.

Commitment is the second element of social bonding. Whereas attachment emphasized the emotional, commitment emphasizes the rational side of participation in any social institution. Commitment stems from a more or less rational calculation of what one must do to achieve goals; in this context, one remains with an institution because it is the pragmatic thing to do. The potential dropout weighs the costs and benefits of staying or withdrawing from the institution. For the committed student, remaining in the school to graduation is essential for achieving internalized goals. It may be necessary to put up with demands that are unattractive, such as meeting the expectations and requirements of courses that are not interesting. However, commitment is expressed through conformity to school rules and demands because continued participation now and in the future provides rewards.

Commitment may be difficult to engender among those who see a bleak future for themselves even if they graduate, or for those who see the route to success in commitment to some other institution or way of life. For the uncommitted student, such as the dropout, calculation results in a conclusion that conformity to school demands does not yield a worthwhile pay-off.

The third bonding element is *involvement*. Individuals involved in activities of an institution are likely to view them as legitimate and valuable. Moreover, if their time is absorbed by institutional activities, it is less likely they will have the time and opportunity to engage in activities that compete for their allegiance. Applied to students, involvement means engagement in school activities. Engagement in academic activities is the first order of involvement, but if an individual's academic success has been limited, it may be necessary to rely on any school-sponsored activities in order to sustain student involvement or engagement.

If school activities fail to engender involvement, or what we call engagement, students drop out psychologically, as evidenced by their passivity and boredom. Leaving school — dropping out in a literal sense — is the next reasonable step on the continuum. Thus, schools must be sensitive to the relative involvement or engagement they can achieve in comparison with other attractive activities. Jobs, peer groups, gangs and street crime may develop greater involvement than does the school. This is especially a problem if the range of activities in school is relatively small, an elite group of students appears to dominate these activities, and success is awarded to a few.

The fourth element, in social bonding, and the bedrock of our theory, is *belief*. It is difficult to be attached, committed and involved if one does not have faith in the institution. If there is no belief in the legitimacy or efficacy of an institution, social bonding ultimately fails. For schools, it is axiomatic that if students believe that getting an education is neither a goal to which they can aspire nor one which will have some pay-off, bonding to the institution will be weak or non-existent. Students clearly differ in their beliefs about the value of school and its potential rewards. For example, one student may see schooling as a path out of poverty, while another chooses highly profitable but illegal street activities as the best means of escape. It is the dropout who questions the efficacy of schooling because it does not appear to lead to his or her valued goals. Generally, there is evidence that even those students who drop out of high school initially enrolled believing in the legitimacy and efficacy of education and expecting to graduate (Wehlage and Rutter, 1986).

Hirschi, in developing his social bonding theory, was concerned primarily about the need to establish social bonds between juvenile delinquents and the norms of conventional society. Bonding, in the context of delinquency, assumes that conventional social norms, institutions and the practices they represent are essentially healthy. Social bonding is achieved when individuals alter their behavior to conform to established norms and institutional requirements. These norms and institutional requirements are not questioned or challenged.

Our concern with at-risk students is very different from this, but the concept of social bonding is useful in providing substance to our definition of school membership. We see social bonding somewhat differently when it is applied to schools because existing norms and practices of some schools are, in fact, questionable when it comes to at-risk youth. As pointed out in chapter 2, some school policies and practices contribute to the problems of at-risk students by inhibiting their development of bonds to the school. The goal of school membership does not suggest that all students in conflict with the norms of public schooling are socially deficient and must change their ways to conform to the demands of the institution. Thus, while it embodies the concept of social bonding, school membership conveys a greater degree of reciprocity between students and school than does the classic definition of the term.

If an individual is to become socially bonded to school, presumably all aspects of the bonding process must be activated. Theory, however, specifies no explicit directives for obtaining this goal, nor does it articulate any logic or order to attaining bonding's four elements. Thus, the question remains: What is the process by which social bonding occurs? What can schools do to stimulate the bondedness inherent in our definition of school membership?

Reciprocity and Membership

Membership for students is established through a reciprocal relationship between them and the adults who represent the institution. In describing membership as it develops in schools, there is a need to capture the social relations between students and adults that exist in the formal and informal life of the institution. Therefore, in addition to identifying and measuring the indicators of social bonding, it is necessary to identify the process through which bonding occurs. Our concept of school membership involves defining and describing the ways in which students and schools interact to overcome the impediments to bonding.

The process of promoting and acquiring school membership requires reciprocity in which the student and the school exchange commitments. Thus, school membership is promoted by the following adult practices: (i) active efforts to create positive and respectful relations between adults and students; (ii) communication of concern about and direct help to individuals with their personal problems; (iii) active help in meeting institutional standards of success and competence; and (iv) active help in identifying a student's place in society based on a link between self, school and one's future. In exchange for this energetic and active commitment from the institution, students are to make a reciprocal commitment that involves: (i) behaviors that are positive and respectful toward adults and peers; and (ii) educational engagement, i.e. a level of mental and physical effort in school tasks that makes their own achievement likely and makes the commitment of adults rewarding.

Reciprocal relations not only require an exchange of commitments and supporting behaviors, but also imply corresponding beliefs about the legitimacy and efficacy of the institution and the student. If, for example, there is a widely-held belief among adults that students are incompetent to engage in institutional activities and reach institutional goals, commitment by the school will be weak or non-existent. Conversely, if students believe that school activities and goals are inappropriate or unrewarding, then student commitment will be weak. In either case, school membership is impaired.

From an educator's perspective, it is important to develop a theory of action that will foster these reciprocal relations. How can schools provide an environment that will trigger the social bonding process? During this study, we became aware of work on college dropouts that paralleled our own, and we incorporated some of its aspects into our analysis. Tinto (1987) analyzes early college leavers and describes the process of becoming a college dropout in terms similar to our findings about high school dropouts. For example, he concludes that the great majority of early college leavers do so voluntarily rather than because of dismissal, and that this voluntary withdrawal is associated with weak academic and social integration. This conclusion parallels our description of weak social bonding and academic engagement among adolescents.

Tinto's research on early college departure is significant in that he describes and labels the process by which students are drawn into institutional membership. The process we call social bonding to the institution, he describes as one in which the college supports students by extending commitment to them. From our perspective, the most important contribution of Tinto's work is his elaboration of a theory of institutional support that attracts and sustains membership. In light of this theory, our concept of school membership has been expanded to include the process by which institutional support produces social bonding.

According to Tinto, the causes of early departure from college are both individual and institutional. Individually, the roots of college departure are grounded in the strength of a person's 'intention and commitment' to acquire a college education, dispositions that are in place when the student enters college. They are, however, strengthened or weakened during the college experience primarily by the student's interaction with the institution. Tinto argues that voluntary departure from college results more from institutional experiences with the college than from prior experiences, preparation or the strength of individual dispositions.

Our understanding of high school dropouts suggests a similar pattern of interaction. Research on the practices of some comprehensive high schools and the testimony of students in our study indicate that schools may withhold the kind of commitment to students crucial to their membership and retention. This lack of commitment often is explained in terms of the family backgrounds, personal problems and anti-school behaviors these adolescents display. Students with certain personal or background characteristics may be seen as unworthy or at least very unlikely to benefit from teachers' efforts; these students are viewed as 'damaged', and cannot benefit from school. Thus, certain personal and background characteristics may make it difficult for some schools to extend themselves to specific students. However the alternative schools we studied often were able to respond constructively to these same youths in spite of their family, personal and school problems. The active commitment of these alternative schools initiated reciprocity between the institution and the students. The response from students was a sense of membership.

Impediments to School Membership

To understand more clearly why many at-risk students fail to experience this crucial sense of school membership, we introduce a set of concepts borrowed from Tinto to identify four common impediments to school membership: *adjustment*, *difficulty*, *incongruence*, and *isolation*.

These terms identify ways in which students are prevented from becoming school members and suggest by implication some constructive responses the institution can make to young people who have been unsuccessful in school.

These terms are useful in our analysis of the process by which students experience school membership in that they provide a way of identifying key impediments to bonding and school membership; they help capture the quality of institutional life by conveying the reciprocal and interactional nature of students' experiences with school; and, finally, they suggest a process by which schools can take an active role in responding to at-risk students to prevent them from dropping out.

Adjustment

Adjustment to school is a major precursor to school membership. The required transition from middle or junior high school to high school means that new demands are placed on students in a larger, more impersonal setting. New peer groups are encountered and the social distance between one group and another may be considerable. Contact with an increased number of adults is required, but these educators often have varying standards and expectations for school work and behavior. Teaching methods often are different from those to which students were exposed in middle school. Teachers lecture more or expect more independent work, and they spend less time checking on student progress or mastery of material. Academic failure and alienation from the institution may result if students fail to adjust to these conditions.

The personal relationships between students and teachers are different in the high school. Many teachers in comprehensive high schools believe it is important to create social distance between themselves and their students as a means of maintaining discipline and helping students to become more independent, responsible and mature. This social distancing is a major source of strain for many students. At-risk students, in particular, need a more personal and supportive relationship with adults than high school typically provides. While the adjustment problem appears to be especially crucial during the transition year from junior to senior high for many of the young people in our study, it was a continuing problem that affected the quality of their ongoing school experience.

A number of schools we studied recognized the adjustment

problem and devised specific and consistent strategies for dealing with it. At the Wayne Enrichment Center (WEC) in Indianapolis, for example, 'family' meetings are held each week to address the problems of adjustment students experience throughout the year. The term 'family' is used to convey emotional closeness and concern for one another; the meetings help to foster a supportive environment and open discussion of students' problems.

The first family meeting in the Fall is devoted to the essential task of learning names; all teachers and students are expected to know one another's names. Some meetings are devoted to solving peer group problems, such as conflicts between individuals. Others are held to clarify and remind students of the 'ABCs of WEC'. 'A' stands for attendance; the attendance rules are spelled out and reiterated from time to time. If a student is to be absent for any reason, he or she must call the school *before* the fact. 'B' stands for behavior; all students must sign an agreement upon admission to the school that they will abide by the school's code of conduct. 'C' stands for credit; almost all of the students are credit deficient. Students must accumulate credits to remain in WEC.

The 'family' meeting helps to communicate an explicit set of strategies and guidelines designed to assist students towards their goal of graduation. Students understand that their continued enrollment at WEC is predicated upon their compliance with specified rules and their completion of a predetermined amount of work each semester. This rather basic institutional mechanism is an example of the way WEC actively seeks to help students adjust. It was, in part, through this help in adjusting that students came to be members of the school and to succeed within its institutional parameters.

Another example of the adjustment process comes from Croom Vocational High School. One of the first things a prospective student sees at Croom is a large brightly colored message painted on the wall near the Principal's office: 'Welcome to Success'. This phrase represents the staff's commitment to make Croom a place in which students will experience school success, perhaps for the first time in their young lives.

In the intake interview just prior to a new student's first day of classes, the Principal reiterates the school's motto:

Do you see these words? What do they mean to you? Do you know that you were picked from a list of applicants? Not everyone gets to go here! Do you think you're a winner? You are, and you can continue to be, if you really want to. What grade are you in, ninth? How long have you been in ninth grade? You know what? As of today, you are a sophomore! Let's look at your grades. Are these good grades? You know, we really don't care about these grades; those days are over. See this empty file folder? This is your record at Croom. What you do from now on will go in this record. You can make this record whatever you want it to be. You get a fresh start here.

This experience with the Principal is extraordinary for most students. For the more than 100 students on the Croom campus, this brief but important experience is part of a ritual of initiation they all share. Their arrival at Croom is both a symbolic and an academic new beginning. A slate clean of past academic failures and a warm welcome by the school's highest authority create a positive and lasting impression on students. Although the process of adjusting to a new environment still may be difficult, some of the negative experiences associated with school are immediately alleviated by the welcoming tone and 'new beginning' message of the interview ritual.

Difficulty

Difficulty in academic matters is a useful way of explaining one cause of academic failure. Although we found literal inability to do the work a relatively rare characteristic of at-risk students, it is the case that increased time and more intensive tutoring were required for many. For some students, the issue has more to do with difficulty in sustaining interest and effort. In talking about their experiences in comprehensive high schools, students complained that teachers made learning 'dull, boring and stupid'. The educational situation students complained most about was the ubiquitous 'lecture-discussion' based on reading assignments.

Academic success in school work is essential if students are to become socially bonded to school. Many at-risk students have difficulty mastering certain kinds of school work and need special help from teachers. Student testimony suggests, however, that some schools consider it their task to determine who can successfully complete difficult work with minimal help. This approach creates winners and losers, performs a sorting function for society, and fosters or exacerbates a difficulty issue for some students, contributing in a major way to their at-risk status.

Many successful interventions designed for dropout prevention offer special courses and pedagogy in an effort to keep students on track in accumulating credits for graduation, and to provide a clearer sense of progress toward stated goals. One of the most frequently used strategies involves breaking courses into shorter units. A semester, or even a quarter, is often too long for students to keep their bearings, and if personal or family problems arise that distract them, an entire semester's credits for one or more courses can be lost. Other strategies include individualized learning packets and cooperative or experiential learning.

Examples of innovative efforts are as numerous as the schools we studied. Sierra Mountain, for example, instituted the '5-1-5' schedule, which breaks the year into seven five-week units, each followed by a week of vacation. While students eventually accumulate the same total in-class hours, these shorter units are viewed as more manageable and compact, thereby helping students attend to the goals and requirements of their courses. Orr Community Academy in Chicago allows students to focus on 'two majors at a time'. Each semester, student time is focused on only two of the four traditional core subjects — math, science, English and social studies. The two majors strategy doubles the number of hours spent on a given subject over half as many weeks and avoids the problem of competing demands from four courses taken simultaneously.

At Sierra Mountain, credit is awarded on the basis of work completed. Students do not fail if they do not turn in all the assigned work during a grading period; they simply earn fewer fractional credits. Likewise, students wishing to earn more than the normal amount of credit for a course can make up lost ground by completing extra-credit assignments. Those in need of remediation can take courses in which grading is based on their improvement and effort, not on the basis of a comparison of their work with that of others. Finally, California has a state-wide program of independent study that allows both regular students and returning adults to acquire credits leading to graduation, an option used by a number of students at Sierra Mountain.

Frequent monitoring of students' academic progress is another strategy used to overcome the difficulty problem in many schools. Daily, weekly or monthly monitoring provides regular feedback on the quality and quantity of student performance. In addition to monitoring by teachers and administrators, a great deal of effort is exerted to encourage students to check their own progress. At WEC, for example, students sign off after each assignment is completed. A personal planning sheet helps individual students track their own progress toward graduation and informs them as to which requirements they have yet to meet. A large calendar posted in a central location keeps students informed as to the number of school days left in which to earn credits. This reminder allows students to monitor their own status and invites them to take responsibility for their own success. WEC teachers consider this a way to avoid 'helpless dependency' that some students display when they rely on continuous adult supervision.

We found that the fourteen schools in our study shared an assumption that most students who failed in traditional high school settings could be successful. These schools adopted a two-pronged approach: students must be helped to adjust to school demands, and, equally important, schools must adjust to students' needs. In all cases, adjustment was aimed primarily at sustaining student effort. With sustained effort, students perceived that they could achieve academically. Most students want to achieve and school membership is contingent upon their demonstrating academic competence to themselves and others.

Incongruence

While incongruence is a more ambiguous term than adjustment or difficulty, we find it captures an important dimension of our data about at-risk students. Applied to schools, incongruence describes the personal and social match between the student and the institution. The quality of that match is reflected in answers to several questions that students implicitly ask about how well they fit into the school: Who am I? Where am I going in the future? How does this school fit into my self-concept and my goals? These questions, which arise out of the family and social background of youth, must be evaluated in the context of family and peer values and experiences.

Incongruence, which applies most clearly to youth from lower socioeconomic status backgrounds, is concerned with the match or perception of fit between the student and the institution. This match is based on the students' understanding of their own values, experiences and projected future; elements of this perception include personal style, social class orientations and racial and ethnic values. The personal and social background of the student can produce a conception of self and the future that seems at odds with the goals and rewards of the school. If there are no opportunities for success in schools consistent with the goals of non-academically inclined students, school will be perceived as incongruent and meaningless.

Incongruence between students and a school affects all who identify themselves as outside the mainstream in some way. Many of the students we interviewed saw themselves as 'outsiders'. Some were 'punkers', while others identified themselves with 'heavy metal' musicians, and still others were simply social outcasts because of physical or personality characteristics. In some instances, race and ethnicity made students 'outsiders'. In general, however, to the extent school represents mainstream middle-class culture, the problem of congruence is most universally associated with youth from lower social-class backgrounds. Fitting into the middle-class value structure of a school is a major issue for many young people.

Most schools, mainstream or otherwise, tend to acquire their own identity based on the peer group that dominates. A school may be run by 'jocks' or middle-class youth, for example, or a school may be known as a 'tough place', characterized by fights and bullying. These labels raise questions about the kind of school an individual student is attending and whether he or she 'fits in'. In addition, students' judgments about the kinds of people valued at a school depend to a large degree on their perceptions of the adults in control. Some schools are seen as places where the teachers and administrators favor the 'brains' or the 'rich and populars'. Students implicitly question how closely they match this favored image.

The Media Academy, an inner-city school serving poor black and Hispanic youth, has made great progress toward creating social and academic congruence with its students. At the Academy, students 'major' in print and electronic media for three years. Prior to enrollment, many students indicate little interest in higher education, and their knowledge of career opportunities is limited. Given the restricted life experiences of many of its students, a program priority is to introduce these youth to the world of the mass media and to a set of opportunities for future work and education that otherwise would escape their attention. Through a network of contacts with professionals in the field, students are introduced to a wide variety of media work. More than thirty professionals, a number of them black or Hispanic, have provided access to their businesses and to their own careers to students of the Media Academy. Students visit the production facilities of newspapers, radio and television. They receive instruction from reporters and cartoonists. They use their new skills to produce an award-winning school newspaper and a locally distributed Spanish/

English-language paper. They also produce public service announcements for radio and television.

The Media Academy is one example of how the apparent incongruence between school and poor black and Hispanic youths has been reshaped into congruence. For the most part, these youths did not readily recognize the connection between school and their own sense of self and their expectations for the future. Overcoming incongruence requires an institutional commitment to provide students with in-depth experience directed by a relatively limited number of adults who can concentrate on the skills, knowledge and dispositions these youths must master for success. Today, many of the students at the Media Academy have developed a sense of confidence in their ability to write well and this has become part of their perception of themselves. The school has created a context in which reading, writing, speaking and thinking critically about issues makes sense. Moreover, the program actively accommodates students without weakening its focus on its central task — which is to teach academics. In turn, this accommodation creates a more congruent match between students and the institution and fosters school membership.

Our study revealed several examples of ways schools are successfully addressing the problem of incongruence. At NA-WAY-EE (Center School) in Minneapolis, where all of the students are Native Americans, the incongruence between students' cultural values and customs and the practices of conventional school is particularly acute. In response, the school takes active steps to integrate its students cultural norms and traditions into every aspect of its approach and activities. Early each Fall, the school hosts a pipe ceremony for all of its students. An elder or a well-known American Indian leader is invited to perform the ceremony and to speak to the student body. Ojibwa is spoken during the ceremony, as is English. At least once during the school year students are invited to participate in a powwow on a reservation. This weekend-long activity enables students to reintegrate themselves into their community and their extended family in an ethnic and spiritual activity. At NA-WAY-EE Native American identity and culture are overarching themes of much of the curriculum. For example, mainstream values are discussed and compared with Native American values and traditions, not with a view to changing the students but as a means of increasing their awareness of their own and others' perspectives. Even as it works to foster in its students a greater respect for and understanding of their own heritage, NA-WAY-EE simultaneously works to incorporate these youths into the broader society, especially in the world of work or in post-secondary education. The school sees this integration or assimilation as an *additive* process, in contrast to the *subtractive* assimilation that many conventional schools promote. This approach distinguishes NA-WAY-EE in a crucial way because many Native Americans perceive that mainstream schools attempt to strip away Indian values, culture, language and tradition. For American Indian students who are struggling with questions of self-identity, NA-WAY-EE provides social congruence in a safe, comfortable environment through a curriculum and pedagogy sensitive to the cultural background of its students.

In similar fashion, the curriculum at the Minneapolis Street Academy focuses on the black experience in America. Many of the materials used in social studies and English classes are from the works of black authors, and the school's library has an adequate, if not outstanding, collection of these materials. In addition, the school hosts special activities, such as 'Black Heritage Night' celebrated in a neighborhood church. This celebration included dinner, a full program of songs, poetry readings of black authors presented by students, a 'rap' by two Street Academy students, a keynote address by a former teacher, and a slide show tribute to Paul Robeson, one of America's great black singers and an outspoken critic of, and activist against, discrimination long before the civil rights movement. About 250 persons attended, including many parents of students and several civic and political leaders.

Black identity is a major concern for many Street Academy students. Special activities, in conjunction with frequent class discussions, help to bridge the gap students perceive between the world in which they live everyday and the daily routines and curriculum of the school.

Loring-Nicollet offers another example of how schools deal with the issue of incongruity. Most of its students possess all the academic skills required for school success, but most of these youths are 'punkers', alienated from conventional schools and to some extent from mainstream society. The school accommodates this unconventionality and cynicism by incorporating them into the curriculum. School staff encourage students to reflect on their values, experiences and circumstances. Rather than exerting pressure to eliminate students' counter-culture identities, the school channels their insights and abilities into political participation and constructive social activities. To nurture their sense of social responsibility, students are required to clean up the building and grounds on a regular basis and to help with repairs and routine maintenance.

The approach to incongruence is markedly different at Croom Vocational High School. Croom students fare poorly in conventional high schools for many reasons, not the least of which is that most fail to see any connection between school and life after school. For most Croom students, low academic performance coupled with a long history of school failure have resulted in low self-esteem and a sense that school offers little in terms of immediate or future rewards. The staff work hard to combat these perceptions by tying school attendance to the very real possibility of employment in the local job market. Students lack fundamental work-related skills as well as work experience, and both are provided. A full-time internship is the culminating experience for students earning vocational certification. The internship guarantees entry into the labor market if students choose to stay in the job.

At the Wayne Enrichment Center, staff make an explicit attempt to connect the experience of school to the workplace. When students arrive at WEC, they punch in at a time clock. Fridays begin with a family meeting. Both events are significant, reflecting two metaphors that guide the WEC program: workplace and family. The workplace metaphor is evident throughout the day. Promptness and regular attendance are stressed. Five tardies equal an absence and five absences during a semester may result in a student being 'fired'. Serious illness or pregnancy are the only acceptable excuses for absence. Even academic success will not save a student from being 'fired' if his or her absences exceed the limit.

Isolation

Isolation, the fourth impediment to school membership, refers to academic and social experiences. School membership requires that students have frequent and high-quality interaction with adults. Of course, isolation from their peers can be troubling to students, but equally serious is isolation from adults, especially as the incidence of family stress and single-parent homes increases. As other social institutions that traditionally provided valuable adult-adolescent contact — church, voluntary organizations — decline in their influence, the school becomes the one place where sustained adult relations can occur.

In explaining early college departure, Tinto identified isolation as one of the most powerful predictors. Of great importance in student persistence is the amount and warmth of faculty-student interaction *outside* the classroom. This finding contributes to his claim that what happens after a student enters college is far more important than what occurred before. The isolation factor is applicable to secondary school student-teacher relations as well. We found that students who had persistent conflicts with adults or who found no teacher with whom to establish a personal relationship were at risk of dropping out. This was true of students in both alternative and comprehensive schools.

One of the comments students made most frequently in making judgements about their school can be paraphrased in this way: 'This school is better because the teachers here care about me'. This caring attitude is revealed in different ways, but it is always communicated by active and demonstrated interest on the part of adults for the welfare of students.

The staff at Alcott Alternative Junior High recognize that one of their first responsibilities is to reach out to students and prevent them from remaining isolated. Most of these young people come to Alcott with a long list of home and personal problems, as well as a history of academic failure. Doug is a typical example. His parents are divorced. He lives with his mother during the week and his father on weekends. He came to Alcott extremely shy and was described by Alcott's Principal, Mrs. Guttierez, as a 'school phobic'. He attended another junior high for a while, but in his own words, 'I just didn't fit in'. In contrast, Doug has made friends with peers and teachers at Alcott. Through the help of a teacher, Doug became interested in flying through the Explorer Scouts. He is now a 'flying buff' who spends weekends with a group that is dismantling and reconstructing an old plane. These associations and activities, according to Doug, were inconceivable when he entered Alcott two years earlier.

We found that isolation was countered when adults expressed explicit interest about a student's academic or personal matters. This interest was seen as an expression of support, and it thereby contributed to a more general belief that all individuals are important and worthy of adult attention. Adult interest sometimes took the form of counseling or mentoring. Teachers, for example, struck up conversations with particular students in an effort to coach them, to help them think through some of the choices that lie ahead. This attention was of key importance in eroding the sense of isolation that many adolescents experience.

Most youth are unable to access and use social services when they need them. In such instances, the adults in the school are the most likely sources of advice and counsel. Close contact with caring, supportive adults is crucial to students avoiding isolation as they face a host of day-to-day decisions. This close adult supervision is an expression of interest and contributes to students' sense of membership in a school.

Although many informal contacts between teachers and students were spontaneous and unplanned, schools formally encouraged such interaction as part of the everyday activities of the institution. Opportunities for interaction were built into the curriculum and school schedule, and informal counseling or advising went on continually in an effort to eradicate the barriers that isolate students from teachers/staff and from other students.

Examples of how some schools worked to combat student isolation vary somewhat, depending on the nature of the student population and of the program itself. For example, at New Futures School, which serves pregnant and mothering teens, the student culture can be a fragmented one. Students come from many different areas of the county and many stay only through a single academic year. Most of the girls don't know anyone in the program when they arrive, and there is no opportunity for extra-curricular activities. In addition, some of the curriculum was individualized rather than taught in a group format.

The staff of New Futures combats isolation in a number of ways. 'Ice-breaking' activities are scheduled for new students. Tours of the school, introductions in classes, and orientation sessions to school facilities all fostered students' feelings of ease with teachers, peers and the physical facilities. Special activities are designed to keep students in social contact with peers and staff, including a Christmas party, an awards assembly, a spring picnic and a trip to the zoo.

The New Futures staff is chosen carefully to provide the kind of adult interaction these girls need. Each staff member is committed to helping the girls turn what may seem like a personal handicap into an opportunity for growth and maturity. Staff members are encouraged to personalize their relationships with students. Counseling, formal and informal, has become a major component of the New Futures program, and nurses on the school staff are in frequent contact with the students. Courses that stress 'parenting' skills provide one of the best opportunities for adult-student dialogue about matters the girls consider significant, and practical training in the day-care facilities has created another such opportunity. Clearly, New Futures has developed an institutional identity and purpose that exceeds helping students continue their coursework toward graduation.

Summary

This chapter has introduced the initial elements of a theory of dropout prevention. This theory applies the concept of school membership to identify a basic student need and outcome that is fundamental to other school goals. School membership is a goal defined in terms of social bonding criteria: attachment, commitment, involvement and belief. At-risk students need schools that deliberately act in ways to show their commitment to helping them overcome the impediments to membership. This active commitment begins with an assumption of reciprocity between adults and students and requires warm personal relations between them.

The concept of school membership helps interpret and explain much of the data about social relations gathered during our study of fourteen schools. School membership is viewed as an intermediate goal for students, the foundation for other goals involving academic achievement and outcomes concerning personal and social development into productive adults. Membership is particularly important for those students who have histories of school failure and who lack the support of strong homes and communities outside the school.

In examining the impetus for, and impediments to, students' social bonding and ultimate school membership, we focused primarily on the needs and experiences of at-risk youth. But any full discussion of educational issues must concurrently consider the professional culture and school climate as they affect teachers. Chapter 6 shifts focus to examine teacher culture and school structure as they impact on programs for at-risk youth.

Chapter 6:
Teacher Culture and School Structure

While this study focused primarily on students and the school programs serving them, we inevitably attended to the characteristics of teachers and the school environment supporting their work with at-risk students. The professional culture and the school climate established by educators were necessarily important to us. In particular, we assumed the set of cultural norms and practices governing educators' relationships with students would be different from some of those found in traditional secondary schools. We also assumed these differences would be crucial with respect to student efforts in school and their responses to teachers.

This chapter presents data about the professional culture established by teachers in the fourteen schools. Those teachers successful in bringing about the social bonding of students practiced their profession based on certain beliefs about students and how best to relate to them. This clear linkage between educators' professional culture and students' school membership merits discussion.

During our study, we attended to conditions promoting teachers' sense of ownership of their school and work, along with shared values, beliefs and activities contributing to a sense of community among adults. We believe that good schools for students will have to be good schools for teachers, if the institution is to sustain its efforts on behalf of disadvantaged youth.

Beyond the subjectivity of professional beliefs and values, however, there are more objective conditions of schools affecting teacher and student behavior. These are the structural and organizational characteristics constraining peoples' choices and actions. Again, we assumed certain school conditions — size, autonomy, degree of teacher self-governance — would either enable or inhibit teacher effectiveness with at-risk students.

Teacher Culture: Beliefs and Behaviors

In educating at-risk students, schools must first address the impediments to their school membership and engagement. Chapter 5 documented strategies that have been successful in helping students to
overcome these impediments and argued that the institution must be
proactive in using them. In such a proactive institutional culture, adults
must share certain beliefs and values about students and their education.
These shared beliefs and values confirm the potential of students and the
obligations of teachers to be successful in their efforts to educate them.

The most fundamental belief among the professionals we studied
was that teacher-student interactions should be governed by reciprocity, a relationship we have identified as integral to school membership. Reciprocity requires both parties to engage in respectful relations,
and in the education of at-risk students, it requires educators to take the
initiative in helping students overcome impediments to social bonding
and membership.

In addition, there are four teacher beliefs and/or values, accompanied by corresponding sets of behaviors, that together constitute a
positive teacher culture facilitating membership and engagement for
students. These beliefs are: teachers accept personal *accountability* for
student success; they believe in practicing an *extended teacher role*; they
accept the need to be *persistent* with students who are not ideal pupils;
they *express a sense of optimism* that all students can learn if one builds
upon their strengths rather than their weaknesses.

Accountability for Student Success

In a positive teacher culture, individual educators believe they are
personally accountable for the success of each student. This self-
imposed accountability means that teachers accept responsibility for
helping each student overcome impediments to success. This belief
inheres a broad obligation to promote academic success along with
personal and social competence.

Carla is a case in point. Carla entered Alcott Alternative Learning
Center at mid-year after being expelled from another junior high for
throwing a book at a teacher. She had a reputation for moodiness,
'crazy' behavior and occasional violence against students and teachers.
Carla's mannerisms and style of dress were very masculine and she
seemed to take pleasure in intimidating younger and smaller students.

As a result, she was systematically ignored by her peers. She was also socially awkward with adults, exhibiting a reluctance or inability to engage in conversation.

Nevertheless, in a briefing session with her teachers, the school counselor reported that Carla probably was academically able, even though her grades did not reflect academic achievement in the past. The counselor told Jan Reed, an English teacher, that Carla was an avid mystery reader. Reed immediately saw this as a possible entree. She began to make casual remarks about interesting mysteries she had read. Carla began to stop after class to talk about particular characters or authors they knew in common. Eventually, these brief exchanges led to longer discussions, some of which provided insights into her anti-social behavior. For example, Carla reported that she was adopted and that she perceived that her parents seemed to 'make a big deal out of it' to other people.

Reed's efforts with Carla began to pay off over the course of the semester. As the school spelling bee approached, Reed encouraged her to enter and offered to coach her. Carla entered and was the school champion.

Despite this success, Carla was not always a likeable or responsive individual. She frustrated her teachers by repeatedly using profanity in class and on one occasion, she threw a book across the room after becoming upset about an assignment given by a teacher. On several occasions she became withdrawn and refused to do any school work. Nevertheless, by the end of the school year, one of our research staff noted a rather remarkable transformation. Carla regularly completed her academic work and was socially more integrated into the school. In an interview, Carla conveyed this notable change in status and attitude by commenting that she wished there were an Alcott summer school because she enjoyed the teachers so much. Carla's case indicates concretely that teacher acceptance of accountability for even difficult students is essential if they are to achieve school and personal success.

Extended Role for Teachers

Teachers who act on their belief in personal accountability often must go beyond the standard set of required teacher activities. In doing so, they practice what we call 'extended role'. They are willing to do more than impart the subject matter they officially have been hired to teach.

Reed was willing to extend herself as an informal counselor, to seek contact with a student who was obviously troubled and in need of attention. She saw her job as more than conveying subject matter; in fact, the job of conveying subject matter could not proceed with much hope of success unless the shell of defensiveness could be penetrated and anti-social behavior reduced. Reed is typical of many of the teachers we observed in her willingness to reach out to students, to bring them into a setting in which adult influence was possible.

Persistence With Students

Persistence with those who are not ideal students is clearly evidenced in the case involving Carla. Profanity, temper tantrums or book throwing individually constitute grounds for suspension or even expulsion at many schools. Many teachers would, with some justification, seek the student's removal from class or even the school, claiming they are not obligated to accept such behavior. They might also claim, again with some logic, that other students have the right to attend class without the disruptions and annoyances caused by students like Carla.

However, one of the characteristics exhibited by teachers we studied was a strong sense of tolerance for young people. Teachers tended to be less quickly offended by student behavior that their colleagues in more traditional schools might see as personally insulting or challenging to their authority. Also, these teachers recognized in their students' undesirable behavior, not so much evidence of defective character but rather the expression of accumulated frustrations and disadvantaged backgrounds. Student misbehavior called not for retribution, but rather for understanding, guidance in appropriate behaviors and a chance to succeed where failure had dominated.

Optimism About Student Potential

Finally, there was a sense of optimism about students' potential for learning. Throughout our discussions, teachers repeatedly expressed their conviction that, despite many students' discouraging records of failure, the right kind of environment and opportunities could stimulate the innate potential buried within each individual. To act on this belief involved the accountability, extended role and persistence already described, but it was best facilitated by the strategy of building on students' strengths rather than focusing too often on their deficits and weaknesses.

This strategy made remediation of academic skills and knowledge far less of a priority for many teachers than one would imagine in light of the records of their students. With Carla, Reed chose to build on her interest in mysteries and her strong reading ability. Efforts to alter her anti-social behavior were more indirect and subtle; behavior modification occurred as a by-product of increased academic success and gradually more stable and rewarding personal relationships with Reed and other teachers.

Literature on effective schools often cites the need for staff to hold 'high expectations' of students. While this has a certain intuitive appeal, it usually is unclear as to what this means in terms of adult beliefs or behaviors. In the schools we studied, the term 'high expectations' inheres a reciprocity, that is, it includes implicit reference to teacher attitudes and behaviors regarding students, as well as expectations for student performance and behavior. The beliefs and behaviors described in this chapter as a positive teacher culture define what we mean by high expectations for teachers. In other words, they are expected to have a strong sense of accountability for student success, be willing to practice an extended role, be persistent with those who are less than ideal students, and hold a belief that students can learn, especially if one builds on their strengths.

School Ownership for Teachers

Most of the fourteen schools we studied shared a similar teacher culture in terms of beliefs and behaviors toward students. A second set of values, beliefs and actions contributed to a common school culture affecting schools as a workplace for teachers. This part of the culture was directed at creating control and ownership of the school, making it a desirable place to teach. Three interdependent elements comprise this dimension of teacher culture: educational entrepreneurship, self-governance and professional collegiality. In day-to-day affairs of the school, these elements intermingle, but we separate them here for purpose of analysis.

Educational Entrepreneurship

One of the most important insights developed from our study of the fourteen schools is the extent to which they provide a context for educational entrepreneurship. Webster's dictionary defines 'entrepreneur' as 'one who organizes, manages, and assumes the risks of a business or enterprise'. Clearly, these schools were not business ventures, but they did require risk taking by individuals. These schools were, and are, vulnerable; they are ventures that can fail, or at least be eliminated by local school districts. Each of the schools in our study was to a large extent the work of an individual or small group of educators who saw a need, developed an idea and acted upon it as an educational venture. It is this vision, coupled with the action that transforms it into a reality, that is intended by the term *entrepreneurship*. In some cases, it was a principal who was the motivating entrepreneur. Carolyn Gaston, Principal at New Futures, is an excellent example. She established a small school in a YWCA and recruited an excellent staff; as the program grew it took over an entire public school building, and eventually a new building was constructed for the school to meet the particular needs of its students, including special day-care and clinic facilities. Gaston also raises funds in the community to support special functions and activities within the school.

At the Media Academy, a teacher is the entrepreneur. Steve O'Donoghue, a social studies and journalism teacher, developed an award-winning school newspaper. He recognized in journalism a vehicle for engaging students in academic work and for training them to think and write in ways they were not likely to experience in the regular curriculum. To provide the Academy with the resources it needed to succeed, O'Donoghue assembled an advisory committee of local media experts. Eventually, more than thirty professionals who work in some aspect of the media were assembled to advise the program and provide student access to their own expertise and to their businesses. Students have toured the Oakland *Tribune*, and attended class sessions with reporters on story writing and job access. The advisory committee also raises additional money for special projects, such as bus trips to colleges and a weekend outing at Yosemite National Park.

The notion that educators should become entrepreneurs blatantly contradicts the staid, and almost universally accepted, view of the role and status of public schools in America. The history of this nation's schools is one of persisting customs, norms and traditions. In general, teacher and administrator culture is dominated by norms of fitting into established structures and routines. While educational innovation is, in theory, considered of value, it is assumed to occur in the face of overwhelming constraints; in fact, schools have typically discouraged staff from creating alternative curricula and structures.

The patterns and assumptions inhered in the traditional, dominant roles for educators were challenged in the schools we observed — and with tremendous results. Entrepreneurship not only produced programs that responded to the needs of students, it had a profound effect on educators, particularly in situations in which teachers were involved. It gave teachers a sense of ownership in their own program, thereby stimulating an adult and professional version of engagement and school membership. Teachers wanted their students to be successful, in part, because they wanted their own ideas and efforts to be successful.

Self-Governance

A second factor that characterized a number of schools was an element of self-governance and democratic decision-making by the faculty. This created an element of control over the school environment and made it a more desirable place for teachers to work. Even programs like the School-Within-a-School and the Media Academy, which were embedded in very large organizations, tended to operate independently through collective decisions. While such self-governance was common, it was not a universal condition. At least two of the schools — New Futures and Croom — can be described as operating under more traditional, top-down models of management. In both cases, however, these were small schools in which faculty had considerable informal influence and the administration was quick to understand and respond to their needs.

Two of the fourteen schools best exemplify self-governance in small, alternative educational settings: Alcott and Sierra Mountain. Alcott's staff consists of thirteen full-time equivalent positions. The faculty meets as often as four days a week to make a variety of decisions. Typically, meetings start half-an-hour after classes are dismissed for the day. Each quarter a different teacher chairs the meeting and another records decisions in a notebook. There is also a designated timekeeper who has the authority to adjourn the meeting at the agreed-upon time. While Beverly Gutierrez, the Principal, is always in attendance, she avoids taking formal leadership at the meetings. According to her, 'This is a *faculty* meeting'.

A typical meeting begins with Bill Colbert, a math teacher, as chair. He entertains a list of topics for the day. The first item is a complaint that the student smoking area outside a back door is a mess. Someone threw milk on the door, and there is litter in the area. After a brief discussion, it is agreed that the school store will not be opened until some student or group cleans up the mess. An announcement to that effect will be made first thing in the morning. The next item of business is choosing a fund-raising activity to pay for the students' spring trip to an entertainment park. One teacher has already researched several possibilities, such as selling pizzas or jewelry. After discussion, the faculty agrees to collect more information.

The final topic is one that is typical of most meetings: dealing with problem students. This exchange is a continuation of previous discussions about Willie, a 16-year-old eighth grader, who is frequently truant. Despite relatively high academic potential (he often achieves perfect scores on spelling tests), Willie has 'floated' in and out of the building for the last month. After reviewing previous, unsuccessful tactics to prevent his truancy, it is agreed that a schedule of weekly conferences with his mother and grandmother are needed to impress upon them, as well as Willie, his need to attend school.

At Sierra Mountain, faculty and other staff participate in the governance process. Members of the clerical staff are included in many decisions because their views and their support for decisions are considered important. For example, the agenda at one meeting included the issue of how to screen students transferring in and out of the school. Earle Conway, the Principal, brought in a proposal that was used as a springboard for discussion by faculty and staff. Several modifications of the proposal were made before a new policy was approved.

Russ Jones, a new teacher at Sierra Mountain, reflected on the governance process, noting that there is a general belief among the faculty that the decision-making process produces 'collective good for the school'. Jones taught at a large comprehensive school before coming to Sierra Mountain, and there he found he had little influence on decisions.

> I feel I've had more impact on decision-making in the last three weeks than I ever had. ... I did what I was told, with a certain amount of my own interpretation, but here I have input. The staff meeting process is remarkable to me.

Principal Conway sees the governance process as responsible in part for his 'high-energy, really believe-in-what-they're-doing staff'. He points out that governance at Sierra Mountain has turned out to be a productive blend of teachers pursuing their own self-interests in the context of serving the interests of students and the school as a whole. Because of the sense of ownership teachers have in the school, they are motivated, for example, to write proposals for grant money to fund new programs they believe will strengthen the school. Success in these ventures is personally rewarding, of course, and it sustains teachers' investment in the school. Teachers need to be committed to students if a school is to be successful, but there also is a need for the school to be committed to the teachers. A key to expressing this commitment is to allow teachers to make important decisions and to invest their talents and energies in a way that is rewarding to them.

Collegiality

Collegiality is the third factor in a productive teacher culture. Teachers in our study defined it as both a feeling of sharing and a set of actions for the common good. Russ Jones at Sierra Mountain describes collegiality when he uses the phrase 'collective good' in discussing faculty motivations at the school. Teachers at Alcott experience collegiality when one 'subs' for an hour while another pursues a special school activity, such as taking a group of students to a drug education conference. At the Media Academy, Steve O'Donoghue and Mike Jackson regularly adjust schedules and curriculum topics to create a team approach. In his history class, for example, Jackson requires students to write a 'newspaper story' about the death of Caesar, using the format and standards taught in O'Donoghue's journalism class. For these two teachers, collegiality and collaboration are a natural approach: their classrooms are in close proximity to one another and they share the same students. It is a common occurrence to see them chatting during the lunch hour or between classes about some joint effort.

Collegiality generally refers to relations among teachers that are supportive of professional efforts. Teachers spoke of enjoying teaching, in part, because they appreciated the close working relations they shared with their colleagues and the spirit of informal camaraderie among school staff. An incident at Alcott is a case in point. Shop teacher, John McEachern, a practical joker, is popular with his fellow teachers. On this occasion the tables had been turned. At one point in a faculty meeting, McEachern asks, 'Who put the grease on my doorknob this morning?' Laughter and vehement denials from each of the accused are punctuated by advice about the need for John to be at work on time to avoid such problems. He promises to 'lay in the weeds' for his chance at revenge, a vow that is greeted with laughter and exaggerated protestations of innocence. It is clear that the faculty at Alcott not only take their work seriously but have a good time doing it.

Enabling School Structures

Twelve of the fourteen schools shared two structural characteristics enabling them to mobilize school membership and academic engagement for students as well as to sustain the kind of teacher culture described in the earlier sections. These twelve schools were alternatives characterized by small size with one-on-one relations and autonomy with flexibility.

Small Size With One-on-One Relations

The largest of the alternative schools, New Futures, enrolls about 250 students at a given time, all of them girls. The other schools ranged from fifty to 125 students. The two comprehensive schools that were part of the study, Lincoln and Orr Community Academy were much larger — 900 and 532 respectively. These numbers connote a specific meaning for the term 'small'. While we concede that our definition is somewhat arbitrary, we believe that any school with an enrollment that exceeds 500 students is no longer small. In the context of effective programs for at-risk youths, small is fundamental in that it facilitates many of the other desirable characteristics we have already described. For example, the difficulties of self-governance increase in proportion to the size of the school. Anonymity for students increases with size, and teachers are less likely to feel accountable for individual students as numbers increase and personal knowledge of students decreases. It is possible that somewhat larger schools might be successful in avoiding these problems, depending on the population of students served and the presence of sufficient resources to keep class size small.

The major point to be made, however, is that adults must serve a limited number of youth because this is the fundamental variable promoting one-on-one social relations between teachers and their students. To promote both school membership and academic engagement, it is essential that students have frequent contact with adults; in particular, it is through frequent one-on-one relations that care, support and personalized teaching are possible, and adults can come to understand students' problems and points of view. For example, some of the most effective counseling we observed was done by teachers, and this was possible primarily because they knew their students well and had time to interact with them.

Small size also has positive effects on faculty relations. It promotes collegiality, makes democratic governance easier and fosters the consensus-building that sustains commitment to school goals. Small size also makes it more likely that teachers can be recruited who share the core values that underlie the school's mission. While it may be possible to promote these personalized, one-on-one relations in the context of a much larger school, we foresee great difficulty in attaining the quality desired. In general, the larger the school the more difficult it is to sustain sensitive one-on-one relations between educators and students, students and students, and educators themselves

Autonomy, Flexibility and Control

The second structural characteristic that enables schools to foster membership and academic engagement is autonomy. Freedom in establishing a curriculum and in determining course context, and flexibility with respect to scheduling and the use of resources are crucial aspects of successful programs for at-risk students. The schools we studied were free from some of the constraints often associated with meeting district guidelines for curricula. Such autonomy gives teachers some level of actual control over the school as a workplace. Obviously, autonomy is relative and always constrained at some point, but it is essential that educators of at-risk students control the school environment to the extent that they are able to carry out their work as they see fit. Autonomy is a prerequisite to entrepreneurship, governance and collegiality in the sense that these qualities of school life are possible to the extent that faculty can exercise a degree of control over their school environment. Without exception, educators cited autonomy as significant in their ability to construct programs that respond to students. It is axiomatic that if schools are to respond to at-risk students, they must act and look different from the institutions at which students were failing and dropping out. Different strategies are needed and these require flexibility in the development of curriculum, in the scheduling of student time and in determining the actual site of educational activities as well as in the evaluation of students and the awarding of credits.

The School-Within-a-School is a good working example of innovation in curriculum, scheduling and awarding of credits. It was possible to alter the structure of the curriculum and the school day because the program was freed from certain conventional constraints. Students can acquire seven credits per year toward the twenty-one-credit graduation requirement. Students in the parent high school typically earn only five credits per year, but additional work-experience and English-social studies credits are routinely acquired by those who are credit-deficient. The School-Within-a-School also offers several non-school experiences for credit that are not available to other students, including volunteer work in day-care centers and homes for the elderly, and renovating public housing. Because the content of core courses (English, science, social studies and math) is not designated by the local departments or the district, the School-Within-a-School enjoys a greater degree of curriculum flexibility than would be the case in many other districts.

At New Futures, the lack of attendance could have been troublesome. Many girls live some distance from the school and public transportation often is unreliable. In addition, some pregnant girls are frequently ill, and young mothers often need to stay at home with sick babies. The school recognizes these legitimate reasons for absence and takes a non-punitive approach. No one fails a course because of absences. Instead, teachers generally respond by helping students make up missed assignments, a process made considerably easier by the school's individualized approach in many classes. The school also has generated funding from private foundations to support a home-tutoring teacher. After a girl has missed five consecutive days, the tutor obtains assignments from each teacher and takes materials to her home for individualized work.

Another important dimension of autonomy involves educator control over the students the school serves. In most of the fourteen programs, admissions criteria were explicit and relatively firm. The School-Within-a-School, for example, accepted students who were credit deficient but had accumulated approximately seven of the twenty-one credits required for graduation. Those with fewer credits were counseled into a different program. Students with the requisite number of credits were then screened in terms of their probable success given the nature of the School-Within-a-School program.

Croom Vocational also was careful to select students well-suited to the program. Students who were disruptive and violent were not likely to be accepted into Croom. WEC also was selective, admitting students for whom graduation could be projected given the framework of the program. WEC staff worked closely with counselors at the parent high school in screening those who appeared to be 'ready'. The School-Within-a-School and WEC both had relatively stringent requirements for remaining in the program. At the School-Within-a-School, students could 'point out' by accumulating five demerit points in a quarter. WEC students who failed to fulfill their contracts were 'fired'. In both schools, it was not unusual for students to be dismissed during the school year because staff believed it was important to visibly maintain program standards and thereby ensure program effectiveness.

Autonomy in most of the schools also involves an attempt to influence new staffing. Time and again we heard that a particular school was successful because the 'right kind of teachers' had been brought together. At Sierra Mountain, there was an explicit belief that existing faculty should play a major role in hiring new faculty as a means of maintaining the school culture the existing staff had developed. At New Futures, faculty gave the Principal credit for excellent judgment in selecting new staff. They said she was perceptive during interviews and was able to choose those who understood the mission of the school and accepted accountability for the girls' success. A number of teachers indicated that staff selection over the life of the school was the key reason that New Futures had remained the kind of place that was good for the girls and good for them as teachers.

Clearly, autonomy in the selection and rejection of students and staff was essential to teachers' sense of control over their work. To ask any of the fourteen programs we studied to accept any and all students who might be labeled at risk would vitiate the concept of matching students with a program and would violate teachers' sense of ownership and control of their environment.

Autonomy also meant flexible use of time, space and resources. The absence of fixed assumptions and rules about how the school should be organized permitted the School-Within-a-School to teach academic courses in the morning and place students in several different kinds of experiential settings outside the building in the afternoon. Their use of community resource people such as day-care directors and carpenters to provide educational experiences is a direct product of program flexibility. Similarly, Sierra Mountain decided to start school earlier and end later in the year in order to operate its schedule of five weeks in class followed by a week of vacation. This flexibility existed in part because the district has allowed the school autonomy over such matters and partly because consensus among a relatively small number of educators was possible. A variation of this flexibility is seen at the Media Academy, where team teaching that focuses on the theme of journalism makes it possible to 'block' segments of the school day. As a result, students can be taken out of school to see first hand how a business uses an international satellite communication system.

Flexibility also meant that these schools were examples of site-based management with decision-making close to the scene of action. The temptation here is to say that a system of democratic faculty self-governance was universal and is therefore a necessary precursor to program success. In fact, our data does not support this. While the autonomy most schools enjoyed did result in variations of democratic governance, two strong programs, Croom and New Futures, exhibited creativeness and responsiveness through a more traditional managerial model headed by a Principal.

In each case, the Principal was a leader with a clear vision of what the students and faculty need to create an effective program. For example, Carolyn Gaston, at New Futures, carved out a significant degree of autonomy for the school within the district. Her own personal style created political legitimacy for the school within the system and with the public at large. Gaston also has generated additional financial support within the community that contributes to the school's success. She has assembled a staff of counselors, nurses and teachers who share a set of values about educating pregnant and mothering teen girls. The result of this leadership is a school with a sense of collegial purpose among its faculty and leadership that is responsive to the needs of staff and students.

A Culture and Structure of Support

What conclusions can we draw about the effects of teacher culture and structure in the alternative schools we studied? We see these factors as essential in providing the support students need to achieve school membership and academic engagement. The structural and cultural factors are interrelated; i.e., smallness and autonomy are linked to teachers' sense of school ownership and their willingness to invest themselves in helping at-risk students. The structural characteristic of smallness promotes one-on-one relations between students and educators, an essential precondition to helping students overcome impediments to membership and engagement. Decision-making in these schools was sensitive to the needs of faculty and students; in most

147

cases, some variation of democratic governance was operating in which faculty made key decisions about such issues as curriculum, scheduling and teacher arrangements.

These structural characteristics made it possible for a specific teacher culture to flourish. This culture has two dimensions: it is concerned with the need to create a satisfying workplace for teachers, and it sets an agenda for responding to students. These educators were interested in being part of an enterprise that was productive and rewarding. Some of them were educational entrepreneurs who valued the opportunity to invest themselves in a program in which they believed. They also valued a degree of self-governance and autonomy that made their efforts pay off for them and for their students.

This culture also embodied a set of teacher beliefs, values and actions concerned with teachers' social relations with students. Teachers accepted personal accountability for student success. They practiced an extended role that involved them in the personal and social concerns of their students. They believed in the necessity of being persistent with difficult students because all students can learn. Frequently, these teachers also believed that the way to engage students is to build on their strengths rather than focusing on their weaknesses. The social relations this teacher culture generated were instrumental in helping students overcome impediments to school membership and academic engagement.

In this chapter, we have presented evidence that certain cultural organizational and structural characteristics were common among the fourteen schools we studied. Moreover, we have argued from this evidence that these characteristics were responsible for bringing students into school membership and educational engagement. The presence of these characteristics created schools that establish support for at-risk students. This picture of schools as communities of support, up to this point, is built primarily upon qualitative data gathered through observations and interviews of students and teachers. The strengths of our methodology and data are balanced against an understandable desire for additional evidence with the features of random assignment, controls and quantitative measures of some of the variables we describe.

Fortunately, there is additional evidence drawn from the High School and Beyond database that confirms and strengthens some of our most important observations and claims. High School and Beyond data have been analyzed by Bryk and Driscoll (1988) in terms of their definition of school as a community. The data they analyze from High

School and Beyond parallel the analysis of this chapter at certain key points. In general, Bryk and Driscoll show that a random sample of schools across the country measuring high on a 'school as community' index are significantly more effective in terms of student achievement and retention of at–risk students, and that these schools have more satisfied teachers.

Bryk and Driscoll hypothesized that schools characterized by a high measure of community provide a supportive environment promoting academic engagement and what we have called school membership. Further, they suggest this engagement and membership should be distributed broadly among groups of students in schools measuring high in community. The effects, they predict, are higher achievement and lower drop-out rates among all groups of students. In testing these hypotheses, Bryk and Driscoll used a random sample of 357 schools from the High School and Beyond database. In addition, they created an index of 'school as a community' using twenty-three variables from this database. These variables were selected using a theoretical definition of community.

More specifically, the twenty-three variables defining school as community include a number of items that have been presented in this chapter. 'Shared beliefs and values' includes teacher agreement on school goals, consensus on beliefs and values, belief that students can learn and agreement on school discipline. 'Teacher collegiality' is built on items about teachers using other teachers' help, shared planning, participation in faculty socials and perception of staff support. The notion of 'extended role' is created out of items about the amount of time teachers spend on activities outside the classroom, teacher knowledge of students, teacher contact with students outside of class, and students' perception of teacher interest in them.

Bryk and Driscoll offer some important findings that supplement our analysis and conclusions. Even in schools with large proportions of lower-class students, teacher efficacy was strong in relation to the school-as-community factor. Teachers' perception of classroom disorder were significantly lower in schools that measured high on community. Finally, teacher absenteeism is lower where the communal school organization exists.

For students, school as a community has a positive effect on student interest in academics. In general, large schools tend not to have the characteristics of community; they are, for example, more likely to be seen as unsafe. Communal schools, on the other hand, stand out as being safe even when they are characterized by racial and ethnic diversity. Class-cutting occurs less frequently in these schools, as does student absenteeism. Mathematics achievement is higher, and this achievement is distributed more broadly across races and social class lines than in schools not characterized by school as a community. Finally, the drop-out rate is significantly lower in communal schools, even among poor and minority students.

Bryk and Driscoll's definition of school as a community closely parallels our descriptions of school membership and a teacher culture of ownership. In their definition of community, they stipulate the need for shared beliefs and values, a common agenda of activities, and certain organizational characteristics that include collegiality and extending teaching roles. They include small size as an important factor that will correlate with higher measures of community. In general, their definition of school as a community and their conclusions about its effects on students overlap with the findings and interpretations we present.

In short, two quite different research strategies, one using a large quantitative data set and the other using largely qualitative data from a handful of case studies, both share a similar conclusion regarding the effects of school as a community. Empirical data broadly supports the hypothesis that certain cultural and structural conditions have an important impact on teachers and students.

Our study indicates that schools can actively help students overcome impediments to school membership and academic engagement. The cultural and structural conditions described in this chapter are necessary in developing schools as communities of support for students and teachers. These cultural and structural conditions provide teachers with the means and opportunities to support students in ways far less likely to occur in traditional comprehensive schools. For teachers and students, schools characterized as communities are good places in which to live and to learn.

In the next chapter, we present quantitative data regarding the impact of the fourteen schools on students.

Chapter 7:
Effects of School as a Community

Seated in front of the small crowd gathered for the school board meeting, Alex taps his fingers on the table and looks at the adults and other students sitting around him. As Sierra Mountain High School's outstanding student during the previous grading period, he has earned the right to give the regular student report about the school. To his right and left are students from Nevada Union and Bear River High schools — a boy in a polo shirt and trimmed hair, whose clean good looks fit the stereotype of class leader, and a girl dressed in white blouse and skirt whose banter and laughter spill out into the audience. Alex's curly, shoulder-length blonde hair is a throwback to an earlier era, and his turquoise T-shirt seems out of place among the well-attired school board members. His girlfriend is seated in the second row, alone; they exchange glances that seem to reassure Alex about the task at hand.

When called on to review recent events at Sierra Mountain, Alex mentions an all-school meeting held earlier in the week to make plans for the end of the year. Two or three field days have been scheduled to provide students with some incentive to finish their classwork and the opportunity to relax with one another before disbanding for the summer. A group of students also will travel to Yosemite over the weekend for rock-climbing, hiking and camping. Although Alex's voice quavers occasionally, his delivery is clear and strong. Still, there is something unique in his inflection; it lacks the smooth and modulated quality of the voices of his audience and recalls the twang of Oklahoma or Nebraska, an accent carried to California during the 1930s that can still be heard in garages, packing houses and small cafes. Like his clothes and hair, his speech sets Alex apart from the polished urbanity of the people around him. Though white, he is clearly a member of a different class, a class whose values and concerns do not always conform to those who manage the public schools.

According to Sierra Mountain staff, Alex was an impossible student in junior high. Before transferring to Sierra Mountain in the ninth grade, he had earned four Fs in a single quarter at Nevada Union. Alex admits hating school in his earlier years because he was always in trouble. He objected to the size of the school and what he perceived to be rigid rules. 'I don't like going to school in a really strict environment because I like being able to cut a little slack. I'm not exactly a goody-goody', he says.

Alex also found that because all of his friends had different lunch periods or classes, he rarely saw anyone he knew. When the one friend who was in some of his classes transferred to Sierra Mountain, Alex decided to make the move, too. At Sierra Mountain, he immediately felt comfortable.

> Everybody seemed so nice and everything, and I liked the fact that they call [teachers] by their first name instead of Mr. Blah-Blah-Blah, and you can't pronounce the last name. At Nevada Union, some of the teachers are really nice, but most of them are snobby ... It seems like they care more about the rules and regulations than they do the students.

At Sierra Mountain, it's the attention teachers are willing to extend to him that Alex appreciates most. After a year at Sierra Mountain, Alex says, 'I don't really consider them my teachers; I consider them my friends'.

Alex is especially grateful for the encouragement he receives from Mike Menzies, his English teacher. 'He says that I'm one of the best students that they have here. He tells me that on all of my report cards, and that just really encourages me to do good.'

And Alex has begun to do very well. He earned a 4.0 average for the fourth quarter of the 1986/87 school year and had raised his cumulative average to 3.06; he had also made up the credits he'd lost from his initial poor showing at Nevada Union. In addition to the Sierra Mountain teachers' interest in him and their encouragement, Alex says the more relaxed atmosphere at the school has also contributed to his willingness to apply himself and conform to the school's rules. For example, at Nevada Union, he and his friend, Jim, were never allowed to work with one another. At Sierra Mountain, this cooperation is encouraged as long as they are quiet and finish assignments.

Alex feels he has learned more in three months at Sierra Mountain than he had in twice that much time at Nevada Union, and he attributes his motivation to the fact that he now enjoys going to school. He has also realized that getting a good education is important so he can eventually 'get a good job and make a living and not have to depend on my parents', a realization fostered by teachers at the school 'trying to make you understand what life's all about'. He's begun to consider further education and is especially interested in learning more about computers. 'If they're there, you might as well use them. If you enjoy it, you can do a lot of fun things by using your brain and your hands.' He figures that with the right training he might be able to get a job at the Grass Valley Group (a local electronics firm that is a subsidiary of Tectronics).

For a boy who had previously been a consistent behavior problem in school, Alex's reaction to rules is also noteworthy. Though he had been apprehended for smoking marijuana at Nevada Union, at Sierra Mountain he takes pains to obey school rules forbidding drugs and cigarettes.

It should not be inferred from Alex's friendships with staff and willingness to assume responsibility that he has become a perfect student. But while he periodically has run-ins with teachers, he finds this doesn't interfere with the relationships he has established with them.

> Like me and Linda have gotten into it twice, and me and Fred have gotten into it twice. It's like they don't hold grudges. Any other teacher at Nevada Union would just hold a grudge against you. And now it's like me and Linda are real close again. ... [Teachers at Sierra Mountain] don't let your attitude get in their way.

Neither could it be said that Alex has become a self-motivated learner. Alex admits, 'I'm not really enthused, I'm not, really. I don't do my schoolwork all the time, but I just do my work and do a good job on it and get it done.' Still, it is this willingness to go along with the school's expectations despite what may be deeper personal preferences that seems most striking about Alex's response to the program at Sierra Mountain.

Alex exemplifies the kind of transformation in student attitudes and behaviors that can result from participation in a special program for potential dropouts. Not all students, of course, make such turnarounds, but many do, and it is useful to summarize briefly the specific effects in evidence after Alex enrolled at Sierra Mountain High School. The most fundamental was a shift in his attitude towards the institution of school itself. What he had previously approached as an aversive experience he now sees as something to be enjoyed. As a result, Alex no longer fights rules and procedures often essential for the smooth operation of the school but instead supports them. Now willing to cooperate, Alex has reversed his previous pattern of disciplinary referrals and course failure and is accumulating the credits required for graduation.

In Alex's case, bonding to teachers and the school they represent has led to improved attendance and academic achievement. It has also led to a reappraisal of his own life options and abilities. The praise he receives from adults he respects has encouraged him to value the importance of education and the doors it can open. Now that he's begun 'to understand what life's all about', he is considering higher education as a means of achieving specific career goals.

Alex's experience at Sierra Mountain raises several themes that will be considered throughout this chapter as we discuss the impact programs for potential dropouts can have on their students. These include the ability of such programs to establish a sense of social bonding to the school, teachers and peers; to support students in their effort to alter previous attendance, behavior, and academic patterns that interfere with school success; to nurture self-esteem and personal control; to improve academic self-concept and to increase aspirations for further schooling; and to extend students' sense of opportunity regarding future occupations. Fundamental to these positive changes, once again, is a commitment on the part of the school to help all students succeed. Such a commitment has led to the cultivation of activities and attitudes aimed at integrating students into the school environment in ways that help them overcome isolation, academic difficulties and the experience of incongruence.

Indicators of Program Effectiveness

Before proceeding, it may be useful to review briefly the elements of our argument covered thus far. We first described the way in which effective programs for at-risk youth often tailor their curriculum to the perceived characteristics and needs of a clearly defined student population. We then discussed underlying commonalities at-risk youth share with all students: the need for group membership, the need for positive relationships with adults, the need to acquire skills and knowledge, and the need to develop a sense of competence. This discussion also documented the central role of school membership in the success of at-risk youths. We described aspects of faculty culture that fostered membership, and we suggested that the maintenance of such a culture is often essential to the effectiveness of school programs. We now investigate the extent to which innovative programs can affect students' sense of social membership and lead to more positive school outcomes.

Assessing Program Effects

Recognizing at the outset the multiple goals and unique structures of the interventions, the complexity of the students' circumstances, and the difficulties inherent in collecting accurate data from and about at-risk youth, we chose to gather data from a variety of sources on a wide range of indicators. Three week-long visits were made to each of the research sites during the 1986/87 school year. During these visits, extensive observations and interviews contributed to our growing understanding of practices that appeared to be successful in reengaging at-risk students in the enterprise of schooling. This qualitative data was supplemented by the administration of pre-tests and post-tests aimed at measuring attitude changes, writing ability and reading level. Attendance and completion rates, changes in student GPA, the incidence of disciplinary referrals, and provision of rehabilitative services also were collected from student files. Summaries of these data appear in tables 12, 13 and 14.

To assess the effects of fourteen programs on students' sense of social membership, changes in eleven selected personal orientations or attitudes, including social bonding, self-esteem, sociocentric reasoning, locus of control, academic self-concept and perception of opportunity were monitored through the use of the Wisconsin Youth Survey.[1] Academic performance was measured through pre- and post-test administration of the Degrees of Reading Power (DRP), the scoring of writing samples collected throughout the school year, and information collected from student files on GPA, attendance and the incidence of disciplinary referrals. In this chapter we present both qualitative and quantitative evidence of the impact these programs can have on the sense of school membership and educational engagement of at-risk youth.

Evaluating Membership in a School Community

Social bonding is measured in terms of the attachment students feel toward school as an institution, their teachers, peers, or accepted societal norms. Proponents of social bonding theory argue that

> ... conditions favorable to social deviancy are rooted in the absence of or weakness of intimate relations with other persons. A youth who is closely attached to and respecting of others feels approval and esteem emanate from others when his/her behavior is in accord with the other's values and beliefs. If such attachments are absent, approval or esteem are either lacking or meaningless. The youth who does not have the love and respect of those significant others will thus be free to reject the normative pattern they attempt to impose (Wehlage, Stone and Kliebard, 1980).

Students who feel a sense of social bonding to school or teachers are less likely to reject school and more likely to conform to certain otherwise unappealing rules and procedures associated with schooling. Students who exhibit a high degree of social bonding tend to identify with the institution, actors or norms and see themselves as having a role, a value and a stake in the outcome of the institution's or individual's efforts.

The sense of social bonding exhibited by students in these special programs for potential dropouts is largely the result of their being drawn into a social environment that encourages the formation of positive relations to peers, teachers and the ethos of the school as a whole. Despite the ideology of individualism and self-reliance that characterizes so much of American discourse about education and social mobility, most people need to feel they are a part of a group to achieve any sense of personal identity. If that membership is denied to them — as it had been denied to Alex — people often respond with defiance or disengagement. An important component of this bonding process involves the provision of a more closely knit peer group. Students who had encountered isolation in the larger and more impersonal environment of their former conventional high schools are able to form sustained relationships with friends with whom they are able to share a majority of their class time. This important social element of the school experience often is regarded as problematic by teachers who interpret this aspect of student life as something that interferes with learning. For Alex and Jim, however, being able to work together at Sierra Mountain laid a foundation for much higher academic achievement as well as more positive feelings about schooling.

David, a student at the School-Within-a-School, spoke of being

Table 12: Indicators of Program Effectiveness: School Membership

	n[1]	Social Bonding to Peers			Social Bonding to Teachers			Social Bonding to School			Social Bonding to Conventional Roles			Social Bonding Composite			Sociocentric Reasoning		
		Δ	s.d.	e.e.s[2]	Δ	s.d.	e.e.s	Δ	s.d.	e.e.s	Δ	s.d.	e.e.s	Δ	s.d.	e.e.s	Δ	s.d.	e.e.s
Alcott Alternative Learning Center	56	.02	.45	.04	.12	.39	.31	-.10	.36	-.28	-.04	.40	-.10	-.09	1.24	-.07	.03	.35	.09
Croom Vocational High School	30	.01	.39	.03	.10	.59	.17	-.18	.49	-.37	-.25	.54	-.46	-.31	1.52	-.20	.11	.44	.25
Loring-Nicollet	26	-.06	.48	-.13	.05	.51	.10	-.08	.45	-.18	-.06	.41	-.15	-.16	1.39	-.12	-.08	.44	-.18
NA-WAY-EE, The Center School	14	.25	.29	.86	.25	.29	.86	.28	.26	1.08	.14	.30	.47	.93	.69	1.35	.23	.24	.96
School Within A School	34	.09	.47	.19	.56	.62	.90	.20	.52	.39	-.01	.42	-.02	.85	1.67	.51	.10	.44	.23
Sierra Mountain High School	18	.15	.59	.25	.10	.50	.20	.02	.47	.04	-.06	.55	-.10	.09	1.76	.05	.14	.39	.36
Wayne Enrichment Center	18	.15	.25	.60	.58	.71	.82	.27	.50	.54	.26	.45	.58	1.44	1.85	.78	.36	.58	.62
Media Academy	37	.14	.44	.32	-.05	.44	-.11	-.07	.39	-.18	.00	.50	.00	.02	.34	.02	.03	.39	.08
Plymouth Christian Youth Center	27	-.06	.37	-.16	.07	.48	.15	-.20	.38	-.53	-.08	.40	-.20	-.26	1.32	-.20	.03	.32	.09
Minneapolis Education and Recycling Center	15	-.05	.37	-.14	.04	.33	.12	-.10	.31	-.32	-.03	.32	-.09	-.14	.84	-.17	.12	.42	.29
New Futures	27	.13	.42	.31	.03	.37	.08	-.01	.33	-.03	-.08	.45	-.18	.06	1.28	.05	.03	.29	.10
Lincoln High School	41	-.03	.47	-.06	.01	.36	.03	-.03	.37	-.08	-.16	.40	-.40	-.20	1.12	-.18	.00	.42	.00
Orr Community Academy	270	-.05	.47	-.10	-.04	.46	-.09	-.06	.44	-.14	-.08	.48	-.17	-.25	1.34	-.19	-.02	.40	-.05
COMPARISON	63	-.03	.46	-.07	.01	.47	.02	-.05	.51	-.10	-.12	.48	-.25	-.22	1.57	-.14	-.05	.45	-.11

[1] n includes only those students completing both the pre and post-tests. Attendance data, disciplinary referrals, and grade point averages were collected from a different sample of approximately 30 students in each program, who were randomly selected from among those enrolled in the program in 1987–88 but who were not enrolled in the program the previous year. NA = not applicable, ND = No data, * = p < .05.
[2] Estimated effect size.

Table 13: Indicators of Program Effectiveness: Academic Engagement

| | Attendance and Behavior | | | | | | Academic Achievement | | | | | | | |
| | Attendance | | Disciplinary Referrals | | | | Degrees of Reading Power | | Writing – Primary Trait | | Writing – Holistic | | Grade Point Average | |
	Prior	Program	Prior 1–4	Program 1–4	Prior 5+	Program 5+	Pre-test	Post-test	Pre-test	Post-test	Pre-test	Post-test	Prior	Program
Alcott Alternative Learning Center	ND	91%	4	3	0	0	39.67	46.31*	4.86	4.14	6.00	5.50	1.22	2.48
Croom Vocational High School	62%	87%	9	11	16	0	35.53	34.44	4.15	4.70	5.45	5.50	.32	2.30
Loring-Nicollet School	80%	85%	ND	ND	ND	ND	72.75	67.88*	5.70	4.70	8.80	8.10	ND	NA
NA-WAY-EE, The Center School	77%	83%	ND	ND	ND	ND	53.64	54.00	4.00	4.11	5.89	6.89	ND	NA
School Within A School at Madison Memorial High School	73%	90%	6	13	0	2	54.43	60.23*	5.01	5.83	7.82	7.53	.86	2.99
Sierra Mountain High School	85%	91%	11	7	4	0	58.00	48.61*	4.75	4.50	6.50	6.25	1.42	2.70
Wayne Enrichment Center	81%	95%	ND	0	5	0	61.36	53.27	ND	ND	ND	ND	1.53	NA
Media Academy	ND	89%	ND	0	ND	0	54.75	49.94*	4.73	4.91	6.09	6.14	ND	2.50
Plymouth Christian Youth Center	75%	91%	ND	ND	ND	ND	51.05	41.05*	3.91	4.13	5.61	5.17	ND	NA
Minneapolis Education and Recycling Center	75%	87%	ND	ND	ND	ND	48.07	42.93	3.13	3.50	4.88	5.25	ND	NA
New Futures School	74%	79%	10	2	4	0	50.58	53.48	5.24	5.24	7.00	7.08	1.77	2.16
Urban League Street Academy	75%	74%	ND	ND	ND	ND	ND	ND	ND	ND	ND	ND	ND	NA
Lincoln High School	96%	94%	4	3	0	0	62.90	59.90*	5.41	5.21	6.56	7.08	3.12	2.71
Orr Community Academy	89%	93%	9	9	3	3	39.27	44.47*	3.66	3.07	5.41	4.34	1.82	1.90
COMPARISON	ND	ND	ND	ND	ND	ND	62.40	57.43*	ND	ND	ND	ND	ND	ND

158

Program Completion[1]

	% Graduating or Completing Program	% Continuing for Another Year	% Returning to Previous School or Other Program	% Moved Out of District	% Dropped Out or Uncounted For	% Earning a High School Diploma	% Preparing For or Earning a GED
Alcott Alternative Learning Center	7	56	20	4	13	NA	NA
Croom Vocational High School	40	40	1	3	16	40	40
Loring-Nicollet School	14	37	13	2	25[2]	25	17
NA-WAY-EE, The Center School	18	28	11	7	48[2]	6	0
School Within A School At Madison Memorial High School	25	34	10	9	22	31	0
Sierra Mountain High School	NA[3]	31	40	19	5	NA	NA
Wayne Enrichment Center	30	30	26	5	9	40	1
Media Academy	0	96	0	0	4	NA	0
Plymouth Christian Youth Center	6	22	6	0	36[2]	17	5
Minneapolis Education and Recycling Center	3	22	12	0	25[2]	2	7
New Futures School	76[4]	25	10	8	24	25	10
Urban League Street Academy	7	16	10	0	55[2]	9	3
Lincoln High School	0	48	36	0	16	NA	0
Orr Community Academy	19	43	8	3	28	NA	0
COMPARISON	ND	ND	ND	ND	ND	ND	ND

* = p ≤ .05.

[1] These data are for 1986–87.

[2] This information supplied by the Minneapolis Public Schools and does not include all student categories. This is the reason the previous 5 columns do not add up to 100%.

[3] Sierra Mountain serves primarily 9th and 10th graders who complete their education elsewhere. 5% of students in 1985–86 transferred to the county juvenile department school.

[4] One full year of program participation is regarded as completion by New Futures Schools. 21% of former New Futures' students stay at home with their babies or work and are not included in the drop-out figure.

Table 14: Indicators of Program Effectiveness: Other Program Effects

	Self Esteem			Locus of Control			Perception of opportunity			Academic self-concept			Aspirations for further schooling		
	Δ	s.d.	e.e.s	Δ	s.d.	e.e.s	Δ	s.d.	e.e.s	Δ	s.d.	e.e.s	Δ	s.d.	e.e.s
Alcott Alternative Learning Center	.03	.49	.06	.02	.35	.06	.01	.37	.03	.10	.46	.22	.32	2.14	.15
Croom Vocational High School	–.20	.47	–.43	.00	.45	.00	–.16	.42	–.39	–.08	.46	–.17	–.06	1.52	–.04
Loring-Nicollet	.28	.70	.40	.05	.35	.14	–.11	.41	–.27	.09	.58	.16	.04	1.96	.02
NA-WAY-EE, The Center School	.25	.36	.69	.35	.37	.95	.25	.30	.83	.32	.34	.94	–.14	1.90	–.07
School Within A School	.23	.56	.41	.14	.36	.39	.27	.38	.71	.54	.59	.92	.47	1.10	.43
Sierra Mountain High School	.22	.58	.38	.07	.38	.18	.07	.34	.21	.22	.49	.45	.28	1.80	.16
Wayne Enrichment Center	.26	.49	.53	.28	.48	.58	.30	.41	.73	.16	.51	.31	1.05	1.21	.87
Media Academy	.05	.55	.09	–.03	.45	–.07	–.06	.37	–.16	–.04	.53	–.08	.29	1.65	.18
Plymouth Christian Youth Center	.09	.50	.18	–.04	.35	–.11	–.12	.27	–.44	.06	.53	.11	.97	1.55	.63
Minneapolis Education and Recycling Center	.05	.21	.24	.14	.29	.48	.09	.28	.32	.11	.36	.31	–.20	1.45	–.14
New Futures	.06	.43	.14	.02	.34	.06	.02	.31	.07	.18	.41	.44	.19	1.68	.11
Lincoln High School	–.16	.49	–.33	–.08	.43	–.19	–.07	.41	–.17	–.06	.45	–.13	–.32	1.66	–.19
Orr Community Academy	–.02	.50	–.04	.04	.42	.10	–.01	.36	–.03	–.04	.53	–.08	–.15	1.93	–.08
COMPARISON	.02	.56	–.04	–.03	.43	–.07	–.08	.46	–.18	–.04	.51	–.08	–.09	1.80	–.05

able to learn more effectively in a class in which he could feel relaxed with his fellow students. 'My reason for that is you feel more comfortable if you make a mistake on something. I mean, all these people know you anyway, and everyone's entitled to mistakes.'

This feeling of being more comfortable with other students and teachers means students begin to allow themselves to take educational risks. Risk taking is essential for academic growth, but it can be severely inhibited by the feeling that even a simple mistake will label one as deviant or unfit. Teachers play a central role in creating an environment in which students are accepted and cared for. Nick, a student at Sierra Mountain, observed that for the first time in his life he looks forward to going to school. Asked why, he was quick to point to his teachers. 'They're just there when you need them. If you were walking to school after missing a bus, you wouldn't see a teacher from NU [Nevada Union] pull over and pick you up. Teachers here would do that.' This sense that teachers are 'there when you need them' leads many students to adopt a different orientation to the values school adults are attempting to convey. The delineation between student culture and teacher culture becomes blurred.

Russ Jones, a staff member at Sierra Mountain, described what can happen when teachers not only treat students as friends but are treated as friends in return. On occasion, he or another teacher will encounter oppositional behavior from a student new to the school; when this happens, older students will respond, 'Hey, that's not cool. We don't do that. There's no need for that', or 'Mike's [a teacher] a great guy. What are you hassling him for?' Jones says such support makes it clear that

> ... our relationships with the kids are important to them, too.
> They value our friendship, and if somebody else is picking on
> us, then frequently there's another student who will come to our
> defense. It's really nice instead of there being the 'us and them'
> it's the 'us and us'.

This willingness to support the school is demonstrated by the respect students in a number of schools exhibit toward the school building and grounds. Alcott Alternative Learning Center, for example, is notably free of graffiti, despite the program's location in an ageing former elementary school building. At Sierra Mountain, the maintenance man, Rick, compared the extensive vandalism and graffiti at the local comprehensive high school with the neat, clean appearance of this school primarily for ninth and tenth graders, most of whom had been viewed as behavior problems. At Sierra Mountain, students think of the school as their home, and without adult prodding are careful about disposing of cigarette butts and litter. The fact that they or their peers have had a hand in building fences, planting lawns and caring for the flower and vegetable beds may also contribute to their sense of ownership of the school.

At Croom Vocational High School, students are similarly involved in maintaining the school plant and grounds; there, as well, young people experience the school not as an alien institution but as their own. After the graduation ceremony at Croom, one parent pointed to his weeping son and asked whether the school would be willing to take him back for another year; he didn't want to leave. The importance of the experience of being party to a shared educational venture cannot be overemphasized. Students come to know education not as something that is done *to* them, but as something they do for themselves and for one another. Such membership counters isolation and incongruence in ways that encourage students to become committed to one another, to their teachers and to their schools. It turns an aversive experience into a positive one. As Nick at Sierra Mountain observed, 'It's like coming here makes me want to wake up in the morning'.

Quantitative Indicators of Program Effects on School Membership

From our data in the fourteen schools, estimates of effect size[2] were computed for pre- to post-test changes in student mean scores for social bonding to peers, social bonding to teachers, social bonding to school, social bonding to conventional roles, and for a composite measure. Changes in sociocentric reasoning were also computed. Not all of the programs in our study, however, had identified increasing school membership as a primary goal. In determining whether programs for at-risk youth can effect students' attitudes, it may be inappropriate to include those programs where enhanced school membership was not a dominant focus. Seven of the fourteen (Alcott, Croom, NA-WAY-EE, Loring-Nicollet, Sierra Mountain, School-Within-a-School, Wayne Enrichment Center) made significant efforts to facilitate school membership.

Of these, six programs showed notable improvements in student attitudes. Four had substantial effects on students' sense of social bonding and sociocentric reasoning. At Wayne Enrichment Center and NA-WAY-EE, students' scores increased on all six measures, with estimated effect sizes ranging from .54 to .82 standard deviations for

WEC and .47 to 1.35 standard deviations for NA-WAY-EE. At the School-Within-a-School and Sierra Mountain, student scores increased on five of the six measures. At Sierra Mountain, estimated effect sizes ranged from .04 to .36; at the School-Within-a-School, estimated effect sizes ranged from .19 to .90.

Of the remaining three schools, Alcott and Croom students increased on social bonding to peers, social bonding to teachers, and sociocentric reasoning, while Loring-Nicollet students increased only on social bonding to teachers. While Loring-Nicollet utilizes camping trips and school meetings to facilitate a sense of school membership, the impact of the peculiar nihilism of punk culture makes these results very difficult to interpret.

It is useful to compare these results with three schools (Lincoln, Orr, and a comparison group made up of randomly-selected juniors in an award-winning midwestern high school) that are structured like most conventional American high schools. At Orr, students' scores declined for all six measures, while Lincoln and comparison students reported only small positive changes in social bonding to teachers.

Even in the remaining four programs (PCYC, MERC, New Futures, Media), which did not explicitly focus on enhanced school membership, the presence of caring, compassionate teachers resulted in increased social bonding to teachers (estimated effect sizes ranging from .08 to .15 standard deviations) in three of the four programs. In addition, student scores on sociocentric reasoning increased in all four of these programs with estimated effect sizes ranging from .08 to .29 standard deviations. In two of these schools, social bonding to peers increased over .31 standard deviations.

Together, qualitative and quantitative data from the schools involved in our study suggest that programs that respond to students' need for school membership can enhance students' sense of social bonding to peers, teachers, school, conventional roles and sociocentric reasoning.

Evaluating School Performance

Because school performance is difficult to measure directly, a variety of indirect measures of academic engagement were used. These include attendance data, disciplinary referrals, reading and writing ability, and grade point average. Presumably, the school performance of students who attend more regularly and who are not disruptive will improve.

Attendance and behavior

A sample of thirty students was randomly selected from among those students who were enrolled in each program during the year of the study but had not been in the program the previous year. The attendance rates and frequency of disciplinary referrals for these students during the year prior to program enrollment and the year of program enrollment were collected and compared.

Attendance rates improved markedly in ten of the twelve programs for which the previous year's data were available. Notable positive changes included 62 per cent to 87 per cent for students at Croom Vocational, 73 per cent to 90 per cent for School-Within-a-School students, 75 per cent to 91 per cent for Plymouth Christian Youth Center students and 81 per cent to 95 per cent for students at WEC. The attendance of students in two programs (Lincoln and the Minneapolis Urban League Street Academy) declined slightly (96 per cent to 94 per cent and 75 per cent to 74 per cent, respectively).

In addition, average daily attendance as reported by the programs compared favorably to overall district attendance rates. Although program average daily attendance exceeds district average daily attendance in only two cases (Lincoln and WEC), the program average daily attendance is often very close to that of the district. In one program (Orr), the attendance rates are identical; in three other programs (Media Academy, School-Within-a-School and Croom) the differential ranges from 2 to 8 percentage points. In the remaining programs, the larger discrepancies can be explained by their open admissions policy, which allows large numbers of students to enroll although many do not attend regularly. While this policy provides students maximum access to schooling, it tends to distort true attendance patterns. In one school (New Futures), the fact that virtually all of the students are pregnant or caring for their own children accounts for their considerably lower attendance rate compared to the district average daily attendance rate.

We were able to collect comparative data on disciplinary referrals in seven of our fourteen programs. In six of these seven, the total incidence of disciplinary referrals declined. The increase in disciplinary referrals in the seventh program (School-Within-a-School) can be attributed to the implementation of a point system as part of the program intervention and a more restrictive definition of acceptable behavior and/or academic performance.

Academic achievement

Our attempts to document the academic growth of students in these programs were only partially successful. The Degrees of Reading Power test was administered at the beginning and end of the school year as a measure of students' reading ability. In all but five of the fourteen programs, the raw DRP score was lower at post-test than at pre-test. Because it seems unlikely that students would read less well at the end of a school year than they did at the end of the previous summer, we are highly suspicious of these results. We suspect that student motivation played a powerful role in determining post-test scores.

A careful examination of the individual test results for students in one program shows how low motivation may contribute to the lower post-test means reported in eight of our schools. The raw DRP score represents the number of correct answers chosen by students out of seventy-seven possible responses. The test is not timed and students are not penalized for guessing. The students' raw score is therefore highly dependent on the time and attention he or she is willing to devote to the test, as well as on individual ability.

Several students' scores dropped by as much as sixty points, a fact which could only be explained by student motivation. In fact, seven of the eighteen students' scores declined at post-test by thirteen points or more. Although ten students' scores also increased during the period of observation, over a one-year period, the magnitude of the increase (ranging from one to seventeen points) is likely to be considerably smaller than these large decreases (ranging from thirteen to sixty points); consequently declines are likely to outweigh increases and depress the post-test group mean.

It is possible that some post-test increases could be explained by low motivation at pre-test. It seems even more likely that post-test decreases could be the result of diminished energy at the end of the school year. Especially given that some students had to take numerous competency exams in addition to our surveys, and others had pressing publication deadlines, it seems reasonable to speculate that their motivation to perform well on a personally meaningless test of reading ability would be low.

Students also were asked to submit writing samples based on a common prompt. These samples were analyzed by an independent panel of experts using primary trait and holistic scoring (see appendix B for a more complete description of this process). The experts did not know that the samples were written by students in programs for at-risk youth. Data were available for twelve of the fourteen programs. Using primary trait scoring, the quality of student writing samples was higher at post-test than at pre-test in six of the twelve programs; quality was lower in five programs and remained the same in another. Using the holistic method, the quality of student writing again improved in six programs, although not in the same six programs.

Comparative data on grade point averages were collected for seven of our fourteen programs. These data could not be collected from six of the remaining seven programs (WEC, Plymouth Christian Youth Center, Loring-Nicollet, MERC, NA-WAY-EE, Minneapolis Urban League Street Academy) because these programs do not assign letter grades. GPA data for the previous year were not collected at the Media Academy. Although changes in GPA from one program to another cannot be taken as a firm indicator of academic growth, significantly higher grades do indicate an increased willingness on the part of students to cooperate with the academic expectations of teachers. In five of the seven programs for which data were available, mean grade point averages increased markedly. Notable changes in mean student GPA include Croom Vocational (0.32 to 2.30), School-Within-a-School (0.86 to 2.99), Alcott (1.22 to 2.48), and Sierra Mountain (1.42 to 2.70). Average GPA declined from 3.12 to 2.71 among students at Lincoln and improved only slightly (1.82 to 1.90) at Orr Academy. The substantial increases in grade point average experienced by students in many programs is encouraging. Mean grade point averages between 2.00 and 3.00 suggest that many students are earning As and Bs in some of the classes.

The support of caring teachers and a renewed sense of connection to the school may well contribute to improvements in attendance, behavior, achievement and GPA. Kelly, a student at Sierra Mountain, found that the willingness of her teachers to deal with personal problems contributed to her engagement in classes. She described her teachers as 'sisters and brothers', and said that the absence of this closeness had interfered with her learning at a previous high school. 'I needed to get where I could grow close to somebody because I can work much better if I don't feel pressured.' At Sierra Mountain she took pride in the fact that she was now earning As and Bs, a significant improvement over the Cs and Ds she had become accustomed to earlier on in her school career.

Rickie flourished at the Media Academy, in an environment in which teachers were willing to reach out to him as a person. 'I learned more this year than any other year of school', he said of his first year at the Academy. What had changed more than anything else for Rickie was his attitude about school. He confessed to not liking junior high school very much because there was so much competition among students for favoritism and 'the teachers were not close to the students'. He perceives the Academy as quite different. 'I had never experienced this before where the teachers are close and encourage me. I was just a C + /B − student, but now I am an A/B student.'

Another way to assess student achievement is to look at program completion and/or high school graduation rates, although these data are hard to interpret because of the open enrollment policies of some programs.[3] Students graduating from or completing the program range from 3 per cent to 40 per cent of the students enrolled in 1986/87. In addition, the data indicate that about one-quarter to more than one-half of the students enrolled in 1986/87 will return to the program for another year; an additional 6 per cent to 40 per cent will return to their previous school or enroll in another district program. Together these indicators define a range of successful outcomes for programs dealing with at-risk youth. Considered together, these figures suggest that the programs are successful with slightly less than half to more than three-quarters of the students with whom they work.

Although the number of students earning a high school diploma may sometimes appear low (ranging from 2 per cent to 40 per cent), it should be remembered that even fewer of these students would have graduated had they not enrolled in a special program. Furthermore, we should remind ourselves that virtually all of the students enroll in these programs with credit deficiencies; many have earned few or even no credits in their one or two years of high school. For many of these students, high school graduation is not a realistic possibility. Even without the acquisition of a high school diploma, students can benefit from what they are able to learn in these programs.

Evaluating Other Program Effects

Finally, several other desirable outcomes are likely to result from both enhanced sense of school membership and academic engagement. In the following sections we look at program effects on self-esteem, locus of control, perception of opportunity, academic self-concept, aspirations for further schooling and provision of social services.

Building self-esteem

Students' sense of being part of a collective educational enterprise encourages not only better attendance and cooperation, it also leads them to experience an increased sense of worth and competence. Students at New Futures, for example, often felt isolated and negatively judged in the schools they attended prior to entering this special program for pregnant teens and mothers. At New Futures, staff encourage students to accept their situation and to build on their pregnancy or motherhood. 'They make you feel that you're special', Jill said of her teachers. 'They go the extra mile to make you feel like somebody.' Debra commented, 'I feel proud. I had a baby, and I finished school. I had to work harder. I'm proud of it. It gives you a good feeling.' Not only do the girls at New Futures recognize their own sense of pride and self-confidence, but others see it as well. Carolyn Gaston, the school's Principal, reported that students who have participated in the program often are characterized as 'more mature' than other youths their age or other teenage mothers. They also have been described as 'well-grounded'.

Teresa, another New Futures student, spoke of visiting her former school to re-enroll. She told one girl she had been at New Futures and had a baby; the girl would not believe her until a third friend came along to verify it. A boy asked nonchalantly whether it had been a boy or girl and its name. Teresa answered calmly and proudly that she had named him Nicholas.

> It made me feel good to tell them without being embarrassed about it. That would really make it hard, if I felt embarrassed about it, but I don't. ... I think of it as, I know something that they don't. I have a great joy and it's something they haven't felt.

Gina, a former student from the Wayne Enrichment Center, experienced a similar boost to her self-confidence and sense of adequacy after participating in this alternative program in Indianapolis. She had been at the neighboring high school for less than a semester when she decided to drop out. She said she didn't know anyone, that she had entered the school with friends, but she never saw them. She felt the school was too big and that no one cared about her. She started skipping and was then threatened with expulsion for forging notes from her parents. A short stay at WEC reoriented Gina to the importance of finishing school and helped her to touch a reservoir of inner strength she feels will allow her to overcome the isolation she continues to experience at the larger school. She participated regularly in student group activities run by WEC staff members for former WEC students who had returned to the high school. She liked the fact that through the group she could help other students survive in a big, impersonal, uncaring environment.

Students in a majority of the programs experienced similar changes in their perceptions of their own self-worth. Their responses on the Wisconsin Youth Survey indicated that in ten of thirteen programs, student self-esteem increased. Estimated effect sizes for these ten programs ranged from .06 to .69 standard deviations. The three exceptions include the two programs where the intervention differs little from conventional schooling (Lincoln and Orr) and Croom. While this finding is unsurprising for Lincoln and Orr, interpretation of the Croom data is more problematic. While the post-test scores of students at Croom Vocational High School show declines in all but two of the attitudes and orientations measured (social bonding to teachers and sociocentric reasoning), these data differ substantially from the solicited and unsolicited testimony of Croom students and the observational data we collected.

Another factor related to self-worth is called locus of control. This refers to the student's belief that factors that affect his or her life are within (internal) or beyond (external) personal control. Successful programs for at-risk youth ought to empower students by helping them take control of their lives. A more internal locus of control was reported by students in nine programs, with estimated effect sizes ranging from .06 to .95 standard deviations.

Perceived opportunity and aspirations for further schooling

As students begin to feel more confidence in themselves and more in control of their own lives, many come to view their personal potential and future possibilities differently. Students in seven of thirteen programs believed that a greater number of opportunities were available to them and that they had a greater chance of success in the future. Estimated effect sizes ranged from .03 to .83 standard deviations.

Students in eight of thirteen programs reported higher aspirations for further schooling, with estimated effect sizes ranging from .02 to .87 standard deviations. This may be closely tied to the fact that students in nine of thirteen programs reported increased academic self-concept. Estimated effect sizes ranged from .11 to .94 with seven programs having an effect of .20 standard deviations or more.

One student whose aspirations and academic self-concept increased after enrolling in a special program for at-risk youth is Rickie, a Media Academy student mentioned earlier. Rickie, an Hispanic student, had realized higher education was probably beyond his parents' means and had stopped considering college as an option. Now, after his experiences at the Academy, he is thinking about the possibility of initially enrolling in a community college and seeing what might happen from there. Like Alex, he is attempting to determine how he might best support himself and take control of his own future. Frances, mentioned in chapter 3, had expected to drop out of high school when she discovered she was pregnant. After being directed to New Futures by her gynecologist, she was able to earn her diploma and win a scholarship that will allow her to attend the local state university to pursue her interest in engineering. Before entering these special programs, students like Rickie, Alex and Frances would have been written off as non-college material. Support from concerned adults helped them to identify different vocational trajectories for themselves.

Curiously, in two programs academic self-concept increased but aspirations for further schooling declined. These declines may simply represent declines in unrealistically high expectations sometimes held by disadvantaged youth (Wehlage and Rutter, 1986; Newmann and Rutter, 1983). At the Media Academy, academic self-concept declined yet aspirations for further schooling increased. This may be related to the fact that this was the most academically rigorous of the fourteen programs; declining academic self-concept may indicate that students are becoming more aware of how much they don't know and how much they will need to know to succeed after high school. In the two programs most like conventional schools and the control group (Lincoln and Orr), both academic self-concept and aspirations for further schooling declined at post-test.

As we became familiar with many of the youth enrolled in these programs, we began to wonder whether increased perception of opportunity or aspirations for further schooling should be expected or desired in all programs. Where students are unrealistic about their future prospects, programs can perform a valuable service by helping them assess future opportunities in more realistic terms. This suggests that the diminished perception of opportunity reported by students at Plymouth Christian Youth Center, the Media Academy and Croom may not reflect a program shortcoming.

Not all students in programs for at-risk youth possess the skills or proclivities to make advanced academic training a reality. Regardless of this, they are also helped to determine ways by which they might create futures that will be meaningful and satisfactory. Students at Croom, for example, are chosen specifically because of their low academic ability and directed into career paths geared toward local employment. Upon graduating, for example, one former student found a job as a groundskeeper at a large industrial laundry. Because of another employee's illness, he was asked to work inside one day. His performance so impressed his supervisors that they soon found him a permanent inside job. The company eventually offered to pay for additional schooling. Today he is pursuing an associate's degree at a local technical school and handling some sophisticated engineering tasks such as installing new machinery and programming microprocessors. He credits Croom with much of his success.

The Wayne Enrichment Center offers many of its students the same kinds of enhanced job opportunities. Jim, for example, is a hefty, bearded white male who appears somewhat older than his peers. He is the sole means of support for himself and his parents, both of whom are unable to work. Because of his age and lack of a high school diploma, Jim's job options are limited. He works long hours as a mechanic's assistant to compensate for a low hourly wage. When interviewed on a Wednesday, he said he had worked sixty-seven hours the previous week and had already worked forty-five hours that week. WEC is allowing him to complete his high school education. He says he 'would never have gotten a diploma any other way'. The diploma will open up other options for him, including the military, which he intends to enter in order to continue his mechanical training.

Provision of Social Services

Finally, programs often perform the function of linking students to needed social services. Our data indicate as many as 25 per cent of students enrolled in a particular program are receiving drug and/or alcohol rehabilitation services. In addition, programs frequently help students secure counseling, part-time jobs, medical services, child care and even housing or clothing.

Discussion

Our data suggest that most of the fourteen programs we studied have a positive impact on at-risk students' attitudes, academic performance, in-school behavior and attendance rates. In addition, significant numbers of these students are (a) choosing to remain in school by either staying in the program for another year or returning to their regular school; (b) entering the labor market with enhanced skills; or (c) earning a high school diploma. Finally, many students in programs for at-risk youth benefit from personal counseling or other social services provided by or as a result of program participation.

Six programs in particular showed positive impact on many dimensions of their students' lives. Students at WEC reported positive changes on all eleven attitudes or personal orientations, while students at NA-WAY-EE, Sierra Mountain, and the School-Within-a-School reported positive changes on ten orientations. Students at Alcott and New Futures reported positive changes on eight and nine of the eleven orientations respectively. In addition, each of these programs reported consistent positive changes in academic performance, in-school behavior and attendance.

It is important to note that the six schools which most consistently appear to affect student attitudes and academic performance are markedly different from conventional schools in several important ways. In these programs, teachers have assumed the additional roles of counselor, confidante, and friend, and efforts are made to bond the students to the school, to the teaching staff, and to one another. Course content is more closely tied to the needs of the students in these programs, and efforts are made to make the courses more engaging and relevant. Greater emphasis is placed on hands-on and experiential learning and students are given greater responsibility for their own success. More attention is paid to the individual needs and concerns of students, in and outside of class. Teachers work together to govern the school and make critical decisions about curriculum and school policy. As a result, the programs can adapt to new circumstances quickly. A climate of innovation and experimentation is common, and teachers function as educational entrepreneurs.

In contrast, the least effective programs (Lincoln and Orr), as measured by our eleven attitudes and personal orientations, differed little from conventional schools. At Lincoln, a group of academically promising students are deliberately scheduled into courses for the college-bound, but neither the instruction, the content, nor the expectations for student performance changes. Lincoln students report higher levels of social bonding to teachers at post-test, but lower levels of social bonding to school, self-esteem, academic self-concept, aspirations for further schooling and overall perception of opportunity. In addition, students' attendance rates and grade point averages declined while in the program.

At Orr Community Academy, students take fewer courses and the class period is doubled to provide for more sustained and intensive study of selected subjects, but, for the most part, teaching has not changed. The standard combination of lecture and seatwork predominates, although there are notable exceptions. While reading scores and attendance rates improved significantly, and grade point averages improved slightly at post-test, students reported a diminished sense of social bonding to teachers, schools, peers and conventional roles, lower self-esteem, lower self-concept, diminished aspirations for further schooling and diminished perception of opportunity.

Summary

Taken together, our data suggest that while conventional schooling may be successful with many youth, it is problematic for those who are at risk. Conventional schooling assumes all students can give meaning to a complex and fragmented array of academic courses, that all students recognize or are able to construct a congruence between schooling and their lives, that students have similar capacities and motivations for learning, that learning is unaffected by the sense of isolation that some students feel in large impersonal institutions, and that students can shield their academic performance from the pressures of outside influences or life circumstances.

The most successful of these fourteen programs can be viewed as prototypes of alternative structures that respond in diverse ways to both the surface characteristics and the underlying needs of at-risk youth. We have attempted to show through qualitative and quantitative data the extent to which these programs are able to diminish students' sense of incongruity, isolation and incompetence, and to reengage these youth in the enterprise of schooling.

Evidence of increases in social bonding to teachers and school, self-esteem, academic self-concept, locus of control and sociocentric reasoning suggest that programs can respond constructively to students' underlying needs. Evidence of improved attendance and behavior, and an increase in the number of credits earned indicate these positive effects are being translated into improved academic performance.

We have seen how programs can affect student performance when teachers assume the extended roles of counselor, confidante and friend, and efforts are made to bond the students to the school, to the teaching staff and to one another. We have seen how at-risk youth can be reengaged in school when more attention is paid to their individual needs and concerns in and outside of class, when greater emphasis is placed on hands-on and experiential learning, and when they are granted greater responsibility for their success. Finally, we have seen how important it is that teachers feel accountable for the individual success of each of their students, and that they be allowed to work together to govern the school and make critical decisions about curriculum and school policy.

In summary, the most successful programs for at-risk youth appear to link school more closely to the experience and values of the students they serve. In addition, by establishing a climate of trust and support, successful programs for at-risk youth help diminish isolation and enhance self-esteem. Together, these factors allow students to focus less on past failure and present circumstances and more on the relationship between success in school and the possibility of a better future.

Notes

1   The Wisconsin Youth Survey was developed by Gary Wehlage, Calvin Stone and Robert Rutter at the University of Wisconsin-Madison. Although this instrument no longer mirrors precisely our emergent theoretical perspective (examined in previous chapters), it parallels that perspective closely enough to provide valuable information about the impact these programs have on at-risk youth.

2   Estimated effect size is calculated by subtracting the pre-test mean from the post-test mean and dividing the difference by the pre-test standard deviation. Estimates of effect size often are used to provide simple but useful estimates of the impact of a given treatment when restricted scale range in combination with small sample size make calculations of statistical significance difficult to interpret. The impact represented by a given effect size can be understood as follows. On average, students will show a net gain of 34 percentile ranks on a particular attitude scale when the program had an estimated effect size of 1.0. For example, a student who scored at the 50th percentile on the pre-test would now score at the 84th percentile. Similarly, a student, having participated in a program with an estimated effect size of only .50 for a particular dimension, could be expected to increase from the 50th to the 69th percentile at post-test.

3   For some programs (especially Plymouth Christian Youth Center, MERC, and Minneapolis Urban League Street Academy), calculating graduation and continuation rates for regular attenders rather than total enrollment (since many students enroll but do not attend regularly) would yield far higher rates than those that currently appear in the tables.

Chapter 8:
Educational Engagement

In chapter 5, we developed the idea of school membership, one of the central concepts in our dropout prevention theory. School membership occurs through social bonding which is generated by attachment, commitment, involvement and belief in the institution. One of these bonding elements, involvement, is particularly important to any conception of effective schooling. Obviously, students must be involved in schoolwork if they are to achieve desired educational outcomes. In this chapter, we continue to develop our theory by elaborating the concept of involvement as educational engagement. In other words, complete membership in a school requires students to be involved or engaged in the formal work that teachers and the curriculum prescribe. Educational engagement, no doubt, occurs on a continuum, but it is always a prerequisite to acquiring knowledge and skills. As with school membership, there are impediments to educational engagement; this chapter describes these impediments and suggests how schools can take a proactive stance to help students overcome these impediments and become educationally engaged.

Educational engagement is part of our theory of dropout prevention, and it also appears as a central problem in much of what has been written recently about American education. The spate of studies about schools confirms that the problem of low engagement in schoolwork is a general phenomenon and is not restricted to those labeled at-risk. Recent studies have reiterated what Cusick (1973) noted years ago: students are frequently mere 'spectators' of their own education; they stand on the sidelines watching and waiting and expend very little mental effort in the process. According to Cusick, weeks go by in which students invest no more than a few hours of concentrated effort. This lack of engagement is apparent in student absences, the interruption and distractions of non-academic activities and student inattention due to boredom with an uninspired curriculum. It has been suggested that the average teenager spends more time watching television each week than actively pursuing schoolwork. While at-risk students make their lack of engagement obvious, observers generally agree that it is a problem among a majority of high school students.

Goodlad (1984), Sizer (1984) and Powell *et al.* (1985) reported the extent of student passivity in the classroom, and Sizer summarized the situation with his observation that American high school students are 'all too often docile, compliant, and without initiative'. This lack of student engagement is clearly a problem the profession must address. If we are to enhance achievement, we must understand more completely how to minimize student disengagement for the broad spectrum of students, including those at-risk. 'Raising standards', for example, in an effort to coerce students into greater effort may increase engagement for some portion of the population, but what about those who are already doubtful about the value of academic effort? Our research on dropout prevention suggests that the conditions for increasing educational engagement are more complex than recognized by simple, blunt policies such as raising standards for graduation.

Defining Educational Engagement

Educational engagement refers to the psychological investment required to comprehend and master knowledge and skills explicitly taught in school. This investment is indicated by various observable forms of student effort that demonstrate attention to, and involvement in, schoolwork. Levels of engagement are indicated when students answer questions, discuss issues, write papers, complete homework, and perform tasks in a laboratory or at a work site. Engagement can also be indicated by student reports of interest in, and valuing of, completing school tasks. Engagement requires intention, concentration, even commitment by students, but it is not generated by students alone. As with school membership, the degree of engagement is highly dependent on the institution's contribution to the equation that produces learning. Engagement is the result of interaction between students, teachers and curriculum.

We assume that learning cannot occur unless a student exerts effort, and that sustained effort in academic matters can be generated by both intrinsic and extrinsic rewards. Students can be motivated by material reward from parents, social approval and status from peers, satisfying the entrance requirements for college, or the ultimate prospect of a good job and its corresponding life style. But these goals must be valued as important rewards before they will lure students to educational engagement.

Engagement is enhanced by intrinsic rewards when students perceive academic tasks as interesting or worthwhile in themselves. Some students may find it intriguing and personally satisfying to learn about ancient civilizations, religious traditions or the logic of computer programming. Some individuals may find the inherent quality of these subjects so satisfying that they invest themselves in learning. For many, however, intrinsic rewards are more likely to reside in the sense of competence they receive from mastering knowledge and skills, in working closely with peers in a group effort, in sharing a common vision or goal, and in seeing a concrete product result from their efforts. Individuals achieve internal satisfaction when such conditions exist and this stimulates continued engagement in the mastery and completion of additional learning tasks (Newmann, 1988).

The engagement of at-risk students is inhibited by a number of factors, some beyond the control of schools. Engagement is promoted or discouraged by family, peers and experiences in the culture of the larger community. If educational engagement is to be sustained, students must perceive a congruence between the value systems of their own personal and cultural backgrounds and those of the school. Success in school must be nurtured in the cultural context in which young people are reared and develop their sense of self and future. Proactive behaviors by significant adults outside the school are needed to promote educational values and respect for educational success. Parents need to provide time and space for doing homework and to guide students in making decisions about activities that otherwise compete for their time and energy. Jobs, sports, vacations, television and youth activities can interfere with school engagement.

Even where value congruence and proactive behaviors by adults are strong, other distractions can diminish engagement. Peers, by the way they spend their time out of school can reinforce or repudiate the desirability of doing schoolwork. Stressful experiences such as family crises, death or divorce may distract students from schoolwork, as will the debilitating effects of poverty and unsafe communities. Sometimes the excitement and economic opportunities of life on the streets distract students from school engagement.

But the school itself can also contribute to the disengagement of students in a number of ways. While academic success should be honored, if only a portion of students can meet the standards of achievement, or if only a restricted range of talents and abilities are rewarded as success, then only those few who have these competencies will see engagement as worthwhile. Students whose talents and abilities are neglected will find it necessary to defend their dignity by rejecting the legitimacy of educational engagement. Schools cannot reward a select few and continue to expect engagement from the rest.

Educational engagement is a complex process that involves more than simply 'motivating' students. Promoting engagement requires attention to student characteristics, the tasks students are asked to perform, the school environment in which the work takes place, and the external environment that influences the student and the school itself. In a comprehensive effort to increase the level of educational engagement among students, each of these influences must be considered and addressed.

Three Impediments to Educational Engagement

It is our contention that in spite of conditions outside the school that weaken student engagement, there are practices that educators could implement to substantially strengthen it. The level of engagement among at-risk youths could be increased if specific impediments under the control of educators were addressed. These impediments to engagement include: (1) Schoolwork is not extrinsically motivating for many students because achievement is not tied to any explicit and valued goal; (2) The dominant learning process pursued in schools is too narrow in that it is highly abstract, verbal, sedentary, individualistic, competitive and controlled by others as opposed to concrete, problem-oriented, active, kinesthetic, cooperative and autonomous. Because of these qualities, the dominant mode of learning stifles the likelihood of intrinsic rewards for many students. (3) Classroom learning is often stultifying because educators are obsessed with the 'coverage' of subject matter; this makes school knowledge superficial, and also intrinsically unsatisfying, thereby preventing students from gaining the sense of competence that ideally accompanies achievement. Any plan for the reform of school for at-risk students must address these three impediments to engagement. In the next sections, we address each of them in greater detail.

Absence of Extrinsic Reward

From the viewpoint of most at-risk students, there is little reason to work hard in school because there is little or no relationship between academic achievement and subsequent employment after high school. The 'good job' that most students can obtain after high school is tied more directly to local labor market conditions, national economic trends and the network of connections an individual has when pursuing employment than to high school achievement. In short, the 'real world' offers no rewards for academic success unless one is trying for admission to a college, something at-risk youths do not contemplate.

Bishop (1987) argues that linking school achievement more directly to employment would help to increase the level of engagement among all students. Generally, entry-level employees are required only to have earned a high school diploma, and job opportunities are unaffected by grade point averages and academic success. Because employers do not inspect transcripts for grades, or even the subjects taken, employment considerations provide no extrinsic reward factor for non-college-bound students. Thus, Bishop sees low engagement as a direct result of the labor market's failure to reward effort and achievement in high school.

In addition, it has been argued that many minority youths perceive a discriminatory 'job ceiling' that limits their potential status and the monetary rewards within the employment system (Ogbu, 1974). The cultural message among many minorities is that effort and achievement in school make no difference in the job market.

With little or nothing to gain from educational engagement, a widely shared peer culture has developed among secondary school students that actively discourages effort at academic achievement. This culture operates under an implicit assumption that no one will try too hard and thereby raise the level of expectations and performance for others. Disengagement from academics is 'cool' in the peer culture. In some situations, for example, black students denigrate academic engagement and achievement as inconsistent with their identity because it is perceived as 'acting white' (Fordham and Ogbu, 1986; Fordham, 1988).

Educators can respond to the lack of extrinsic rewards in two ways. Schools should develop academic and vocational curricula that more directly connect adolescents to employment. This connection, although it is not completely under the control of schools, can be made more explicit as seen in the curriculum offered by Croom Vocational

High School with its training for immediate employment, or it can be indirect as seen in the Media Academy's development of academic skills and a vision of new opportunities for youth with these skills. In both cases, students perceive that the knowledge and skills taught in these programs can lead to valued employment or additional educational opportunities.

Connecting curriculum and employment could be an important motivational strategy for many at-risk youths. However, making school extrinsically engaging is, in our judgment, only part of the solution. This strategy assumes that young people always recognize their own self-interest and become motivated to act on it. Appealing to people's self-interest is probably a better strategy than trying to coerce them to work harder by raising academic and graduation standards. But neither strategy — nor the two together — is a sufficient foundation upon which to develop school reforms that increase engagement. Other reforms must also occur, and these should have their roots in a more comprehensive and adequate conception of learning, and in a restructured curriculum that is much less fragmented and superficial. These reforms are likely to enhance engagement based on greater intrinsic rewards and also to sustain it when school becomes difficult and requires substantial effort.

The Narrow Conception of School Learning

Reforms that will achieve greater student engagement must be based in part on different assumptions about how learning occurs and the range of competencies that can be developed as part of school learning. One way to examine the assumptions that underlie school learning is to compare it with learning that occurs outside of school. Resnick (1987), by contrasting learning in and out of school, highlights how narrowly conceived school learning is in comparison to learning and knowledge used in non-school contexts. This narrowness gives school learning an air of unreality; i.e., by restricting learning to a formalized style associated primarily with school, it appears disconnected from life beyond school and students see it as useless or even invalid (McNeil, 1986). The consequence of this narrowness is to devalue school knowledge in the eyes of students and to reduce the possibilities that school learning will be intrinsically rewarding to many students.

Further, some kinds of learning that would be intrinsically interesting to students are unavailable; among the range of skills and knowledge that are needed to be successful outside of school, only some are rewarded in school. Students capable of developing competence in areas unrecognized by the conventional school curriculum are denied important opportunities, even though society is likely to value these competencies in the workplace. The experiences provided by School-Within-a-School, Croom, Media Academy and New Futures that challenge students to build, create, maintain, care for others, and communicate are counterpoints to the typical learning experiences in schools.

Resnick identifies two characteristics of school learning that restrict its scope. First, the learning process in school is highly individualistic and ignores the socially shared learning process that occurs and is required in many settings outside the classroom. In school, students are to acquire a specified body of knowledge and skills through a process that requires independent — rather than interdependent — learning. In fact, many schools have gone to the extreme of individualizing learning, and in so doing they have removed the student from interpersonal contexts that provide meaning and purpose to learning. Typically there is no emphasis on group efforts to achieve or to solve a common problem. In contrast, learning outside the school is almost always embedded in some interdependent process in which learning and sharing of information with others is an indispensible characteristic.

Modern organizations exemplify the practice of group learning. Businesses frequently cite the need for workers who are able to work with others in problem-solving situations. Some of the most important recent innovations in manufacturing productivity, for example, in Japanese auto manufacturing, have developed around cooperative work-groups. The assembly line approach is disappearing as flexible, custom manufactured products from carpeting and denim to machine tools and kitchen cabinets are increasingly in demand. Health care is another example of the emphasis on group sharing of knowledge; when a patient enters a clinic to be examined and treated for some malady, there is, by necessity, a cooperative effort in which knowledge is generated and shared by a wide array of professionals.

School learning exhibits remarkably little group or cooperative orientation. Classroom cooperation often is considered cheating. Only recently has research produced a conception of 'cooperative learning' that demonstrates effectiveness in promoting learning among a range of students (Newmann and Thompson, 1987). This approach is not yet widely employed, however, in American schools.

According to Resnick, the dominant definition of achievement also narrows the scope of school learning. Achievement is most commonly defined as the acquistion of knowledge that can be recalled by students. There is no apparent purpose to such knowledge other than answering teachers' questions. Typically, teachers ask students to organize their thoughts on carefully circumscribed subject matter in order to respond correctly to subsequent questions. Teacher questions require students to respond verbally to teacher cues, to mark the correct answer from alternatives supplied on a test, or to write statements that demonstrate that some knowledge has been acquired. Achievement is measured in terms of students' ability to answer teachers' questions rather than their ability to produce a product or engage in a dialogue about some issue or problem. Competence displayed by correctly answering teacher questions is so restricted that it seems unimportant to the present or future of many students. They feel no personal ownership of the knowledge school requires them to learn. Taken together, this restricted conception of learning pursued through a highly individualistic approach that requires responses to teachers' seemingly irrelevant questions results in disengagement for many students.

In contrast, the context for acquiring out-of-school knowledge most frequently involves practical usefulness, whether the field is medicine, law, automobile repair or carpentry. 'Real world' knowledge has practical purpose and social value, both to the individual and to some larger group. The 'test' for most out-of-school learning is successful application in a practical setting. Within schools, educators need to develop a much broader range of assessment strategies indicating the ability of students to apply skills and knowledge. Archbald and Newmann (1988) develop the concept of 'authentic achievement' in their discussion of various assessments now used in some schools that include student portfolios and public performances.

In summary, this section has argued that in-school learning needs to become a socially shared process in which students work together in a cooperative framework to produce socially valued outcomes. Most students are likely to feel ownership of the knowledge they are generating when it is characterized by these qualities. The intent is to increase the chance that students will find intrinsic rewards in their work, thereby enhancing student engagement. This is not to suggest that every lesson must be explicitly 'relevant' to students. Educators can certainly ask students to suspend judgment about the 'relevance' of certain knowledge, but the persistent separation of school learning from learning as it occurs in the world outside of school is maintained at the cost of considerable disengagement.

Coverage and a Superficial Curriculum

Traditional teaching is dominated by an obsession with coverage of vast amounts of information in many different subjects. Coverage is characterized by racing through topic after topic in order to 'expose' students to the key concepts and facts of a broad school subject. The coverage process fragments knowledge, produces only superficial understanding that inhibits gaining a sense of competence from learning, and undermines whatever intrinsic interest that subject matter might hold for students.

Critics have bemoaned the cheapening of the curriculum through a proliferation of courses and the creation of a 'shopping mall' mentality that promotes student choice of courses based on whatever strikes their fancy (Powell, Farrar and Cohen, 1985). While not disputing this claim, we believe a more serious problem is the obsession with coverage that characterizes even the traditional 'solid' academic courses in most high schools. There is no end of good ideas and topics to which students should be exposed. As more and more knowledge is developed, teachers feel obligated to cover this knowledge — to expose students to all the topics, ideas and facts that are important in a subject area.

But this obsession with coverage is a frustrating, losing battle for teacher and student alike. Consider the enormity of the task implied in covering 'United States History: Reconstruction to the Present'. Not only does the course cover a large time span, which obviously gets longer each year, but there are historians hard at work generating more and more knowledge about a myriad of topics within this span of years. And new knowledge does not necessarily replace old; newly-discovered facts and interpretations must be compared with traditional views of what happened in the past. Not only is more knowledge being generated about Andrew Johnson, Teddy and Franklin Roosevelt and John F. Kennedy, but whole new topics are being constantly identified. Increasing interest in, and demand for, a view of history reflecting the roles of women and minorities, for example, have created new bodies of knowledge that must be given their due. Traditional fields of specialization, such as foreign policy and labor history, have been sub-divided to create additional topics beckoning for attention by the textbook writer, teacher and student.

The disciplines of history, the social sciences, literature and the humanities are probably more seriously affected by this proliferation of knowledge than others. Certainly, the sciences, too, have an expanding body of knowledge that teachers feel obligated to cover. State mandates, district guidelines and competency tests further exacerbate the need to cover 'all' of a subject. The blatant reality is that students can never successfully learn all that might be covered in the various content areas, and yet coverage continues to dominate the classroom.

Newmann (1988) sees coverage as a destructive 'addiction' that destroys the curriculum. Teachers feel obligated to cover all of the topics of the book or official curriculum, and yet they realize that much has been left out, not understood, or even misunderstood. Newmann argues that this addiction to coverage is grounded in an illusion that people can master all that might be important to know. This illusion is responsible for wasting a tremendous amount of time in schools since most of what is covered passes out of the student's head shortly after the obligatory exam. But more insidious than the waste of time is the 'mindlessness' that coverage encourages. Newmann states:

> Classrooms become places where material must be learned, even though it may seem nonsensical to students (because there is no time to explain), where students are denied the opportunities to explore related topics they may be curious about (because their interests may wander too far from the official topics to be covered), where teachers' talents for teaching subtle nuances and complexities are squelched. As a result, many students stop asking questions soon after early elementary grades; they passively allow teachers and texts to pour material into their heads to be stored for future reproduction...

Newmann outlines the only feasible alternative to coverage: a curriculum designed to treat selected topics in depth. His conception of curriculum depth is consistent with Sizer's (1984) and is captured by the phrase 'less is more', but the meaning of this phrase must be clarified. Less refers to less mindless coverage and less acquisition of superficial knowledge; more refers to greater mastery of fewer topics. More also refers to greater complexity of understanding and more thoughtfulness about the topics investigated. More does *not* refer to more reliance on a skills-oriented curriculum, but it does imply greater competency in those skills acquired while studying topics in depth. Learning characterized by thoughtfulness and increased competency in the use of skills and knowledge on the part of students is, in our judgment, more likely to be intrinsically rewarding and thus more engaging.

In summary, we believe the problem of engaging the at-risk student in schoolwork is explained to a large extent by the impediments that prevent learning from being extrinsically and intrinsically reward-ing. Weak engagement, in turn, contributes to underachievement for some and dropping out for others. Schools cannot hope to make major inroads into the dropout problem without attacking these impediments, whether in traditional comprehensive high schools or in alternatives intended for dropout prevention.

Some Examples of Educational Engagement

Innovations to overcome these impediments to engagement were sporadic in many of the schools we studied. We found that some of the schools were more resourceful than others in developing a broader range of learning experiences for at-risk students. In some schools the first priority was to promote school membership rather than to develop more engaging learning strategies. There were, however, some out-standing examples of educators overcoming the impediments to edu-cational engagement. The best innovations in curriculum responded to students' need for both extrinsic and intrinsic rewards and provided for a broader range of opportunities for students to develop competence. In this section, we present some examples of successful engagement of at-risk students.

The Media Academy with its focus on skills, knowledge and dispositions required in the electronic and print media, exhibited the most comprehensive effort toward increasing student engagement. This example is especially useful to educators because it suggests a number of thematic variations that could be adapted elsewhere. The generalizable characteristics can be found in clear linkage to the world outside of school through the use of local media enterprises. Daily classroom work frequently centers on contemporary events of interest and meaning to students. Competence is gained as students become familiar with the skills of writing and video production, the course's technical tools. Students produce their own newspapers, editorials and public service commercials, which require in-depth study. Since student work is publicly acknowledged as important, extrinsic rewards are powerful. Frequent feedback from students and adults about the program's successful publications gives whole groups of students both extrinsic and intrinsic satisfaction for their efforts.

The Media Academy is an example of how learning can be a socially useful enterprise. The questions that trigger students' written products are frequently their own, developed out of a personal decision to pursue a particular topic. Students are producing something they, their peers and adults find useful and important in daily life. These characteristics imbue a sense of ownership to school work and make it intrinsically rewarding. A powerful learning process has been set in motion when a group becomes engaged in creating products that can be examined, used and preserved as symbols of success and competence. Some of these rewards spring from accomplishing a group effort that is larger than any single individual. Compelling also is the perception expressed by students that their school work represents 'real work' and has the status of what adults do outside of school.

The Media Academy also provides a good example of how school learning can be constructed to reward a range of diverse abilities and interests. Newspaper production is comprised of a great variety of tasks; among them there is almost always one which a student can successfully perform and gain a sense of competence. Some students are better at interviewing and getting a good story, while others may be more skilled at editing, taking and developing pictures, selling ads, or typing stories into the word processor. All are necessary for a successful product, and contain the potential for extrinsic and intrinsic rewards. This is not to suggest that students are channeled immediately into narrow job specialities, but rather that in the production of media there is a wide range of tasks and skills students can perform. This increases the likelihood of each student finding a niche in which he or she can contribute and thereby receive rewards and a sense of competence within the context of a group effort.

Finally, the Media Academy provides an example of how the typical school's obsession with coverage can be exorcised. 'Depth' is provided by concentrating on skills, knowledge and dispositions that are essential in the media field. Happily, the substantive issues and events that are the subjects of journalism utilize important academic skills and knowledge — reading, writing, oral communication and thinking critically. The media curriculum of journalism, English and social studies continually focuses student efforts rather than dispersing them through a broad coverage of topics that students have to be 'exposed to'.

Surveying feature articles in the newspapers produced by the Media Academy, one is struck by the seriousness and maturity of the writing. Stories and editorials frequently touch on important social issues: AIDS, apartheid, 'date rape', the conflict between teens working and studying, drug abuse, school policies on attendance and tardiness. Steve O'Donoghue and Mike Jackson, the lead teachers in the

Academy, make explicit attempts to push students toward critical or higher order thinking. The teachers repeatedly call upon students to think and write about topics in complex ways. This challenge to students is responsible for much of the engagement that can be observed in classes.

An example of a class from the Media Academy offers some insight as to why students are engaged and the quality of their engagement. The following account is from Mike Jackson's English class. The students have been reading Richard Wright's *Native Son*. Coincidentally, an issue of *Newsweek* magazine carries a long article about 'Today's Native Sons' who live in the nation's urban centers. Jackson seizes the opportunity to compare Wright's work with this contemporary journalistic version of 'native son'. Generally, his purpose is to help his students to think critically about issues affecting them by using history, literature and contemporary accounts.

The magazine article depicts a scene of young black men who are unemployed drop-outs and criminals. The litany of depressing social conditions is not unfamiliar to the youthful readers. Students take turns reading the article aloud. Some struggle with the words, mispronouncing them or are unable to give their meanings when asked. 'Who can help Jimmy with "paradoxical"?' asks Jackson. Sometimes he uses an idea from a paragraph to launch into an historical comparison with Richard Wright's experiences several decades earlier. He pulls no punches about racism, but many of the students seem ignorant about the historical context of the examples used in the article. Jackson tries to fill in the gaps in their knowledge. For example, no one appears to know what a 'Jim Crow' law was, and he gets blank stares when he asks for the meaning of *'de facto* segregation'. Jackson is most successful in generating student discussion when reference is made to local conditions. For example, students can identify and discuss the conflict of values exemplified by Oakland's recent funeral parade given by some local citizens to honor a slain drug dealer.

In Steve O'Donoghue's journalism class, the style is different but engagement is also high. One particular class finds students assembling at the beginning of the hour for an attendance check and a few instructions and reminders. The class then scatters as individuals head off across campus in pursuit of various stories they have selected to write. One student was to interview the senior class president, another the captain of the basketball team, and others sought out various leads about upcoming school events. One boy returned, crestfallen, to complain that a teacher with whom he had made an appointment had canceled. It was surprising to find a student disappointed at not being able to pursue a school assignment; most adolescents would be delighted to find an excuse for not continuing their work.

This kind of coursework was typical of what occurred in a journalism class and it generated a substantial degree of engagement. It was characterized by concrete tasks to perform, such as interviewing and writing, and these called upon students to be active and relatively autonomous in their work. Students produced articles that had meaning in the context of school life and could be evaluated in terms of shared standards. Increasing competency could be observed and it was rewarding to students when they saw themselves improving in skills essential to being a better writer. By emphasizing a core of skills in journalism, English and history, the problem of superficial coverage was reduced. When articles were published, students received extrinsic rewards in the form of recognition from peers and adults.

Sustaining student engagement in educational tasks is a significant problem. Teachers need help in this, and developing a student peer culture that supports educational engagement is an important form of help. The Media Academy differs from a typical high school in that younger students have frequent contact with their older, more experienced and competent peers. Sophomores in the Academy encounter juniors and seniors as the latter take primary responsibility for publishing the two newspapers. This contact occurs primarily in the production room where concrete tasks are performed. The sophomores see the older students in the most responsible roles associated with the papers. Younger students are able to acquire the culture of the Media Academy as they gain an image of the work involved in newspaper production. This setting creates an induction process in which the norms and skills are passed on from one group to the next. This peer culture serves to re-enforce and sustain the engagement of students when not in direct contact with teachers.

In addition, the Media Academy's three-year curriculum provides long-term or extended contact between teachers and students. Such extended contact provides two benefits that enhance engagement. First, teachers and students are able to develop close personal relationships over the three years of the program. Academy teachers can become mentors and coaches much more readily than those in conventional high schools where students tend to pass from teacher to teacher, one semester at a time.

Second, the three-year curriculum allows teachers to take a 'developmental' view of students. For example, O'Donoghue mentioned that a particular student is 'only a fair writer now, but when I get through with her she'll be a lot better'. Taking a developmental view of students contributes to a feeling that these teachers can invest themselves in students and that there is a good chance this investment will pay off. Students will get better at their writing, editing and critical-thinking skills. From a teacher's perspective, it is possible to anticipate satisfaction that comes from working with students as they improve. Moreover, there will be proof of this improvement in the concrete products of newspapers and other media productions.

A similar long-range view of school has been internalized by a number of the students. They spoke about a sense of progress, about seeing themselves improve as they move from simpler to more complex tasks in writing and production. Older students who had been in the Media Academy for three years testified that keeping a group together over this span also builds a sense of community among them. They talked about the closeness they felt for one another that had developed through cooperation required to produce newspapers. The Media Academy builds the kind of school membership that is the foundation for educational engagement.

The Media Academy challenges a number of conventional assumptions about what it means to learn in school, and provides some insights into the program's success at engagement. How unlike traditional school to have students, particularly those who are at-risk, in active roles, producing socially useful products such as a Spanish/English-language paper for a local community and creating public service announcements and commercials for radio and television. How unlike school to have students working cooperatively on a group project and at the same time becoming competent in the necessary academic skills of reading, writing, speaking and critical thinking. How unlike school to engender a sense of school membership through academics rather than extracurricular activities such as sports or music.

Other schools we studied developed curriculum that provided some of the same intensity of engagement. New Futures, for example, places a significant emphasis on courses concerned with child development and parenting, a curriculum developed by the staff at the school over a number of years. This instruction is seen by the young mothers as providing important knowledge related to their own and their children's futures. Acquisition of this knowledge is intrinsically rewarding. In addition, this knowledge is linked to their experiences in the day-care centers as well as to their own children. Engagement was high in such courses and experiences regardless of students' academic skills and previous school performance.

A number of schools were successful in producing strong engagement in vocational and experiential components of their curricula. School-Within-a-School developed significant out-of-school experiences that provide rewards to students and tap diverse abilities and inclinations, but most importantly, achieve success in relation to schoolwork. All SWS students did volunteer work in either day-care centers or nursing homes, and all helped in the reconstruction of old houses which are then sold to low-income families.

These experiences are part of a vocational preparation curriculum designed to provide students with experiences in socially useful work. Success in such work tends to build a sense of self-esteem for having accomplished concrete tasks of value. 'Real world' experiences such as those found in house reconstruction, day-care centers and nursing homes are selected because they place students in contact with mature and skilled adults. The rationale is not primarily to teach these young people the vocational skills necessary to be day-care workers or carpenters, although they may choose to pursue one of these fields. Rather, the intent is to provide them with experiences in adult roles and to help them begin to make the transition to the world of work. In addition, this experiential learning provides students who have a history of academic failure with an opportunity to be successful and to develop new competencies that are socially valued.

Students who have nothing but failure and frustration to show for their work in academics often blossom in working in non-school settings. Lucinda, one of the poorest readers in SWS, was unlikely to find success in traditional schoolwork, but her energy and positive attitude were responsible for much of the success she found working in a nursing home. The residents there were taken by her enthusiasm and friendliness. Lucinda completed her time at the nursing home with a new sense of competence previously unavailable to her in the context of traditional academic work.

Rolando, one of the least academically engaged boys in SWS, enjoyed a similar success. He immediately took to the work involved in reconstructing an old house. Within a few weeks, his energy, skill and common sense about the tasks that needed to be done were noticed by the carpenter who headed the student crew. Rolando was made 'sub-foreman', which carried with it additional responsibilities such as making sure the crew was on task and that supplies and equipment were put away at the end of the day. For the first time in his school career, Rolando had been singled out for his responsibility and competence, a student to be emulated.

Croom students also performed socially useful work as part of their vocational curriculum. In shop courses, students performed routine maintenance on the school's buildings. In the building construction and maintenance course, students repaired screens and windows, sanded and resurfaced floors and rebuilt porches. The groundskeeping students maintained the extensive and attractive lawns and gardens that are considered a mark of distinction at Croom. The students in the food service course prepare the noon meal each day for the student body. These kinds of experiential learning produce a natural engagement that is often lacking in conventional courses, where students read about rather than experience various topics. Although Croom, the Media Academy and SWS differ in some important ways, each introduces students to a range of activity they consider 'real work' and is likely to produce extrinsic and intrinsic rewards.

Experiential learning opportunities of the type described can provide students with a chance to develop and display abilities that conventional schooling has ignored. To the extent that these experiences provide students with success and a sense of enhanced competence, educational engagement will be substantially higher than is typically found among at-risk students in the contemporary high schools.

A Theory of Dropout Prevention

Educational engagement, the second major component in our theory of dropout prevention, has now been presented. Educational engagement and school membership comprise the central concepts in the theory modeled in figure 1.

The theory focuses on school factors associated with dropping out and directs attention to those conditions over which practitioners have some control; i.e. social relations within the school and forms of learning and curriculum. These school factors include the quality of relationships between adults and students and the amount of extrinsic and intrinsic rewards students can be expected to derive from learning. Social relations address ways in which educators can actively assist students in becoming bonded to the institution. There is some overlap and redundancy in these theoretical concepts, but this is not necessarily

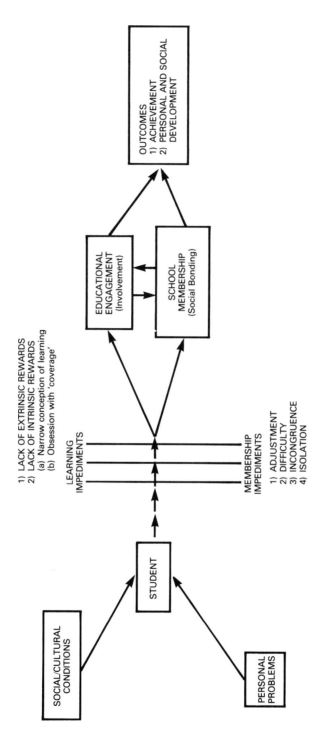

Figure 1: Dropout Prevention Theory: School Factors

a problem. Instead, it further demonstrates that the dropout problem involves a number of interacting and interrelated factors that constitute a complex phenomenon.

The theory hypothesizes school membership as the foundation upon which educational engagement is built. Interaction between these two concepts is indicated. Engagement and membership are shown as intermediate goals that schools must promote as a way of helping students arrive at the outcomes of achievement and personal and social development. The specific impediments to both engagement and membership are the leverage points for practitioners — adjustment, difficulty, incongruence, isolation and lack of extrinsic and intrinsic rewards. It is this notion of impediments that makes the theory helpful to practitioners. By identifying impediments within the school, educators can focus on those conditions that block students' movement into membership and engagement. Educators can use this theory to analyze their school and to invent ways of altering the experiences of students.

Underlying this model is another set of school factors concerned with enabling educators to work effectively with at-risk students. Chapter 6 described the teacher culture and structural conditions identified in the various alternative schools. These can be seen as necessary conditions for educators, if they are to help students overcome impediments to membership and engagement. In other words, educators must be in a position to alter school conditions for students. They must have the authority and resources to shape school practice and policy in response to at-risk students.

Briefly, these underlying and necessary conditions include a professional culture characterized by personal accountability for student success, a willingness to extend the teaching role beyond traditional practices and concerns and a spirit of optimism and persistence with students characterized as difficult to teach. We also found a high degree of teacher ownership of their schools, a factor encouraged by staff collegiality, a strong role in self-governance and opportunities for educational entrepreneurship. Finally, an essential characteristic of effective schools was their small size, which permitted educators a degree of flexibility and control over school conditions. More importantly, small size facilitated frequent one-on-one interactions between adults and students. This appears to be the crucial characteristic of social relations in the successful schools we studied.

Any complete theory of effective schools with at-risk schools will need to incorporate these underlying conditions into a model. At this point, we cannot determine exactly how these conditions interact with other factors in the theory, but they appear to be necessary in order to develop a theory of effective schools.

Summary

Promoting school membership appears to be the primary effort of many alternative schools, and they are relatively successful in this endeavor. Promoting educational engagement is more difficult and requires innovations in curriculum and instruction that many educators are now beginning to develop and implement. Despite this, we presented examples from the Media Academy and other schools in which there was a high degree of educational engagement.

The concept of educational engagement, together with school membership, constitute the central concepts of our theory of dropout prevention. The theory explains how educators can induce alienated students to become active in the educational process. Theory argues that students who are school members and engaged in school work are likely to be better achievers and to develop personal and social characteristics valued by the society.

The next chapter takes a critical stance with respect to the schools we studied. It considers a number of persisting issues about alternative schools serving at-risk students. It also raises several important questions about the very factors that make these schools effective.

Chapter 9:
Continuing Issues

Many of the fourteen schools we studied have achieved a degree of success in reconnecting detached, estranged or alienated students to the process of formal education. Even so, their successes often are offset by two realities that affect all educational programs. It remains the case that many students are unable to overcome the behavioral or attitudinal patterns which formerly contributed to their initial school failure. And, secondly, even those students who graduate from high school may be unable to achieve satisfactory educational or occupational outcomes once they leave the supportive environment provided by these alternatives. A number of issues place constraints on the degree of success achieved by these programs: some are generic to most public schools, while others are more unique to alternative programs created for this specific student population.

We have argued thus far that success with at-risk youth is tied to overcoming impediments to their social membership in the school and their engagement in formal education. The creation of programs specifically suited to the problems students have encountered earlier in their educational careers or that have arisen from changes in their outside-of-school lives often is a first step to reconnecting them with the school. Schools like New Futures, the Media Academy and Croom Vocational display an element of transparent practicality that is immediately obvious to most students, particularly those who have consciously chosen to enroll in their programs. This match offers an initial vehicle for eliciting a student's commitment to a particular educational format. Sustaining that commitment often depends upon the formation of a social environment that helps youth overcome earlier patterns of resistance or apathy. The support they receive from caring and interested teachers can assist them in dealing with problems related to maladjustment, incongruence, isolation or difficulty that previously may have interfered with their educational success. As a result, alternative programs for potential dropouts are able to retain these students more effectively than would conventional schools.

It must be recognized, however, that alternative educational interventions created for at-risk students should be viewed more as experimental models than as defined and tested approaches guaranteed to eliminate school failure, reduce dropout rates and result in higher academic achievement. These programs are very much in process, struggling with individuals and issues that prevent them from achieving many of their goals.

It is the aim of this chapter to explore some of the difficulties faced by those who work with at-risk students, difficulties that may be encountered by others who attempt to create comparable programs. Our intent is not to critique the fourteen schools in our research project, but to discuss several continuing issues that confront all educators who embark on the difficult but essential task of reconnecting at-risk youth to schooling. This chapter will present a number of interrelated issues that appear to influence student performance in special programs and that impinge on these programs' ability to develop pedagogical and curricular innovations more likely to result in meaningful social and academic learning. The initial three sections of the chapter will touch on issues that arise in the programs themselves as teachers and students construct an educational environment that accords with individual and collective intentions.

Long-term Educational Issues

Perhaps one of the most difficult problems faced by teachers in these programs is that the emphasis they place on social bonding and school membership is not always attractive to potential dropouts. Some students choose not to respond to the interpersonal overtures of their teachers and refuse to accept the behavioral norms that accompany participation in a formal institution. By remaining withdrawn from adult members in their school community, such young people never experience the support that might enable them to reverse previous patterns of disaffection and, on occasion, resistance. This is the first issue that educators contemplating the innovations we have described here must confront.

The second is that despite becoming socially engaged in the life of the school, many at-risk students continue to view academic work as either meaningless, onerous or unworthy of sustained attention. Though they may fulfill the academic tasks required for continued membership in the program, they refuse to become committed to the process of learning. This reluctance is shared by the majority of American students, who even in comprehensive high schools remain disengaged from the educational process (Sedlak *et al.*, 1986). This common failure to develop the dispositions characteristic of more self-reliant learners places serious limitations on students' ability to find adequate employment in a labor market that increasingly demands some level of post-secondary training.

Contributing to student disengagement is the tendency of teachers in many of these interventions to be concerned primarily with the social and emotional problems their students bring to school. Their attention often is directed to encouraging adjustment to the institutional requirements of the school or to fostering more positive student self-esteem. They see their students as immature or emotionally injured and concentrate their efforts on these issues rather than on the very real need of at-risk youth to acquire the knowledge and the personal skills required to make their way in a highly competitive and demanding occupational environment. While drawing such students into the experience of membership in a school setting appears to be essential, this school-based membership is no guarantee that at-risk youths will make a satisfactory transition to the workforce after they have graduated.

Combined with their emphasis on emotional support, programs for at-risk youth also must attend to the more difficult task of fostering students' willingness and ability to take charge of their own learning and personal lives. Failure to do so means that special alternatives for this population run the risk of becoming sophisticated and compassionately run warehouses for students deemed undesirable by conventional schools. This kind of tracking, however, well intentioned, will not train or help these disadvantaged youth to construct decent lives for themselves. Educators who work with these students must consider both their short-term and long-term needs. They must impart to their students an understanding of the critical role further educational training, whether vocational or academic, will play as students attempt to construct adequate and meaningful occupational roles for themselves in the larger society. This can only occur when teachers create curricular programs that inspire sustained engagement and cultivate in students an independent desire for further learning.

The remaining issues discussed in this chapter relate to ways in which a concerted emphasis on curricular innovation might result in more educational engagement and improve life chances for students in these interventions. The most successful programs for at-risk youths address the problems of educational and social engagement in ways that favor neither one nor the other. Educational engagement becomes a natural outgrowth of the more collective social environment fostered at the school. In addition, these programs often present intellectual or vocational training in ways that seem purposeful and socially valuable to students.

Though such a curriculum may be viewed as philosophically desirable, the practicalities of implementing it are another matter. The lack of institutional legitimacy experienced by many of these programs often precludes the development of new curricular responses that challenge traditional conceptions of 'appropriate' classroom learning. As a result, though many of the fourteen programs we studied succeed in creating supportive social environments, few have developed academic or vocational offerings capable of eliciting the educational engagement of the majority of their students.

Programs for at-risk youths are thus faced with a variety of problems that impinge on their ability to help more of their students attain satisfactory educational or vocational goals. These problems include resistance from students themselves, unnecessarily limited expectations of teachers, and constraints imposed by the institutional environment in which these programs operate. Nonetheless, some programs have begun to develop curricular and instructional as well as social practices that draw students into a more sustained commitment to learning. Addressing their attention to students' strengths rather than weaknesses, teachers in these schools demonstrate that youth often regarded as incompetent in conventional classrooms are capable of sustained effort, academic and/or vocational mastery, and social cooperation, particularly when learning is linked to the completion of collective tasks. School environments that elicit the creativity and involvement of such students deserve to be more widely emulated.

The Limitations of Communities of Support

These alternative programs reach many, but by no means all, students with whom they come into contact. One hears of the students who fail to be reached when staff at Sierra Mountain express their frustration over students who 'stay in a bubble', who remain isolated and impervious to teachers' overtures and expectations for changed behavior. Some students spurn staff attempts to establish a personal relationship; teachers' commitment to those students' continuance in the program is lowered as a result. A teacher at the School-Within-a-School acknowledged that she felt much more supportive of, and committed to, a difficult student who had opened up to her than she did to his friend who had never shared his thoughts. Thus, we see that continued commitment on the part of teachers is predicated upon a reciprocal response from students. Even in programs that attempt to be sensitive to the characteristics of a variety of students, teachers find it difficult to sustain care for students who reject their expressions of concern. Asking them to do more may be asking the impossible (Noddings, 1984).

Students who withhold a positive, personal response to staff overtures are most likely to be recommended for transfers to other schools or dropped from a program. These 'failures' tell us about the limitations of communities of support. School membership meets many of the underlying needs of at-risk youths; when combined with a more personally relevant curriculum, many students respond to the respectful treatment by teachers, the development of competence, and the increased congruence between themselves, schooling and their future. But a closer examination of those whom these processes fail to reach reveals that supportive communities cannot succeed with students who refuse to respond to the offer of membership and who are unwilling to accept the rules that accompany such membership.

Every school has its own set of norms, values and expectations that define a 'good' student. Similar to comprehensive secondary schools, programs for at-risk youths expect that students will listen to what their teachers have to say and entertain the possibility of personal change in order to conform more closely to educators' expectations. Teachers in many of these programs see students' behavioral changes as the primary indicator of their own professional effectiveness. But some students resist becoming more congruent with the expectations of their teachers and the rules of the program. Such resistance is not infrequently connected with regular drug use, as described in chapter 3. But student incongruity with the aims of the school also can arise when the program's expectations for personal change imply a denigration or repudiation of a student's sub-cultural identity (i.e., an identity related to membership in a particular class or racial or ethnic group). The story of Bob Schwartz offers apt illustration of this point.

Bob dropped out of the School-Within-a-School in the middle of his senior year, the culmination of a process of conflict during which he was unable or unwilling to achieve congruence with the program's staff, methods or goals. Bob's sense of self, including his habit of making jokes in class, was unappreciated by the teachers. His own summer job experiences working with his father as a roofer made him unwilling to fulfill the program requirement of finding and keeping a minimum-wage job. Finally, Bob bridled at the imputation that he was a loser, that his life demonstrated failure.

Bob, who is over six feet tall, always cut an imposing figure in dark glasses, black leather jacket, motorcycle chaps and boots. He remained aloof from the impromptu, informally friendly conversations between School-Within-a-School teachers and students, and he appeared unwilling to participate in the conviviality of the program office. Yet it was this very marginality to the program and its attendant low status that were implicated in Bob's 'disruption' of classes. A particularly striking example of Bob's resistance to membership occurred during an English class in the fall of his senior year.

After a quiz on *The Merchant of Venice* and a short lecture introducing the next scenes, Mrs Kinder, the English teacher, went to the cassette player to start a recorded version of the play and discovered the tape was missing. She asked, 'Who has the tape?' No one answered; finally, Bob said he did. He sauntered to the front of the room, inserted a tape and turned on the cassette player. Heavy metal music consumed the room's silence for a few seconds as Bob performed a quick, gyrating dance for his classmates. Mrs Kinder quickly turned off the player and confiscated the tape. Grinning, Bob returned to his table by the window. The girl sitting next to him produced the tape of the play, saying, 'Can't you take a joke, Mrs Kinder?'

Earlier in the same class, Mrs Kinder had told a story about a friend who had recently returned to the university and feared not succeeding at this new endeavor. Mrs Kinder's friend had been encouraged after meeting an older woman who had retaken a college algebra class three times before she was able to earn a C. The point of the story was that people don't fail until they stop trying. Bob responded to this homily by saying, 'I've never failed in my life except classes', clearly indicating a firm sense of his own identity and strengths that went unacknowledged in the narrow world of school achievement.

This series of events is closely akin to the school 'resistance' of girls and boys documented in British studies of deviant students (Davies, 1984; Willis, 1977). Students with contrasting cultural values, low status and little power in schools demonstrate their ability to control events by disrupting lessons, especially through the use of humor. Bob's orchestrated 'play' for his classmates took advantage of the class routine of listening to a cassette tape of Shakespeare; he surprised the teacher by interrupting her smooth lesson plan with heavy metal music. Students whose identities, whose values, pasts and futures are incongruous with the expectations of teachers often resort to illegitimate, short-lived usurpations of power. They temporarily invert classroom roles so they are in control of events. Bob's marginality to the informal social life of the program and his disruption of classes suggest that he saw himself as a low-status outsider.

Given his low-status position, Bob was especially sensitive to further insults to his competence or to his sense of identity. Teachers commented about Bob's appearance; one lunch hour Mr Dams, a teacher, complimented Bob on his purple underwear, which was showing through a six-inch rip in the rear of his jeans. Bob laughed the comment off. All students received lectures from teachers regarding the need for an appearance (for example, short hair for boys, respectable clothes) in keeping with the expectations of present and future employers. Bob's long hair and ripped jeans demonstrated his resistance to these admonitions.

Bob similarly resisted the program requirement to hold a job for which a student was granted vocational educational credits. During a conversation with Mr Nidy, the program's lead teacher, Bob was reminded he needed to find a job if he hoped to earn credits for the vocational component. Bob said he was hoping to get a position at an auto-body shop but that nothing had as yet worked out. When Bob was again reminded of his failure to fill this requirement, he challenged Mr Daman, the business education teacher: 'Whose idea is it to work during the school year? Nobody had to do this last year.' Mr Daman explained that this requirement for seniors had been part of the program since its inception. Bob said he only wanted to work at Christmas, but Mr Daman told him this would not count toward the basic requirements of the course. Employed by his father as a roofer the previous summer, Bob hoped to utilize the work hours he had accumulated then for the course as well. He had become accustomed to a sizable wage, and employment in the minimum-wage positions his classmates had accepted was unappealing.

Bob was last seen at the School-Within-a-School the day he arrived with his hair cut, wearing a fresh white shirt. He was sullen and defensive, and when Mrs Kinder complimented him on his appearance, he blew up and left school. Shortly thereafter he also left home. Bob eventually returned to the program, but by that point he was so far behind on work experience credits, he dropped out.

The story of Bob Schwartz illustrates that a single program for at-risk youth may not elicit a desire for membership on the part of all potential dropouts. The School-Within-a-School's emphasis on learning work habits characteristic of conventional occupational settings was inappropriate for Bob, who knew that he could maintain his independence and behavioral style and still make an adequate living as a self-employed laborer. Such positions are no longer common, and Bob was fortunate to have access to one; this access to employment also meant that he could afford to reject the learning that the School-Within-a-School offered to him. Another program that respected his independence and imparted skills useful for running a small business might have been more likely to elicit Bob's commitment and interest.

No single model can encourage membership or respond to the specific educational needs or desires of all at-risk youth (Ghory and Sinclair, 1987; Sinclair, 1983). A multiplicity of interventions is required. Even then, however, some students may continue to resist the efforts of teachers whom they see as representatives of an opposing culture (Erickson, 1987; Waller, 1932/1961).

Social Bonding Without Academic Engagement

As articulated in chapter 7, however, many students are in fact willing to enter into the relationships with their teachers that foster social membership in the school. They become partners in the experience of 'us and us' valued so much by staff and students at Sierra Mountain. Overcoming their sense of incongruity, formerly at-risk youth discover that teachers can also be friends, and schooling can thus be a positive rather than an aversive experience. For some students, however, school membership remains limited to the social dimension. They thrive on the warmer interaction with adults and peers or the more supportive structures that set these programs apart from many conventional secondary schools. But they refuse to accept their teacher's academic demands and implicitly utilize the threat of dropping out as a means of limiting the expectations for work and involvement placed upon them by the school. Though they experience increased commitment towards these special programs, they remain reluctant to accept totally the school's agenda.

At Loring-Nicollet in Minneapolis, for example, strikingly able students often refuse to participate in class discussions, take notes or exert themselves academically. They acquiesce to the school's required math and science classes but avoid topics that might be confusing or frustrating. The classes they like most are those that give them the opportunity to talk about lifestyles, sexuality, relationships, drug use, and so on, although even in these courses their participation is often desultory. What these students claim to appreciate about Loring-Nicollet are the social and personal benefits they encounter there. Coursework is tolerated, but these students fail to become truly engaged.

This tends to be the experience of a number of students at the School-Within-a-School as well. Jason, mentioned in chapter 3, is characteristic of students who could do better but who remain distanced from the requirements of formal education. While his performance at the School-Within-a-School improved dramatically, Jason did as much as necessary, but no more. The School-Within-a-School offered him a less taxing and more supportive setting in which to complete his education. Unfortunately, it did not draw upon either his imagination or commitment, and it failed to alter the distaste he had felt towards formal education since grade school, a distaste that led Jason to refuse to consider any training past high school.

Like Jason, several students at Sierra Mountain invested only a fraction of themselves in their coursework. The father of one able student expressed uneasiness about this aspect of the program and worried aloud whether its students were being prepared for the more rigorous expectations they would encounter if they chose to pursue higher education. While recognizing that Sierra Mountain teachers faced the difficult task of eliciting any involvement from young people who had previously rejected schooling altogether, this parent feared its students were being tracked into occupational roles with limited futures.

Teachers in programs for at-risk youth must grapple with the dilemma of tempting students to school but then not driving them away with demands they may refuse to tolerate. The primary lure offered by many of the programs we studied is the opportunity to belong to a supportive educational community where tolerance, respect and care are more in evidence than in most conventional secondary schools. But teachers fear that their students will refuse to tolerate the inevitable requirements of formal education and the frustration of failure. As teachers in regular schools reduce academic expectations in order to win the cooperation of potentially resistant students (McNeil, 1986; Sedlak *et al.*, 1986), so educators in programs for at-risk youth are cautious about asking too much of their students, suspecting that if pushed, at-risk youth will simply leave.

In many of the fourteen schools, teachers' commonly held beliefs about why at-risk youth are in danger of dropping out made this accommodation acceptable. With some frequency, teachers ascribe their students' earlier school failure to personal flaws or difficult home and community backgrounds. To address these problems, teachers see their task to be quasi-therapeutic. Some assume that helping students adjust to the institutional requirements of the school and workplace will enable them to graduate and make a successful transition to the labor market. Others hope that by providing a safe environment with supportive counselors and teachers, students will begin to confront personal problems and be able to construct a stronger sense of themselves. It is not uncommon for the same educators to interpret their work in both ways at different times.

Jim Nidy at the School-Within-a-School articulated the concern about adjustment in the following way:

> I guess we really are a behavior modification program. If these kids can't get their acts together, no matter now much factual material we teach them, they're still not going to be successful in life. They've got to improve their self-concept or they're always going to be seeing themselves as losers and their marriage relationships are also not going to work for them. They have to learn how to get along with other people, which a lot of them haven't been able to do. They have to learn some respect for law and the society; whether they agree with it or not, they have to learn how to function in that society.

To facilitate this end, the School-Within-a-School is structured in a way that requires students to adopt the behavior patterns of responsible employees. A similar emphasis can be found at the Wayne Enrichment Center, the Minneapolis Education and Recycling Center and Croom Vocational High School.

Addressing personal problems and providing a shelter for non-conforming or troubled adolescents are seen as primary goals in other programs. Teachers view their schools as one of the few places where students can obtain kindness, warmth and, occasionally, food. Less insistence is placed on institutional adjustment; more energy is directed towards creating a safe and inviting environment. Earle Conway, the Principal at Sierra Mountain, indicated he knew of several students who had run away from home but continued attending classes. For such students, school becomes a place where for five or six hours each day they can experience a degree of fellowship, tolerance and physical security that may be absent in the remainder of their lives. Teachers commonly believe that creating and maintaining such an environment entails avoiding learning experiences that can lead to frustration or failure. Few students at Sierra Mountain are 'nagged' or even pushed. Making school attractive and comfortable is a primary means by which the program seeks to retain its students.

New Futures, Alcott, NA-WAY-EE, the Minneapolis Urban League Street Academy and Loring-Nicollet also focus on providing a safe and supportive learning environment in which educators consciously attempt to help students deal with personal issues that interfere with their learning. While these programs often succeed in improving their students' attendance and sense of school affiliation, this preoccupation with student problems rather than strengths has tended to divert teacher attention away from the creation of curricular offerings more likely to lead to educational engagement.

Perhaps most problematic, this deemphasis on eliciting educational involvement on the part of at-risk students ignores the changing economic environment beyond the school. Prior to the early 1970s, graduation from high school was considered an admirable and sufficient goal for at-risk youth because there was adequate work in the industrial sector for students with only a high school diploma. Such jobs are becoming increasingly scarce. *The Forgotten Half: Non-College Youth in America* (William, T., Grant Foundation, 1988) chronicles the economic plight of the 50 per cent of 20- to 24-year-olds who, because they lack post-secondary credentials, are being denied access to employment that pays a living wage. Between 1973 and 1986, the real wages paid to this group declined by 28.3 per cent. The situation for drop-outs is significantly worse; their real wages have dropped by 42.1 per cent. In comparison, the real wages of college graduates have dropped by only 6 per cent. Given the changing economic structure of our post-industrial society, it is unlikely that the situation will improve.

The tendency of educators in programs for at-risk youth to mute academic demands in order to sustain a less threatening and more embracing school climate is thus of serious concern. Teachers limit the scope and value of their programs and may unintentionally consign their students to low-paid jobs by imagining that nurturing personal and social growth is incompatible with the creation of a challenging and engaging learning environment. Social and intellectual or vocational growth, however, need not be viewed in conflicting terms. Though most American schools, including many for at-risk youth, present learning as an isolated, competitive and abstract task, this formulation of the nature of education reflects a limited understanding of how learning takes place in non-school settings. As Resnick (1987) has indicated, learning outside of formal classrooms is generally a collective process focused on the acquisition of skills and knowledge related to the completion of specific tasks. People learn in order to interact with one another in socially purposeful ways. In such settings, intellectual growth and social interaction are conjoined. Learning becomes a source of personal or group empowerment, a means for altering what may be aversive economic and social circumstances. [1]

We suspect that the abstract and isolated learning that continues to occur in most of the programs we studied, particularly in the academic subjects, fails to encourage students to accept formal educational requirements. By dwelling on the encouragement of social membership to the exclusion of sustained educational engagement, these teachers have neglected the curricular and pedagogical experimentation that might enable their students not only to adjust to school and feel better about themselves but become engaged learners in the process.

The key to bringing about this reorientation to learning need not entail the rejection of the supportive social environment already established in these schools; rather, that social environment could become the matrix in which more challenging educational experiences are developed. The task for educators will be to create curricula and pedagogical practices that make use of that environment instead of standing in opposition to it. In this way, more students may be encouraged to become involved in their own educations and to leave school better prepared to make the transition to further schooling or the workplace.

Matching or Tracking

It is clear, then, that shaping educational interventions in ways that primarily address students' emotional needs can result in a diminished emphasis on formal learning. Concern about matching what are thought to be the unique educational requirements of a specific student population also can lead to tracking and reduced expectations. Students with histories of poor academic performance traditionally have been assigned to remedial classes and vocational training; the recurrent emphasis on remediation and vocational studies in many of the fourteen programs is thus not a fresh response. It has been held up as an alternative to college preparatory education since the Cardinal Principles of Education were framed in 1918.

The great danger in this response is that it has typically involved reduced teacher expectations about future occupational possibilities for the students assigned to such classes. Students are presented with coursework that allows them to fulfill institutional requirements for graduation, but they are not encouraged or challenged to acquire knowledge or skills that will help them gain other than entry-level positions in the labor market.

Teachers in many of the fourteen programs expressed the belief that the materials taught are less important than accumulating the credits required to graduate and acquiring the habits of promptness, dependability and deference to authority. A teacher in one of the schools we studied gave voice to a commonly shared attitude towards formal learning:

> ... it really doesn't make much difference what we're teaching. I'm not a person who feels real strong about subject content because, you know, it's different if you're training a person who you know is going to go out and be a molecular biologist ... then you can really teach them stuff that's going to help them. A lot of these kids, we have no idea where they're going, what they're going to do. We try to give them the basic skills they're going to need when they're out, but what I teach in science really isn't as important as how I teach it and whether the kids feel that they're getting something out of it.

While this teacher's concern about how students respond to the curriculum is commendable, his assumption that their educational needs are different from those of a future microbiologist is troubling. Most students enrolled in regular or advanced high school science and mathematics courses will not pursue careers in these fields. Nonetheless, their access to further education often is predicated upon whether or not they have been exposed to the fundamental concepts and modes of thinking characteristic of these disciplines. To become 'educated' they must be willing to master this material.

By suggesting that the content he teaches makes little difference, this teacher reveals his expectation that most of his students face a limited future of low-paying and low-prestige occupations. He shares with many educators a tendency to see at-risk youth as fundamentally uneducable with respect to the material that is truly necessary or relevant to further schooling (Page, 1984). Unlike their peers in an academic track, these students receive a symbolic kind of education: Their transcripts will show the required courses in math and science, but little of the learning upon which further schooling may be predicated will have occurred. This problem is not limited to programs for at-risk youth but appears to be a widespread phenomenon in American education (Goodlad, 1984; Metz, 1988). It is this proclivity to label a proportion of students as incapable of mastering more challenging academic material that turns matching into tracking.

Teachers can eliminate this two-tiered system of education by refusing to accept the lack of motivation and vocational clarity demonstrated by many at-risk youth, and by developing educational programs more likely to demonstrate to students the interrelationship between their classwork and 'real' life in an increasingly specialized and complex economic environment. It should be the goal of all educational programs that students not only comply with the minimal course and institutional standards required for graduation but exhibit a more thorough and ongoing commitment to the tasks of learning.

It is in this context that the curricular and pedagogical innovations of the Media Academy seem so important. Though teachers in this program do not expect that all of their students will pursue careers as media professionals, their classroom approach unfailingly demonstrates the close interrelationship between formal learning and adult occupations. The program also provides students with the opportunity to experience the personal satisfaction and affirmation that come from committed involvement in work that is collectively organized and socially purposeful.

The Media Academy helps students to understand the extrinsic and intrinsic values of educational engagement and allows them to perform tasks that require the demonstration of maturity and responsibility. While teachers in this program recognize and respond to the unique characteristics of their students, they have avoided creating an educational experience that reifies negative characteristics, such as minimal aspirations and low motivation; instead, the Media Academy challenges students to grow beyond their previous behaviors and assumptions about their own vocational futures. In this instance, matching has not led to tracking but to the development of learning experiences that stretch students beyond their current circumstances and nurture a new form of involvement with school.

For many at risk youth, such involvement will not be elicited by a curriculum focused on the acquisition of communication skills. It may, however, be fostered by coursework that has a comparable payoff in terms of involvement in school-based enterprises and future occupational opportunities. The Peninsula Academies model, which allows for training in a variety of vocational areas (Dayton *et al.*, 1988), could provide a route to adequate employment for young people for whom a four-year college education may not be an appropriate or acceptable option. Particularly if this training were linked to more advanced vocational programs in local community colleges (see Parnell, 1986), students disinclined or unable to complete a college-preparatory curriculum would have options and incentives that could lead to increased educational engagement and improved post-graduation employment possibilities.

Croom Vocational High School incorporates elements of such an approach in its two-year vocational training program. This program would be further strengthened if students received more broadly-based instruction in an environment that more closely approximates the world of work, with many of its attendant responsibilities and opportunities for learning. If shops at Croom were organized as collective enterprises (i.e., as catering or janitorial services), for example, students could be trained not only in the more fundamental skills required to work in food services or building maintenance; they could also be introduced to skills related to management, bookkeeping, business correspondence and advertising. All students in the program might not be interested in, or capable of, assuming these responsibilities; those who did, however, would be exposed to additional vocational possibilities that would offer greater opportunity for economic advancement and personal development, possibilities they might then seek to pursue upon finishing their studies at Croom. The program would thus acknowledge students' histories of academic failure and frustration but also challenge them to move beyond individual characteristics and patterns of behavior that had limited their options in the past.

It could be argued that such a program still constitutes a form of tracking. There is no way to deflect this charge. But the provision of more expanded opportunities seems likely to enable more students with histories of school failure to develop the talents and interests required to find adequate employment upon high school graduation than is the case now. Though these students still may not have the options available to their more advantaged, college-bound peers, their career futures will be significantly brighter than those of high school dropouts or even many high school graduates who have not received such practical, broad-based training.

Similar challenges can be offered to students in non-vocational settings as well. At issue is the need to help students realize their own potential to acquire skills and assume responsibilities they may have considered beyond their capabilities. Community-based and in-school service projects have been highly effective in leading at-risk youth to extend their vision of the possible. At the Wayne Enrichment Center, for example, an extracurricular leadership training course offers students the chance to organize community service projects. Some WEC students assumed responsibility for planning and holding a Christmas party for disadvantaged children and a clothing drive for needy families. Others were also involved in providing entertainment for participants at a summer International Youth Conference. Teachers were careful not to direct these activities but allowed students to discover what they were capable of accomplishing.

Such activities provide another form of collective effort and give students the opportunity to develop different social and academic skills. Research has shown that young people who participate in service activities value being treated as adults and being involved in learning experiences that are active rather than passive; as a result of these experiences, participating students also seem to exhibit a higher sense of social competence and responsibility to the non-school community (Newmann and Rutter, 1983). Community service programs assume that young people are capable of giving to others and of behaving with maturity. These opportunities offer another route for drawing at-risk youth into a recognition of their own possibilities as mature and contributing adults.

Cross-age tutoring programs, which provide a school-based rather than community-based form of service, have been successful in eliciting increased engagement and participation from at-risk youth. An evaluation of such a program involving potential dropouts from four San Antonio high schools showed students involved in the program exhibited higher rates of school retention, improved self-image, more positive orientation to the school, decreased incidence of misbehavior, more solid acquisition of academic material and a concern for the future (Intercultural Development Research Association, 1986a). The findings of this study parallel those of Cohen, Kulick and Kulick's meta-analysis of cross-age tutoring (1982).

As at the Media Academy or at WEC, where teachers believed that students were capable of fulfilling their responsibilities and performing conscientiously, nearly all participating students met those expectations. Here again, work was socially situated and purposeful, and it resulted in increased motivation and commitment to the process of learning.

Such commitment and motivation can also be elicited for academic work when teaching and learning occur in an educational environment that gives students the freedom and support to pursue their own interests and yet interact with others in a dynamic school community. The Jefferson County Open High School in Evergreen, Colorado (described in Gregory and Smith, 1987) incorporates work experience and community service into its program. It has expanded the experiential learning that occurs in such activities to include academic coursework as well. Serving at-risk students as well as other youth disenchanted with conventional schooling, the Open High School requires its graduates to complete six passages based on the Walkabout educational model developed by Gibbons (1974 and 1984). Students must fulfill projects in the areas of practical skills, logical inquiry, creativity, personal adventure, career exploration and global awareness. Projects can be completed away from the school or as part of group activities. Transcripts are composed not of grades but of extensive reports regarding the learning experiences students have created for themselves. Approximately two-thirds of the school's graduates seek further education.

The Open High School demonstrates the powerful impact that enabling young people to shape their own education can have on their engagement and desire for further schooling. This openness to curricular and pedagogical experimentation needs to become more widespread among educators of at-risk youth. Many at-risk students are capable of becoming genuinely engaged in learning; they need only to be helped to see how learning can contribute to their own sense of meaning and identity. When that learning occurs within a community framework, their engagement is often enhanced as a result of involvement in collective tasks.

While we continue to believe that matching educational programs to the characteristics and needs of particular populations of at-risk youth can make a significant contribution to their educational success, we strongly caution educators to avoid the construction of interventions that do no more than help these students to acquire basic skills, to accumulate course credits or adjust to institutional necessities. While these issues must certainly be addressed, it is crucial that students be challenged to master skills and knowledge required for participation in our increasingly sophisticated labor market. Programs that fail to rise to this challenge may be routing their students to jobs that have only slightly more potential for personal satisfaction and advancement than those available to students who have dropped out.

Educators of at-risk youth must not simply accept their students' learning difficulties, lack of motivation or outright resistance to the tasks of learning. They must instead develop curriculum and pedagogical practices that will demonstrate to their students the benefits of educational engagement, today as well as in the future. In this way, matching educational offerings to specific groups of students can be used as a powerful tool for encouraging their participation in the classroom *and* enabling them to link their participation to occupations that promise more than the minimum wage and bare subsistence.

Constraints on Curricular Innovation

Initiating such curricular reforms is not simply a matter of imagination or will. Though teachers of at-risk youth may grasp the importance of this form of innovation, institutional factors may preclude more fundamental educational experimentation. Most alternative programs already exhibit significant differences from more conventional schools in that their social environments are more tolerant, personal and supportive; such innovations themselves can prompt questions about the legitimacy of alternatives for potential dropouts. Attempting more radical changes might jeopardize the survival of the program altogether, particularly if these changes do not conform to the course of study required for graduation in other district schools. Beyond the problem of maintaining academic legitimacy, teachers in such programs are rarely given the permission or the resources to develop curricular or innovative pedagogical practices that set aside conventional assumptions about appropriate teaching and learning. There is a tendency for teachers, administrators and members of the public not associated with programs for at-risk students to view these special interventions as either unnecessary frills or as educationally suspect. By espousing an educational philosophy that asserts the importance of academic success for all students, such schools challenge the competitive and individualistic nature of much American education. When fostering that success entails creating more personal and informal school environments, school district patrons in some instances suggested that programs for at-risk youth do nothing more than coddle troublemakers. They assert that such youth should be punished for their misdeeds or lack of conformity rather than understood or supported. If the academic progress of these students is dependent upon participation in courses that embody the kinds of innovations discussed in chapter 4 — innovations such as shortened grading periods and variable credit — teachers in other district schools may call into question the standards and coursework developed by educators in these programs.

Staff members in alternative programs for potential dropouts often encounter ongoing skepticism from their colleagues in regular high schools about the legitimacy of their work. It is difficult for some of these conventional teachers to acknowledge that other educators may succeed where they have failed. Other teachers cannot grasp why anyone would wish to work with this element of the student population and occasionally assume that those who do have done so simply out of a desire for smaller classes or less demanding preparations.

This kind of criticism often leads to a deep anxiety among staff about the longevity of programs for at-risk youth. Teachers and administrators often are called upon to defend their schools in ways that personnel in more conventional programs rarely encounter. This tension inevitably necessitates careful consideration of the political consequences of any program innovations. The lack of widespread institutional or community support for these interventions clearly impinges on the amount of experimentation their staffs are willing or able to entertain.

The board decision to adopt a '5-1-5' calendar at Sierra Mountain, for example, was made many months after the idea initially arose among staff members. The superintendent, realizing there would be substantial resistance from other district administrators, counseled Earle Conway, Sierra Mountain's Principal, to wait until the school had proven itself for another school year before proposing this innovation. While politically sensible, this kind of advice is indicative of the careful strategizing educators in these alternatives must engage in if they hope to develop the kind of program they see to be valuable and appropriate for their students.

Even well-established and apparently secure programs such as Croom and New Futures continue to feel that they are in jeopardy and must carefully present themselves to their constituencies in ways that will foster support rather than doubt or skepticism. Croom has existed since 1966, and New Futures since 1970, but administrators in both programs suspect that if and when budgetary constraints must be imposed, their alternative programs will be the first to go. While these programs enjoy a degree of autonomy over the shape of their curricula, that autonomy depends upon the maintenance of widespread public support for their work. In order to sustain that support, Dr Edward Doyle, the Principal of Croom, cultivates a close relationship with the local media to ensure that favorable stories about Croom are presented regularly to the public. This public relations effort is intended to strengthen taxpayers' tenuously positive perception of Croom and to counter the assumption that special dropout programs share the moral failings of the teenage drug abusers or juvenile offenders they often serve.

At New Futures School, Principal Carolyn Gaston approaches the same dilemma in a slightly different way. There, public support is cultivated by school personnel, who are expected to participate in numerous community organizations. Teachers volunteer to be Girl Scout counselors or after-school tutors, or to serve on the boards of various civic groups. They do so as staff members of New Futures, thereby maintaining a highly visible public profile. Teachers at New Futures also are encouraged to remain aware of changes in local civic and school politics. They determine explicitly the positions of school board candidates vis-à-vis their program and then assume an active role in election campaigns. Panels of New Futures students also make frequent presentations before civic groups. As at Croom, such efforts are aimed in part at sustaining a positive public impression of the school so that, in the event of a budget crisis, a groundswell of local support can be drawn upon to protect the program. When compared to the legitimizing activities of personnel in more conventional schools, these efforts seem extraordinary and demonstrate the attention and energy frequently required to keep alternative programs afloat.

One consequence of this struggle to achieve even limited levels of legitimacy is that personnel in these programs are cautious about venturing too far afield from conventional curriculum. Nearly all of the fourteen programs we studied continue to follow district or state requirements for graduation. A common result of these requirements is limited curricular experimentation, particularly in the academic component of the program's offerings. A teacher at Sierra Mountain observed that the school's academic program was, in fact, conventional, that the program differed only in its small size and informal, personal social environment. At the Wayne Enrichment Center, the need to match courses at the local secondary high school led to the development of a series of instructional learning packets that parallel the parent school's offerings. These packets tend to demand little more than fact-finding from students. Except in the areas of business or home economics, the process of learning becomes mechanical and isolated with little social interaction and no independent problem-solving or inquiry.

As indicated earlier, these constraints on innovation serve only to confirm many students' impression that academic classes have little to do with their own lives or interests. Though alternative programs may provide a more supportive and enjoyable social environment than their traditional counterparts, they still may not encourage or instill a commitment to learning. When instruction is based on a simplified or mechanical version of course offerings determined by conventional schools, at-risk students are deprived of the vitality of genuine intellectual inquiry.

It is not surprising that an education that may consist of little more than a series of curricular hoops leading to graduation fails to engage or inspire at-risk students. These students need educational experiences that draw them into the learning process by igniting their imagination, interest and commitment to others. An emphasis on remediation or the mastery of isolated facts or skills seems unlikely to alter their less-than-positive orientation to learning, yet it is just this orientation that must be changed if at-risk youth are to carve out a satisfactory place for themselves in our increasingly demanding economy.

If alternative programs are to develop the kinds of curricular reforms discussed earlier, districts and the public must grant them permission to transcend commonly accepted assumptions about the kinds of teaching and learning that are appropriate for public schools. At present, that permission is restricted to the domains of altered social relations aimed at developing school membership, remediation and vocational training. And even this permission is tentative. The constant need to legitimize their activities and approaches prevents such programs from instituting the kinds of curricular innovation that could lead their students to increased levels of motivation and engagement.

Beyond the question of sustaining legitimacy, other institutional factors also inhibit curricular experimentation. In most school systems, there is little room for the teacher-entrepreneur. The evolution of the curricular innovations discussed throughout this book has almost always involved struggle and determination to circumvent or scale bureaucratic hurdles. The Media Academy in Oakland is a case in point.

Though the Academy has received support from the school district's central office and has the backing of a number of influential community members, program staff have encountered varying levels of resistance from middle-level administrators and other teachers at Fremont High School. This lack of support has also led to the delayed receipt of important equipment, criticism of student newspaper reporting that is seen as potentially damaging to the school's image and uncertainty about the hiring of staff needed to implement the program's stated goals. Not all teachers can be expected to possess the commitment, persistence or thick skin required to create and sustain programs that do not conform to the institutional guidelines and expectations that govern so much of what happens in schools.

School administrators and the general public must be willing not only to suspend some of their notions about what constitutes a legitimate educational experience, but to consider greater organizational flexibility as well (Chubb, 1987). Not all teachers will take advantage of that flexibility, but if those who are inclined to do so are encouraged to experiment, schools could well become more vital and exciting places. The availability of resources will, of course, affect the extent to which innovative teachers will be able to translate their ideas into programs, and a narrow resource base often has been the excuse used by school administrators to limit educational experimentation. As teachers identify funding sources beyond the school, however, this excuse loses its force. Particularly in the face of widespread interest on the part of foundations, corporations and local businesses in supporting school reform, the lack of district funds does not need to preclude innovation; an enterprising teacher is likely to seek out appropriate resources elsewhere in the community. What often does prevent such innovation, however, is the inability of the institutional structure of specific schools or entire districts to absorb the kinds of changes we have described and advocated here. A spirit of innovation and experimentation must be not only allowed but engendered, and creative teachers must be encouraged to translate their visions into reality.

With such freedom and encouragement, teachers in programs for at-risk youths might feel the approval and support they need to entertain the forms of curricular innovation discussed earlier. This, in turn, would enable them to identify ways to use their programs' more communitarian social environments to enable their students to experience a collective and socially purposeful education. Learning need not be seen as an essentially individualistic activity focused on the manipulation of symbols and the mastery of a predetermined body of information. It should instead be conceived of as a joint exploration of the world, an exploration in which students are urged to contribute their own skills and insights into an ever-changing and broadening understanding of their shared experience. This is the nature of the out-of-school learning that Resnick describes, the kind of learning that might indeed elicit more commitment from not only at-risk students, but all students.

In their creation of learning communities, programs for potential dropouts have laid the foundation upon which such a curricular reform can and must be built. Rather than purveying simplified versions of the isolating and abstract coursework characteristic of conventional classrooms, such programs could take the next step and construct their academic offerings in ways that might also draw their students into an experience of school membership that includes educational engagement and commitment.

Conclusion

The programs involved in our study are notably successful in helping at-risk youth to achieve a more positive relation with the school and school adults. As indicated in chapter 7, higher attendance rates and grade point averages, the reduced incidence of behavior problems and the increased experience of social bonding to the school, teachers and peers all point to the success these programs have achieved in overcoming the isolation, alienation or estrangement of many potential dropouts. Though unable to help all at-risk students, particularly those who cannot or will not accept the school's institutional norms, these programs have created a more embracing and supportive social environment that is appealing to many young people who had rejected the competitive and impersonal classrooms encountered during their previous education. The opportunity to continue their schooling in such settings has enabled many students who would have otherwise dropped out to graduate.

The problem remains, however, that special programs for at-risk youth often limit their sense of responsibility to a focus on high school completion. Teachers assume that if their students can learn to adjust to the school's institutional requirements, develop more positive self-images and earn a diploma, they will be adequately prepared to take their place in the larger community. Achieving such ends is without question essential for these young people; twenty years ago, doing so would have been enough to guarantee an adequate place within our national economy. Unfortunately, this is no longer the case. Not only must the young graduate from high school, they must also acquire the skills and dispositions required to seek and successfully complete further training if they hope to find employment that offers anything more than a subsistence wage.

Educators involved with at-risk youth must recognize that the labor market has become much more unforgiving of those who are unwilling or unable to continue their schooling. Not only must they help their students complete secondary education, they must also encourage them to adopt a new orientation to the demands of formal learning. It is not enough that at-risk students complete their coursework in a resigned and detached manner. They must instead come to understand that education is vitally important to their own well-being and that they are capable of shaping schooling in ways that will allow them to create decent lives for themselves.

In constructing educational environments that are more supportive and caring, teachers of at-risk youth have eliminated the cause of some of the frustration that has led potential dropouts to reject schooling. They do not, however, show these students how dealing with the difficulties of learning, particularly academic learning, can be challenging, personally validating and socially rewarding.

As indicated earlier, programs like the Media Academy elicit a notable level of involvement and motivation from at-risk students. Their willingness to accept the program's demands appears to be predicated on the way in which student work is situated within a collective context. Effort is experienced as a social rather than an individual phenomenon. Within this setting, students become willing to give of themselves in ways that rarely occur in conventional classrooms. It is important to realize that simply increasing demands upon at-risk youth in classrooms where learning remains an isolated task is likely to do nothing more than further alienate them from formal education. Those demands must instead be presented in a situation in which motivation is socially generated and maintained. In this kind of setting, a student's failure to overcome frustration and sustain effort has more than individual consequences; it has implications for all others involved in the learning environment as well. This form of communal support for learning has great power and should be more widely tapped. It seems particularly important to foster such collective learning among students who have failed to become engaged learners in the individualized learning environments encountered in most schools.

To reiterate, many programs for at-risk students have succeeded admirably in creating schools that overcome social isolation and alienation. The communities of support they offer do draw students back to school. Now these programs must find ways to transform their communities of support into communities of learning and labor, communities in which students learn to value exerting effort and overcoming challenges through working on shared projects that are clearly meaningful and useful to themselves and others. If such learning and labor were contributed to the welfare of the broader constituency responsible for supporting the school, even plaguing questions of legitimacy might be assuaged. If successful in achieving this balance between the social and academic tasks of the school, programs for at-risk youth might well serve as models of an educational process that could revitalize schooling for all students.

Note

1 We recognize that the availability of adequate employment can have a profound impact on student engagement and school retention (Ogbu, 1978). The task of eliciting students' commitment to education must thus be seen not solely as the school's responsibility. Communities as a whole, but especially their business leaders, have a grave responsibility to assure that there are enough jobs for the young. Without such assurance, economic and social deterioration is inevitable (Wilson, 1987). Schools, however, can do much to demonstrate to students that they need not be passive victims of circumstances considered beyond their control (for example, class position or lack of employment opportunities). Changing those circumstances will almost certainly require individual initiative and collective action. Acquiring the knowledge and skills available in schools may be essential to bring about such changes both on a personal level and within the broader community.

Chapter 10:
School Reform and Beyond:
Policy Implications

The literature on at-risk students indicates that dropping out of school is a complex phenomenon. Background conditions arising from family, social and economic circumstances all can contribute to an individual's decision to leave school. Poverty, discrimination, joblessness, crime and conflict-ridden neighborhoods take their toll among many youth. Some students, regardless of their race, class or family status, develop personal problems that make continued schooling difficult or impossible; physical health problems, drug abuse, pregnancy and psychological depression prevent these students from staying in school. It is also the case that some school policies and practices lead students to quit school. Some schools are characterized by massive student course failure, frequent use of suspension, high rates of grade retention and lax attendance policies encouraging truancy and poor achievement. Each of these school conditions indicates not only ineffective practices but a lack of concern and accountability with respect to at-risk students.

The 'causes' of dropping out — family background conditions, personal problems and school practices — present a complex set of problems. It also seems reasonable to assume that these factors interact with one another in ways not clearly understood. This web of conditions surrounding those at risk of dropping out makes intervention a formidable challenge for all educators.

Most of the description and analysis in the previous chapters concerned school-level events and conditions involving students, principals and teachers. Much of this description is intended to suggest reforms to the building-level practitioner. But we believe our findings also have much to say to a broad group of individuals involved with policy-making somewhat removed from day to day school events. The reforms recommended in this chapter are addressed especially to policymakers at local and state levels. This group includes state legislators and boards of education, state superintendents and their departments, along with local school boards, district superintendents and middle-level administrators. Many of the implications of our research must be recognized and acted upon by these people if there is to be any change in school conditions for at-risk students.

These policy recommendations are aimed at three goals. First, there is a need to encourage the development of more and stronger alternatives for at-risk students. Alternatives should be an integral aspect of a comprehensive strategy of dropout prevention in most school systems. In some communities, however, alternative schools still are considered illegitimate by the profession and the public. This perception of illegitimacy can make it difficult, if not impossible, for these programs to carry out the important functions of offering high quality programs to students and providing leadership in innovation.

Beyond the need for strong alternatives, educational policy must promote *systemic* school reforms. A systemic approach is recommended on the assumption school systems comprising of centralized bureaucracies along with large middle and senior highs will continue to exist. The systemic approach requires schools to implement policies and practices affecting a broad range of students whether they can be labeled at-risk or not. The concept of systemic change contrasts sharply with piecemeal approaches that attempt to identify, label and treat a group considered at-risk while maintaining the status quo for other students. Systemic reforms should be preventive in nature and reach most or all students, especially those who are unlikely to be served by alternatives targeting particular populations.

Finally, there is a need to go beyond school reforms and establish a community partnership strategy of intervention with at-risk youth. We believe communities should establish a coordinated youth policy drawing upon the broadest range of constituents and their resources. Such youth policy would recognize that some of the problems contributing to students' at-risk status arise outside the school and are best addressed with the aid of community resources directed at social and employment conditions.

In a community partnership, interventions should be initiated on several fronts. One focus is the set of local economic conditions constraining young people. A second focus is on access to the social services disadvantaged young people need for additional support in their lives. This community-based strategy requires linking school with a range of resources and opportunities in response to the identified problems of at-risk youth. To promote collaboration among different interests and institutions, communities will need to be proactive in building consensus about the need to work together in the interests of at-risk students.

Before spelling out in detail the substance of these policy recommendations, we offer a review of the key finding from our research. It is this finding that provides the context for our recommendations.

The Key Finding: School as a Community of Support

The key finding from our research is that effective schools provide at-risk students with a community of support. School as a community of support is a broad concept in which school membership and educational engagement are central. School membership is concerned with a sense of belonging and social bonding to the school and its members. Educational engagement is defined as involvement in school activities but especially traditional classroom and academic work.

The strength of school membership and educational engagement for students is due primarily to the way in which the schools interact with them. Schools successful at dropout prevention created a supportive environment that helped students overcome impediments to membership and engagement. Conditions that accompanied this environment were a professional culture among educators that accepted moral responsibility for educating at-risk students, and sufficient autonomy and resources to encourage educational entrepreneurship in the development of new programs for students.

Several impediments to students' educational engagement can be identified. For non-college bound students, one is the apparent absence of any payoff for working hard in school. Academic achievement makes little difference in terms of their entry-level employment, and they have no plans to continue their education. Engagement is further reduced for many students when the conception of learning in school is too narrow. Abilities necessary in the world of work are little used or recognized in the classroom. School learning is constricted in methods and content to such an extent that intrinsic interest is squeezed out. Finally, engagement is weak for many students because the curriculum is trivialized by an obsession with 'coverage'. Because course-taking in high school means students are asked to cover superficially a wide variety of topics and information, the material itself becomes meaningless; as a result, learning does not convey to students a sense of competence or intrinsic reward.

Given the diversity of problems at-risk students encounter, the schools in our study developed strategies in response to these impediments based on two insights: Programs should be matched to student needs and problems, and strategies should take advantage of student interests and strengths. Thus, some students needed a haven from serious home or personal problems where they could receive adult guidance. Others responded to vocational experiences that provide a sense of competence and a road map to the future by linking school and employment. Others, such as pregnant and mothering girls, responded to a curriculum and environment emphasizing child development and the importance of being a good mother. Still other students responded to the challenge of rebuilding old houses, producing newspapers or learning a marketable trade.

One implication of our research is that schools are successful with at-risk students when the institution accepts a proactive responsibility for educating these youth. This responsibility derived in part from a teacher culture characterized by a moral obligation to serve youth other teachers were likely to reject as unworthy. This form of 'professional accountability' was sustained by certain attitudes and practices that fostered a positive school culture and caring approach, thereby making student success more likely. We believe it was the strength of teachers' sense of professional accountability that was the fundamental strength of these schools. Whatever their technical features, schools without this basic commitment will remain ineffective with at-risk youth.

Policy Recommendations for School Reform

In developing a broad attack on the problems of at-risk youth, especially that of dropping out of school, we offer policy recommendations in three arenas. As suggested earlier, policy-makers should focus on three arenas of action as they work to improve schools for the benefit of at-risk students. Strategies in each of these three arenas should address the problems of school membership, educational engagement and the conditions enabling schools and adults to serve at-risk students. The first arena concerns the development of strong alternative schools and programs. The second calls for systemic reform of policies and practices within existing comprehensive secondary schools. The third arena goes beyond good alternative and comprehensive schools to create community partnerships that address the broad range of needs of at-risk youth. Taken together, these reforms establish a youth policy agenda for states and communities.

Strengthening Alternatives

Recommendation 1

Districts should establish strong permanent alternatives as part of a comprehensive strategy of dropout prevention. Alternative schools should be high-status organizations receiving resources commensurate with the tasks they undertake and the success they demonstrate.

Alternative schools, especially those that target at-risk youth, occupy a marginal position in many school systems. Even the most successful long-lived alternatives in our study often were troubled by a sense of being in jeopardy. Educators in most alternatives spoke of having to fight for their existence each year as they saw their school a possible target for 'budget cutters'. In contrast, they pointed out, traditional high schools were funded automatically without being asked to provide evidence of their success or to explain their failures. Alternatives were constantly asked to justify their existence, as if they were a 'frill', or there was a suspicion they failed to 'pull their weight'. Their insights about the education of at-risk students often went unrecognized. When their success was publicized, it often was denigrated by fellow professionals under the assumption that alternatives must operate with inferior standards. Evidence of success was sometimes dismissed as 'giving into an undesirable element in the school', or that alternatives provided a form of 'coddling'. In addition, a degree of 'guilt by association' was projected on teachers of at-risk students; it was assumed that these teachers must be inferior and incompetent or they would not work with such inferior and incompetent students. As a result, the professionals in these schools felt isolated, rejected and defensive about their work.

Marginality for alternative schools extended to their status within the administration of the system. Some were pathetically under-funded despite the herculean task assigned them. As one central office administrator said, 'We don't want to make these programs too good or a lot of kids will want to get into them'.

Despite this resistance to alternatives for at-risk students, many school systems today offer high quality alternatives to gifted, talented, special interest and highly motivated students. Thus, magnets and other schools of choice are seen as legitimate and offered in recognition of different student interests, abilities and the need to desegregate schools.

However well magnets serve these purposes, in some systems they may unintentionally provide a new form of sorting and tracking that is deleterious to the quality of schooling for the at-risk. Moore and Davenport (1988) found that magnets attract the most successful students, leaving at-risk students to flounder in low quality neighborhood schools. To promote their success, magnets often are given prerogatives in selecting staff matched to the students and receive extra resources that enhance the school climate and staff morale. Enrollment limits and selectivity allow magnets to plan more accurately than other schools who will be attending and what resources are needed. The emphasis on creating special schools that recruit and select students with clear abilities and interests deflects attention away from improving the quality of education for at-risk students. The attitude across many systems is that magnet school students are educable, but the remainder are losers and probably undeserving of much effort.

High quality alternatives for at-risk students were not part of the plan in a number of the districts we studied. Central office administrators sometimes conveyed the view that alternatives for at-risk youth were at best only temporary measures to provide a stop-gap response to a pressing problem. Some gave the impression their alternative schools were viewed as businesses about to go into bankruptcy. The opinion expressed in one district was that 'early intervention' efforts with at-risk students, when finally in place, would surely eliminate the need for such alternatives. In other words, it was assumed that prevention efforts based on early identification and intervention will eliminate the population of at-risk students in the early grades. Alternatives for at-risk youth at the secondary school level will become unnecessary.

In our judgment, this point of view is naive. Some at-risk students will remain at risk to some degree throughout their stay in school and will need or benefit from alternatives. While early intervention within mainstream schools may respond to some conditions, students can become at-risk later in their school years for reasons not detectable in the early grades. A number of factors other than competence in basic skills leads to dropping out. A divorce or death in the family, drug abuse, a family move, pregnancy, or a traumatic conflict with the school each can push some individuals into rejecting school. Alternatives provide an important way the system can respond to such students who become at-risk later rather than earlier.

In addition, alternatives are inherently good, if they are of high quality. By high quality alternatives, we mean organizations that have sufficient resources and autonomy to define and act upon a clearly organized agenda for staff and students (Chubb, 1987). Even if there were no at-risk students, school systems should provide a range of high quality alternatives as a way to maximize the educational possibilities of young people. It is misguided to assume one form of schooling must be acceptable to all in the system. Alternatives providing curriculum and organizational variations for a broad range of students — at risk and otherwise — are important. Such variations provide a diversity of environments and opportunities for the diversity always present among students and educators.

Recommendation 2

Districts, in cooperation with state departments of education, should establish special alternative schools for at-risk students with a clear mission that includes experimentation, curricular innovation and staff development.

Alternative schools should perform three important functions. First, these organizations should provide high quality education to at-risk students. Second, these schools should be places of innovation providing models of curriculum and teaching particularly effective with at-risk students. Third, these schools should provide staff development programs to increase the number of teachers effective with at-risk students and provide for diffusion of curricular innovations developed in alternative schools.

To carry out these three functions requires state and district policy to free alternatives from some of the existing constraints on curriculum and teaching. It may also require negotiation of union agreements allowing modified work rules. It will certainly require a change in thinking on the part of district and state administrators.

The curriculum innovation and staff development functions can be viewed as a package. In addition to the permanent staff of an alternative, teachers from other schools could rotate through the school based on a 'sabbatical' system. The permanent and sabbatical staff would work together with students. Those on sabbatical would come to the alternative to learn about a new strategy, such as experiential learning, or to work with existing staff on the development of a new curriculum, such as a field-based vocational program. Such district-wide participation by educators is likely to increase the status of alternatives, and to establish them as environments characterized by collegiality and opportunities for professional development.

In California, the legislature has taken a different approach in funding a series of 'academies' throughout the state. The thematic 'major' of each academy is both academic and vocational; current offerings include programs focused on health-related subject matter and occupations, electronic and print media, food services, business and finance and electronics and computers. A careful evaluation concluded that, in general, the academies are successful. According to an evaluation report, 'When viewed against matched comparison groups not participating in the academy programs, academy students recorded higher grade point averages, and failed fewer courses' (Dayton *et al.*, 1988).

California is an important example of how states can generate local experimentation and program development. Unless such authorization and attendant resources are forthcoming, however, it is unlikely that alternatives will receive the full legitimation and support they need. Our observations suggest two reasons that local districts experience difficulty establishing innovations of this type. One is the inertia and vested interests controlling central school administrations. The second is a belief at the school building level that programs must not deviate from the status quo. Educators view success in generating strong alternatives as unlikely given real or imagined official constraints by district and state regulations.

Systemic Reforms for Secondary Schools

A systemic approach to school reform must involve five principles: (1) the need to have good information about students; (2) the need to have good information about the effects of school policies and practices on at-risk students; (3) the recognition that personal and smaller environments are more likely to produce school membership and educational engagement for at-risk students; (4) the recognition that more of the same kind of curriculum and teaching is not likely to succeed with at-risk students; (5) the need to have a mechanism that will hold schools accountable for success with at-risk students. It is our prediction that if these five principles guide state and district policy, traditional, comprehensive high schools will become substantially more effective with their at-risk students and dropout rates will decline significantly.

Recommendation 3
State policy should require each school system to establish a Management Information System (MIS) that provides basic and common data on all students.

A common problem facing school systems is an inadequate definition of the term 'dropout', a lack of systematic data on enrollments and withdrawals from school, and a consequent inability to provide an accurate account of their dropout rates. At minimum, a state-mandated definition of dropout along with the implementation of an MIS will provide school systems and states with accurate data on the dropout problem. A common definition and an accounting procedure shared by all school systems within a state will provide indicators of relative school effectiveness. An operational definition and accounting procedure already have been elaborated by Williams (1987).

An MIS in each school district would accomplish two distinct but related tasks. Such a system makes it possible to keep track of students throughout their stay in a single system and as they move to other state systems, thereby maintaining accurate records of their educational histories. Second, an MIS allows districts to establish student and school profiles based on various indicators of student characteristics and school quality. Data can create descriptive profiles of schools based on dropout rates, student achievement, attendance, mobility (school transfers), limited English proficiency, out-of-school suspension, in-school suspension, course failure and grade retention, and any other category a system deems important.

An MIS is essential to establishing the information base a school needs to understand its population and to track students' progress within a system. Schools serving different populations will likely produce somewhat different achievement and dropout rates. An MIS allows for the disaggregation of data by various categories such as gender, race/ethnicity and other relevant categories. Generating district and school profiles of student populations provides a basis for informed policymaking at the local level. At the building level, it will provide systematic data on a number of variables crucial to understanding at-risk students. These data can then be used by the district, and ultimately the state, in identifying problems and in establishing indicators of school progress.

Recommendation 4

State policy should require schools to examine the effects of course failure, grade retention, out-of-school suspension and other practices that appear to impact negatively on at-risk students.

The absence of an MIS should not deter a school system from gathering data on key variables known to be highly correlated with dropping out. An examination of institutional practices should begin with course failures. Minimally, every school should have data on the number of failing grades assigned students, as failure is highly correlated with dropping out. Such data should indicate whether there are particular grade levels, departments or courses in which students consistently experience academic trouble. In effect, schools should investigate whether 'bottlenecks' exist at certain points that restrict students' progress toward graduation.

Schools should maintain high academic standards, but such standards should not result in the massive failure of students. In general, large numbers of course failures indicate a problem with much more than students. Individual schools and school districts should openly investigate the issue of failing students to determine why they are failing and what can be done about it. Schools also should examine the extent to which faculty believe some students must fail in order to maintain academic standards for the rest.

State departments of education can play a role in bringing this issue to public attention and helping schools examine their practices. Policy regarding the use of course failure should be established at both the district and building levels. In developing this policy, teachers should be encouraged to create standards they believe are appropriate for their courses, but they must be able to defend their grading practices in light of the impact of failure on students and the range of alternatives to failure that exist.

If there is evidence that some students are unprepared to learn what teachers believe is appropriate material for a given course or grade level, then some alternative to failure should be developed. It makes little sense to continue to teach material that is too difficult for students at a particular grade level to master. For students who are having difficulty succeeding academically, there should be help in the form of remediation, tutoring and optional paths to satisfactory completion of requirements along with alternative methods of teaching.

Beginning with the middle school/junior high, the practice of retaining students in grade should be carefully monitored at both the district and building levels. Data needs to be gathered on the extent retention is used, along with evidence of its effect on the dropout rate. As a form of academic remediation, there is little evidence retention in grade for adolescents results in improved academic performance (although it may help some students in the primary grades). Conversely, there is considerable evidence grade retention is associated with dropping out. In addition, retaining students typically impacts negatively on teachers and other students. Overage students in a class are often disruptive, further complicating life for all concerned. Again, it makes little sense to retain large numbers of students in the absence of any proven benefits for the students.

The question of grade retention also raises the issue of academic standards. Schools are loathe to promote students who have clearly not completed required academic work, either because they are unable or unwilling. But social promotion is not the only alternative to retention. Districts should develop a policy regarding the acceptable rate for grade retention in various secondary schools. To reduce retention rates, school systems can provide additional support services for students who are having difficulty passing coursework. It should be noted, however, that this strategy should entail more than a remedial approach to academic learning. A more effective approach is to utilize a support team of teachers, counselors, administrators and social service professionals to work with failing students and their families. One team member is formally vested with responsibility for monitoring each student. If these additional support services appear to be ineffective with students who are failing systematically, there should be an alternative program available beginning with the junior high grades.

Data also should be kept on the number of out-of-school suspensions at each school. The practice of out-of-school suspension should be a focus of policy discussion at both the building and district level. Clearly there are occasions when the only responsible action for a school is to suspend a student; it is necessary to remove a student when he or she is incorrigibly disruptive or a threat to others. On the other hand, it probably is not productive to suspend students for cutting a physical education class, or for using a four-letter word when talking with a teacher. Alternatives to out-of-school suspension should be an important consideration.

Recommendation 5

State and local policy should encourage the decentralization of large schools and school systems, creating smaller units characterized by site-based management.

Decentralization is intended to permit educators more autonomy and flexibility in creating the personalized educational environments proven to be effective with at-risk students. The alternative schools we studied offered valuable insights into the importance of small size and the degree of autonomy and flexibility needed by educators. Small size permits personalized face-to-face relations between adults and young people; it is through such one-to-one relationships that impediments to school membership can be overcome. Autonomy and flexibility permit educators to invent the kinds of programmatic strategies that allow them to act on behalf of students. Educators in such programs are in a position to respond constructively because they know their students well from frequent one-to-one contact.

Minimally, junior and senior high schools should be based on a 'house' system in which there is close contact between students and a small, consistent group of adults. A variation of this system uses an even smaller 'family' unit for junior high and early high school; in this system, a team of four or five teachers is responsible for a group of students for an entire year including counseling and monitoring their academic progress. The school-within-a-school model is another way of breaking large high schools into smaller units. Various alternatives within a larger structure should be undertaken with the intent of increasing school membership and developing a curriculum more engaging. This strategy also can allow students some of the advantages of a larger organization.

Good schools for students must also be good schools for teachers. Good schools for teachers are places where collegiality rather than hierarchy and bureaucratic demands define the interaction among people. If schools are not good places to work, there is little chance good ideas about teaching at-risk students will generate action for very long. Good places for teachers extend to them the opportunity to govern many of the day-to-day conditions affecting their worklife. Self-governance is important in developing the sense of empowerment and professionalism, and it also provides an opportunity for teachers to develop the kinds of day-to-day support they so frequently cite as important. The autonomy and flexibility of smaller schools permits adults to cooperate and collaborate in ways that can enhance their impact on students.

Many school systems need to invigorate and encourage initiative. In part, the answer lies in smaller more flexible school environments that encourage educational entrepreneurship as part of a culture of responsiveness in teaching at-risk students. Successful entrepreneurship should be rewarded; those teachers and administrators who do a better job with students, who are willing to invest and commit more of themselves to young people, should receive additional benefits. Rewards can include more opportunities for program leadership and development, as well as additional teaching resources, including opportunities to travel and share with colleagues in other school systems.

Recommendation 6

State and local policy should encourage the development of new curricula and teaching strategies designed for diverse groups of at-risk students.

Creating new curricula and a broader range of experiences responsive to at-risk students should be seen as a long-term, developmental effort. There is much to be done in creating the kinds of curriculum that are likely to produce academic engagement within diverse groups of students. Such curriculum should develop what we generally recognize as basic skills and knowledge, but in the context of a broad range of human activities and interests.

Curriculum must move away from superficial coverage of information to a focus on in-depth understanding that produces in students a sense of competency and an innate reward for learning. It should also avoid narrowly tracking youth into vocational slots. Without these changes, curriculum will fail to produce in young people the dispositions toward further learning and pursuit of additional training that are essential in an age of increasing change and high technology.

State and local policy can promote the development of such curriculum and teaching in several ways. First, there is a need to reduce the over-regulation of curriculum that produces standardized, lock-step requirements, textbooks and course content. Second, state and local testing should not dictate specific content or objectives that ultimately force educators to teach to the test. Instead, states' efforts should focus on the development of indicators of students' ability to use information and think carefully (Newmann, 1988).

States could make a major contribution to educational improvement by helping to develop and implement a variety of ways for students to indicate mastery and competence. New directions in testing and evaluation should be encouraged, including student exhibitions such as portfolios, and public displays through performances, presentations and products. The emphasis here is on what students can do as a result of their studies, not just on the mastery of a pre-specified body of knowledge and skills. This evaluation strategy does require mastery of bodies of information and sets of skills in sufficient depth to use them in applied and problem-solving situations, but it allows for the application of knowledge in a variety of ways.

State policy can contribute to the development of new curriculum and teaching by sponsoring model school programs; California's academy model is one example. States also could target particular schools with additional money and personnel to aid in program development. It is important that states and local districts signal educators that innovation in curriculum and teaching are authorized at the highest levels.

Policy also should reflect a high priority for educating teachers about successful interventions with at-risk students. As suggested, alternative schools could be used as sites for staff development. States and districts should explore a variety of ways of providing in-service training for their faculty. The need for consciousness-raising about at-risk students among some teachers should be confronted. Faculty culture in some schools needs to be redirected in terms of its sense of accountability, the need for adults to play the 'extended role', and to establish an ethic of persistence and optimism with at-risk youth. It is probably a truism that unless teachers and administrators believe they can and should be successful with at-risk students, other efforts at school reform will ultimately prove unsuccessful.

Recommendation 7
State and local policy should develop mechanisms to hold schools accountable for their dropout rates through a system emphasizing outcomes and results.

The teacher culture in effective schools, characterized by teachers' sense of personal and professional accountability for at-risk students, is the most important locus of accountability. Where a culture with this character exists among staff it should be valued and preserved, and where it is absent, its development should become a central priority.

Beyond individuals' sense of accountability, schools as institutions also must be accountable for responding effectively to their at-risk students. Currently, most schools are not accountable for either high dropout rates or the practices that produce them. To establish such accountability, three conditions must be satisfied: 1) Reliable data, such as generated by an MIS, must be available. 2) Some goal or outcome is needed against which to compare the existing state of affairs; i.e. is there a discrepancy between the existing dropout rate and the specified goal for that rate? 3) Accountability systems require the designation of explicit incentives and consequences for either success or failure in meeting specified goals.

Schools also must have the authority, opportunity and resources to work with at-risk students in ways that are likely to be successful. Many schools are not only short of resources, but hamstrung by local system and state regulations that prevent their effective intervention. These regulations, which tend to focus on schools' processes and procedures rather than their effectiveness, discourage staff initiative, incentive and responsibility.

In a bureaucratic and procedure-regulated system, there is only the weakest conception that school policy and practice should be driven by positive outcomes for at-risk students. The major question in such systems is whether the school, its teachers and students have conformed to the regulations for hiring certified personnel, according to contract language, teaching specified courses, and acquiring stipulated credits as established by state and local hierarchies. Sanctions are not brought to bear against schools that fail to reduce high dropout rates, or fail to increase the achievement of the lowest achieving students. Sanctions are reserved for those who violate procedural rules.

To alter this system, state and local agencies should establish data-gathering systems that allow close monitoring of outcomes concerned with at-risk students. This should include, in addition to dropout rates, a range of achievement measures and information about students' successful transition to employment and/or post-graduation education. Information about these outcomes will permit both the public and school agencies to focus on indicators of school effectiveness.

These indicators should be the products of a process that respects local conditions and input. If the criteria are mandated in a purely 'top-down' fashion, such as state department of education regulations, they are likely to be resisted by local districts. Public dialogue in local communities is necessary in developing consensus on criteria about the indicators of school effectiveness with at-risk students.

The establishment of indicators and goals of effectiveness also can lead to the use of incentives and disincentives for school success and failure with at-risk students. It is only when good information, established goals or outcomes, and incentives are used in combination that schools are held accountable for the education of at-risk youth.

Community Partnerships

Our research on at-risk students concluded that school factors, family backgrounds and personal problems are the three broad contributors to a student dropping out. Of these, schools typically can influence only the first — school factors. Community partnerships represent a way in which a critical mass of resources can be brought to bear on some of the additional non-school conditions that make young people at-risk.

Our concept of community partnership is a second generation variation that goes beyond the popular school-business partnership. Community partnerships are a step toward the development of local youth policy, a necessity in many communities where it is no longer reasonable to assume that young people will grow up 'naturally' with the support of an extended family, friends and voluntary organizations such as churches and youth groups. As many of these traditional institutions are weakened, new strategies of support for young people must be developed. The alternative is to abandon many youth to the streets and the influences they will inevitably find there.

The Annie E. Casey Foundation's New Futures Initiative (Wehlage and Lipman, 1988) provides concrete examples of such partnerships. With the financial assistance of the Casey Foundation, five cities have developed plans for collaboration based on a study of their local conditions. The five cities are: Dayton, OH, Lawrence, MA, Little Rock, AR, Pittsburgh, PA, and Savannah, GA. The Casey Foundation's guidelines require each of these cities to plan a partnership that brings resources to bear on the problems of dropping out, teenage pregnancy and youth unemployment. Each city has created an umbrella New Futures organization to oversee the partnership's various efforts. It is this comprehensive concept of community intervention that underlies the next recommendation.

Recommendation 8

Cities should develop broad-based community partnerships aimed at serving at-risk youth.

A wide range of local institutions and public and private interest groups should be brought into partnership to affect the lives of local youth. Partnerships should bring together schools, the economic structure represented by major business and industry, the political structure, higher education, unions and the various human services provided by social welfare agencies and voluntary organizations. Community partnerships will be effective only if they require public commitments in which each organization formally agrees to coordinate efforts and contribute resources in pursuit of specified goals. Partnerships are intended to increase the effectiveness of existing resources by coordinating disparate institutions. The assumption is that a coordinated and collective effort will have greater impact than the sum of institutions acting individually.

A number of principles guide the creation of community partnerships, and policy at the state and local level should be sensitive to them. The first principle is that partnerships establish a broad 'owner-ship' of the problems facing youth. This means that mainstream and middle class institutions and people need to accept some responsibility for those problems that are disproportionately identified among the poor and minorities. Such ownership can begin with an awareness of the problem, an awareness founded in accurate information about how many, who, and why youth are dropping out, becoming pregnant and unemployed.

'Owning' the youth problem also involves a broad community recognition of the need to respond constructively and avoid 'blaming the victims' by seeing them as incompetent and recalcitrant. Such ownership sometimes can result from a sense of moral obligation to disadvantaged people. It also can develop out of a sense of 'self interest': Citizens can come to recognize that ineffective schools, high dropout rates, heavy welfare rolls and unemployed youth on the streets are not only expensive to the community, they also present an unattractive picture to those considering economic investments and development.

A second principle behind a conception of partnership is the need to establish community membership among disadvantaged people. Our view about the importance of this sense of belonging is a logical extension of our argument that school membership is crucial for students. Youth and their families must believe they are part of the community, that they have a legitimate part to play in organizations, that they can share in decisions affecting them, and most importantly, that there is an economic future for them in the community.

A community partnership model also should reaffirm youth as valuable members of a community. In the short run, students and their parents can be involved in decision-making within the community partnership structure. In the long run, young people will see themselves as having a future if, in fact, job opportunities are available to them as a culmination of their schooling and participation in the partnership.

A third principle is the need to establish an organizational structure creating collaboration, coordination and effective action among the partnership's various constituents. An independent 'lead agency' is necessary to achieve coordination and maintain accountability. In the absence of this kind of agency, coordination of youth services may be the exception rather than the rule. A study of Pittsburgh, for example, found a condition probably typical of most urban areas. The city's youth services were described as 'a vast array of isolated programs', unconnected with efforts being made by schools, business, higher education, and neighborhood groups. All were well-intentioned, but the inevitable result often was duplication of effort or, worse, no services for some needy youth.

A fourth principle of community partnerships is that school and community must be integrated. Integration means bringing community resources and experiences into the school, or taking students into the community to experience first-hand things learned only abstractly in classrooms. Such integration responds to some of the impediments to academic engagement and assumes an opportunity to provide disadvantaged students with experiences they would not ordinarily enjoy.

A fifth principle is the need to establish accountability for effectiveness with at-risk students. Accountability exists when individuals or organizations are held responsible for attaining agreed-upon results. For schools to be held responsible for affecting the dropout rate, it is necessary to establish the existing rate, to specify the interventions that will be used to alter it and to specify a time within which a specified goal will be met. A similar process of data gathering, intervention strategies and goal setting is used in addressing youth employment, teenage pregnancy and other problem areas.

Accountability is more likely to be achieved when an over-arching lead agency establishes the ground rules within which the various organizations operate. Commitments must be put in writing and the agency must monitor those promises. Ideally, the lead agency would include members with sufficient political and economic 'clout' that they can command the resources and insure delivery of promises. Accountability can be further insured through case managers who would have intimate knowledge of individual at-risk youth, would be close to the scene of action and in a position to make calls regarding the effectiveness of various youth-serving agencies. He or she would report directly to the lead agency and indicate when and where programs are or are not effective. Finally, the lead agency would utilize a community MIS to provide good data on the extent to which goals have been met regarding dropout, employment and pregnancy.

Accountability is the Achilles Heel of most educational programs. A central issue that has bedeviled education, as well as social service agencies in general, is establishing accountability for the effective delivery of services. How can schools and other public service agencies be measured against some standard of effectiveness? There is no simple answer to this question. But progress toward such accountability is possible where communities have good information about the conditions of their youth, authorize schools and other agencies to deal with the major problems that are identified, provide local organizations with sufficient resources, including direct assistance from the most powerful political and economic sectors, and then have reasonable measures and standards to judge effectiveness. These accountability standards need not be the same in every community. It seems reasonable that communities should discuss local conditions and negotiate the 'acceptable' percentage of dropouts from a school system at a given time. It seems equally reasonable to negotiate the number of jobs that businesses will promise to successful graduates of local high schools. Once established, these and other goals should be public standards to which organizations are held accountable.

Dropout Prevention: A Cost-Benefit Analysis

The recommendations for reforms of policy and practice presented here are potentially far-reaching in their effects on educational institutions. While the impetus for reform originates with the dropout problem, the recommendations can also affect a larger segment of the school population and change the professional lives of educators. Are these unmeasurable benefits and a lowered dropout rate worth the effort from an economic perspective?

Intuitively we believe the benefits will far out-weigh the costs. It is generally assumed that reforms leading to lowered dropout rates will produce benefits for individuals and for society. For individuals, graduating from high school is associated with enhanced opportunities, and a more fulfilling life for individuals and their families. From a societal perspective, dropouts are associated with crime, low wages, unemployment and a cycle of poverty that affects their children. In addition, the dropout is seen as contributing less in taxes than graduates and diminishing the economic productivity crucial to the nation's competitiveness. While these claims make intuitive sense, does a cost-benefit analysis support this argument? Can a case be made that the benefits of spending money on at-risk students will outweigh the costs of the accompanying interventions?

In answering this question, we rely on the small amount of literature in this area. The Intercultural Development Research Associates (1986) of San Antonio conducted a cost-benefit analysis related to dropouts in Texas. The economic assumptions about the social costs of dropping out were those established by Levin (1972) and Catterall (1987) and were applied to a single group of ninth graders entering Texas high schools. Using data on dropout trends in Texas, IDRA estimated that about 86,000 students would drop out of the 1982-83 ninth grade cohort. The model estimated the lifetime loss of wages and tax revenues resulting from unemployment associated with dropouts, the impact on social welfare services, unemployment compensation costs, crime, and prison costs. To these socially undesirable costs were added the costs of educating potential dropouts.

Included in the category of dropout prevention costs was a 25 per cent increase in expenditures over that normally calculated as per-pupil costs in Texas. Their conclusion was that even if schools added a quarter more expenditures to the normal costs of educating students, there would still be a substantial social benefit. The benefit categories amount to about $17.5 billion while the costs total $1.9 billion; benefits exceed costs by over $15 billion. According to the IDRA analysis, 'for every dollar expended on prevention and the education of the would-be dropout, nine dollars will be returned'. IDRA points out that the lost tax revenue each year from the 86,000 dropouts would by itself quickly overtake the costs of dropout prevention. IDRA concludes dropout prevention should be seen as more than funded by the gains in additional tax revenues.

Conclusion

Our research offers evidence that special attention by educators can make schools successful in preventing students from dropping out. To make major inroads on the dropout problem, however, requires substantial reforms and initiatives by states and school systems. The three arenas for policy initiative — strengthened alternatives, systemic school reforms, and community partnerships — can be seen as a comprehensive strategy inhering a broad range of interventions. This set of strategies is not a continuum of good to best; rather it is a series of ideas, each of which offers a different locus of action and creates its own opportunities for addressing youth problems. Each has its legitimate place because each attacks problems that can place students at-risk.

Alternative schools offer the possibility of responding directly and personally to students who have not been well-served by mainstream schools. These settings also provide opportunities for educators to invent a 'better way', one in which they believe and are willing to invest themselves. Systemic reforms focusing on better information about students and enlightened practices affecting the treatment of students are desirable even without the dropout problem. Community partnerships will need to incorporate alternative schools and systemic reforms into their general strategies, as well as bringing to bear the resources of private and public institutions in developing a youth policy for each local community.

Our research also argues that beneath issues of policy and program are more fundamental issues concerning problems of school membership and educational engagement that affect each individual student. These are fundamental educational issues in the sense they persist across schools and classrooms whether students are in alternatives or comprehensive schools. These fundamental issues persist whether a teacher is offering traditional academic content or some variation of vocational or experiential curriculum. Community partnerships will also need to extend the notion of membership and engagement to broader social and economic participation of youth in the community. Without opportunity for good jobs and some influence over the conditions within a community, students are unlikely to believe even the best school programs will have some pay-off for them.

Effort at school reform on behalf of at-risk students can reduce the dropout rate. Moreover, expenditures to bring about reduced dropout rates appear to be overwhelmingly cost effective for a cost-conscious society.

Appendix A: Fourteen Schools

Alcott Alternative Learning Center, Wichita, Kansas

Alcott is a junior high school serving about 125 students who have exhibited serious academic and behavioral problems. Student records for late elementary and early junior high school indicate course failure, truancy, delinquency and drug abuse. Represented, too, are a number of students who are foster children and who have suffered from abuse or neglect at home. Many Alcott students are from single-parent homes, have moved several times, or have parents who suffer from drug abuse, alcoholism and/or depression. Since enrollment is open and students attend Alcott by choice, they represent a cross-section of the district. The majority of the population is white, but there are also blacks, Native Americans, Hispanics and Asians. Some parents seek out Alcott with the hope of finding a more successful school experience for their child. Some students hear about the school from friends and elect to transfer from another junior high. It.is also the case that some students have been told by administrators and counselors in other schools that they should transfer to Alcott, that it is the best 'choice' for them.

The school's basic intervention strategy entails offering an alternative environment that is highly personalized and provides strong counseling and basic-skill components. Since almost all students arrive at Alcott feeling alienated from school with a self-perception that they are academic failures, heavy emphasis is placed on reducing their defensiveness. More than most schools, Alcott attempts to involve parents by offering speakers on a variety of topics such as alcoholism and the family and communication between teenagers and their parents. The school tries to access a variety of community social services to reach students and families perceived as in need of assistance.

Croom Vocational High School, Upper Marlboro, Maryland

Since opening its doors in 1965, Croom Vocational High School has occupied the site of an abandoned Nike missile base, seventeen miles from the urban environment where its students have grown up and previously gone to school. A lack of fundamental work-related experience and limited academic ability are the two most salient characteristics of the 120 students who attend Croom. The poor academic record of these young people might be overlooked by employers if they were able to demonstrate some expertise in the entry-level jobs they seek. Unfortunately, Croom students are unable to offer this kind of compensatory expertise. As a result, they are among the least likely to be hired.

To be enrolled at Croom, students must be at least 16-years-old. They enroll in a two-year program. Some students will be able to earn a regular high school diploma by the end of the two years, but most will obtain a vocational certificate or GED. First-year students spend mornings in academic classes (reading, English, mathematics, science and history) and afternoons in shop courses. The academic courses share a clear basic skills orientation. The student/teacher ratio at Croom officially is 11:1; but the entire staff, including the Principal, aides and secretaries, function as teachers and counselors for all of the students as a way of providing positive and successful experiences in a caring environment.

The shops (groundskeeping, food service, building trades, auto mechanics, building maintenance, business occupations, child care and geriatrics and painting) reflect the labor market of the surrounding county. In general, the shops are designed to provide students with basic employment skills. First-year students rotate through six of the eight available shops, spending about four-and-half weeks in each. At the end of their first year, students choose their primary shop. They will spend three hours every morning of their second year working in that shop; their afternoons will be spent in academic classes. Near the end of their second year, students are placed in full-time jobs. Although the work students do at Croom varies greatly, certain principles are consistent across all shops. The instructors employ a 'coaching' style of teaching and seek to develop a positive orientation to work in their students. Several of the shops use the school as a laboratory (for example, the food services shop prepares lunch, the groundskeeping shop tends the school grounds).

Lincoln High School, Atlanta, Georgia

Lincoln (pseudonym) is located in the inner city of Atlanta. It serves poor black students, all of whom are considered at risk by the school. There is a significant teenage pregnancy problem. Many of the students are from single-parent homes, live in public housing and are supported by welfare. Low educational and occupational aspirations characterize the students and the community from which they come.

Despite this background, forty-seven out of a student population of approximately 650 were identified soon after entering Lincoln as having 'academic potential'. This group became the target of special attention with the intent of helping them not only graduate, but also to assure they would receive the kind of education that would allow entrance into higher education. Included in the plan for this group were a commitment by parents to be involved in their child's education, special enrichment activities, counseling and a college preparation curriculum.

Little reference is made to Lincoln in the text because this program was found to be indistinguishable from other conventional comprehensive high schools. The special program's impact on students was minimal or even negative.

Media Academy (Fremont High School), Oakland, California

The Media Academy, an alternative program serving black and Hispanic youth from Oakland's inner city, centers on the fields of electronic and print media as an academic and career theme. Up to fifty students may elect the program when entering the high school in the tenth grade and 'major' in media for three years. Students take a normal sequence of courses leading to a regular diploma, but the program's core courses — journalism, social studies and English — focus on skills and knowledge related to the media. Writing, critical thinking and public speaking are stressed, both in the classroom and in a variety of experiences with professional journalists and media-related businesses.

A large and diverse advisory committee from the community provides additional resources to the Academy. Many members of this group give students access to their employees and work sites. Some of these professionals come to the school to teach about the media, and students are invited into local television and radio stations, advertising agencies and newspaper offices to experience first hand the range of opportunities in the media. In addition, students write for their school newspaper, yearbook and a Spanish-English paper distributed to local residents. They also have access to radio and television stations, which use student-produced public service commercials.

The Minneapolis Federation of Alternative Schools, Minneapolis, Minnesota

The Federation is comprised of six small alternative schools, five of which participated in our study. They are funded by a combination of private and public financial resources. The private agencies include the Urban League, Lutheran Church and United Way, among others. A broad range of students is served by these schools. Though no public school facilities are used by these alternatives, students who meet the city and state requirements for graduation are issued a Minneapolis Public School diploma.

Loring-Nicollet School

Loring-Nicollet School enrolls approximately forty-five students who are academically capable, but nonetheless unsuccessful in conventional high schools. Many of the students are 'punkers' and are alienated from conventional peer groups and mainstream society; they find little relevance in what is taught in traditional classrooms.

Loring-Nicollet School responds to these students by orienting its curriculum to their needs and concerns. The curriculum is a mixture of standard and unique course offerings, all with clever or curious titles. Many of the courses deal with serious personal or social concerns of youth. Some classes are small and emphasize personalized instruction, but large group instruction, similar in many ways to that found in a more typical high school, is common.

The students appear to tolerate here what they did not tolerate in their former schools. This may occur because the staff do not seek to rid students of their counter-cultural identities, but instead help them to channel their insights and abilities into constructive social action. In this way, adults encourage students to reflect on their values, experiences and circumstances, and to break down some of the barriers that impede their participation in mainstream society.

The Minneapolis Education and Recycling Center

Housed in an old factory/garage building near a freeway, the Minneapolis Education and Recycling Center (MERC), as its name implies, combines practical work experience with instruction in the basic skills of reading and math. About twelve students work in the recycling facility; six during each of two shifts. These students attend school upstairs during the shift they are not working. Average enrollment in the school is about thirty-eight students. Students who are not employed by the recycling center are required to be employed elsewhere. The academic staff includes one full-time lead teacher, two part-time teachers (one morning, one afternoon) and a part-time secretary. Three classes are offered in the morning: English, math and careers. The students alternate English and math; all students are enrolled in a career exploration course. The afternoon schedule is more varied. In addition to English and math, students can take science, art or a course called 'Rated R', which deals with sexuality.

The Minneapolis Education and Recycling Center combines simulated entry-level work experience and schooling. This combination is particularly appealing to students who need a source of income but have been unable to secure a job, and to students who find conventional abstract classroom instruction problematic. By working a half shift in the recycling center each day, students acquire an income and a variety of work-related skills and attitudes, such as being on time and interacting productively with fellow workers. At workers' meetings, they learn to voice their concerns about worker safety and the overall operation of the recycling plant. After a successful probationary period, some students will have the opportunity to gain supervisory experience. In classes, the students acquire the basic skills necessary to pass the city competence tests and earn a high school diploma.

NA-WAY-EE – The Center School

NA-WAY-EE (Ojibwa for 'centered' or 'on balance') is an accredited alternative high school for Native American youth. In operation since 1972, the school serves approximately 100 students a year through a curriculum that includes a culturally-based education program; individual, group, and family counseling; employment opportunities; culturally-based field experiences and projects; and chemical health education, counseling and referral.

NA-WAY-EE students are Native Americans who have dropped out of conventional schools. Most of them come from poverty settings and lag two or more years behind their public school peers in reading and math; many have been involved in the criminal justice system. There is a high incidence of drug and alcohol abuse among students.

A racially mixed (white and Native American) staff instruct students in the basic standard areas of English, social studies, math and science. A special emphasis in math and science started in 1987 with the goal of providing opportunities for students in post-secondary education or in jobs that require science/math/computer backgrounds. Staff also provide formal and informal counseling to students on a daily basis. The search for cultural identity is a theme at the school.

NA-WAY-EE offers a safe atmosphere and a curriculum and pedagogy that are sensitive to the cultural backgrounds of its students. Its small size allows a familial interaction among students and staff. The school offers a viable educational option for Native American youth whose very high rates of school leaving reflect the inability of the city's high schools to accommodate the unique needs of this cultural/linguistic group.

Plymouth Christian Youth Center

Located just one block from one of Minneapolis' most notorious streets, Plymouth Christian Youth Center is a neighborhood school dedicated to serving the youth of the city's North-east side. The school has an average enrollment of approximately 112 students. In addition to a lead teacher, the PCYC staff consists of five teachers, one of whom is a social worker who teaches courses to stay in touch with the students. From time to time the staff is supplemented with volunteer teachers. PCYC also has a work coordinator who helps PCYC students find jobs. In addition to his contacts in the community, he works with a JTPA job developer in securing positions for PCYC students and graduates.

Most distinctive about PCYC is the quality of student/teacher relationships and the obvious impact this has on students' willingness to achieve academically. In many ways PCYC illustrates what a 'bare bones' intervention can accomplish with competent and very dedicated teachers who are convinced they can make a difference in the lives of their students. They convey a caring attitude and are more accepting of students' language, dress, behavior, learning disabilities and personal problems than teachers in conventional high schools.

Urban League Street Academy

The Street Academy began in 1971 as an Urban League-sponsored educational alternative for black youth who were alienated from traditional schools. It now annually serves about 100 students whose academic skills and personal circumstances make success in conventional school settings unlikely.

Most of the Street Academy's students are referrals from the city's high schools, especially the one in the neighborhood. Judging by test results in reading comprehension, writing and math, the students' skills are very limited and many are chronic truants. Several male students have been in trouble with the law and have been referred to the school by the courts. A small number of pregnant students attend, as well as several teen parents. Alcohol and drug abuse is common.

A remedial focus characterizes the curriculum, which manifests itself in the school's pervasive emphasis on the basic skills in all commonly taught subjects. As an all-black school, the Street Academy emphasizes black awareness and studies of the black experience. Typical classes enroll fewer than fifteen students, half to two-thirds of whom attend regularly. Rewards and incentives are used to promote behavioral changes among students. Much time and effort are spent by staff in dealing with the personal problems of the students.

New Futures School, Albuquerque, New Mexico

New Futures School is an alternative public school for pregnant and mothering girls from 12 to 21-years-old. Its comprehensive program offers health care, parenting classes, day care, academic classes and a jobs program to the 250 girls typically enrolled. However, average daily attendance is about 100 and the nurseries accommodate seventy-five children.

Girls typically enroll when they are four or five months pregnant; they are required to take three parenting classes that include working one period each day in one of the nurseries. Parenting classes teach female anatomy, nutrition, the stages of foetal development, the steps of delivery, child development and exercises for pregnancy and after childbirth. Health care is provided at the school by three staff nurses, as well as in weekly clinics with physicians from the University of New Mexico. Emotional health also is carefully tended by counselors who meet regularly with students to discuss the emotional issues surrounding pregnancy and motherhood. Academic course offerings help students move toward high school graduation. New Futures also offers a GED preparation program and a preparation-for-work class with job placement. The program is 93 per cent funded by the school district and the remainder comes from private and other public funds.

New Futures is distinguished in its comprehensive approach to teenage motherhood. Its staff see students as capable of being good mothers, good students and successful adults. This positive outlook helps the girls adjust to their pregnancies and go on with their lives. Small classes and attentive teachers help girls improve their academic performance, which further boosts their self-esteem and belief in future possibilities. Regular interactions with counselors also promote self-reflection, goal setting and problem solving. Students credit New Futures as essential to their finishing high school, considering post-secondary schooling and going on with their life plans.

Orr Community Academy (TMAT), Chicago, Illinois

Orr Community Academy serves a student body that is 85 per cent black and 15 per cent Hispanic. A 70 per cent drop-out rate at Orr Community Academy provided the impetus for the initiation of the 'Two Majors at a Time' (TMAT) program. TMAT attempts to reduce course failure by scheduling students into two academic courses per semester, each of which meets for two periods a day. Staff at Orr believe that absenteeism causes much failure, and the TMAT program seeks to reduce the number of absences and cuts by monitoring attendance closely and scheduling students in double periods. Once a student is in class, the eighty-minute period promotes the completion of required coursework. Additional support services augment the TMAT schedule. Reading, math and science tutorials have been initiated, and a general tutorial service operates before and after school. Dropout prevention specialists have been assigned to monitor student attendance, grades and homework so that more students will pass more courses. Staff members contact parents by telephone or mail when absences accumulate.

The TMAT program was initiated during the 1986-87 school year with more than 300 ninth-grade students. During the first semester, 29 per cent of non-TMAT students passed all classes while 50 per cent of TMAT students passed all classes. The second semester 20 per cent of non-TMAT students passed all classes and 30 per cent of TMAT students passed all classes.

School-Within-A-School (James Madison Memorial High School), Madison, Wisconsin

The School-Within-a-School is designed for students who are seriously credit deficient after two years of high school and therefore unlikely to graduate. About sixty-four students, mostly white, are in the four semester program. Most of these students are competent in their academic skills, but they do not function well in the large parent high school with its relatively impersonal social relations. The program contains a sequence of academic and vocational courses and successful completion of all components, including extra credit courses, results in a regular diploma at the end of two years. There are three full-time academic teachers, several part-time vocational teachers, along with a half-time secretary. Emphasis is placed on close monitoring of students' attendance, academic progress, and behavioral problems. The vocational component relies heavily on placements in a variety of job sites around the community. Juniors rotate through four vocational areas during the year: building trades, child care, health services and business skills. Three of these areas involve volunteer work in day care centers, nursing homes and in reconstructing old houses in the community. Seniors take either a marketing or foods services class and then find paid part-time employment in these areas.

Together, the personalized academic setting and the students' vocational experiences are aimed at helping them achieve positive records of school attendance and punctuality, increase their knowledge and skills in academic subjects, develop occupational skills and credentials and earn the credits needed to graduate from high school.

Sierra Mountain High School, Grass Valley, California

Sierra Mountain High School is a small 'school of choice' located outside of Grass Valley, one of the numerous towns scattered in the foothills of the Sierra Nevada Range in California. A staff of fifteen are responsible for creating and maintaining a daytime alternative program for approximately ninety to 100 ninth- and tenth-grade students; the same educators also operate an independent study program in the late afternoon and early evening for students who have rejected conventional classes altogether and for adults trying to complete high school. Some students enrolled in the daytime alternative are referred to Sierra Mountain primarily because of their poor attendance or unwillingness to cooperate with the behavioral standards and procedures of the district's two comprehensive high schools. Other students voluntarily choose to attend Sierra Mountain because of its reputation as a more open and caring institution.

The program is distinguished by its emphasis on informality, the creation of a sense of community, a high level of participation among staff over decisions governing the school, and curricular innovations in a number of areas aimed at personalizing teaching and learning. The school is especially successful with students who respond positively to adult attention. Classes are often structured as workshops in which student and staff interaction is frequent and ongoing. Teachers use a variety of instructional strategies but tend to emphasize lessons that demand the active involvement of their students. From this base of frequent communication and cooperative participation, relations between teachers and students achieve a degree of intimacy and mutuality generally absent in more traditional educational settings.

A central element of the program at Sierra Mountain thus involves eroding the boundary between student and staff cultures. The school works best when students have been drawn into its ethos of care and mutual respect. When, as one teacher phrased it, the 'us and them' is replaced with the 'us and us', formerly at-risk students come to demonstrate a commitment to the school's mission and its teachers. This commitment is frequently translated into increased academic engagement and achievement.

Wayne Enrichment Center, Wayne Township, Indiana

Wayne Enrichment Center (WEC) serves a variety of purposes. It acts as a structural and curricular alternative for non-traditional students; it allows pregnant teens to return to the comprehensive high school with no loss of class time or credit; it offers some students a second chance by giving them the attention and help they need to get their personal lives in order; it provides opportunities for ongoing counseling and drug therapy; and it teaches students basic vocational skills. In general, the difficulties WEC students have coping in a conventional high school are related not to low ability but to low self-esteem, passivity, family crisis, pregnancy or pressing financial obligations.

WEC operates morning, afternoon and evening sessions. It is staffed by five teachers (four full-time, one part-time), a counselor and a secretary. Approximately 100 students are enrolled, fifty in each of the morning and afternoon sessions. When students arrive at WEC, they punch a time clock. Every Friday, the day begins with a family meeting. Both events are significant, reflecting two metaphors which guide the WEC program: workplace and family.

Students earn credits toward graduation by completing course packets, which include various assignments considered, in total, to be the equivalent of one semester's worth of work. Because students concentrate on only one or two subjects at a time, and because there are few teacher lectures or other group activities, WEC students can progress through courses more quickly than typical students in typical classroom settings.

Appendix B: Research Methodology

Research reported in this volume used qualitative and quantitative methods to investigate and describe the impact of school programs on students' attitudes, behaviors and achievement. This appendix addresses the choice of schools, our background assumptions, and the qualitative and quantitative research techniques employed; it also acknowledges certain limitations of our study.

Selection of Schools

Schools in the study were selected during the spring of 1986 from nominations meeting six criteria: (i) a school should serve a subset of the broad population of students at risk of dropping out of school, such as urban minorities, poor rural whites, Native Americans; (ii) school selection should provide the project with a range of age groups as well as dropout prevention and dropout retrieval strategies; (iii) a school should demonstrate an innovative program for students, such as the use of experiential learning or a new approach to vocational education; (iv) all schools should have some evidence of their effectiveness, such as higher attendance, credit accumulation or reduced dropout rates; (v) schools should have the potential to serve as a model for other districts; and (vi) school sites had to be willing to accept the presence of researchers and provide access to teachers, students and data.

The Danforth Foundation, the National Association of Secondary School Principals, a number of state departments of education, members of the National Dropout Prevention Network and a variety of professional contacts around the country facilitated the identification and nomination of potential research sites. In all, about sixty schools were nominated. Most of these sent descriptive material about their programs, and telephone conversations provided further information about the extent to which each met the six criteria. Twenty schools were selected for final consideration. A one-day visit to each of these schools was made and, after further consideration, the fourteen described in this book were selected. Anonymity was promised one school to secure its participation.

Assumptions and Hypotheses

The study was conceived with the assumption that practitioners have developed effective strategies with at-risk students and the profession could benefit from learning about them. One task of the study was to describe these 'naturally occurring' strategies as a way of stimulating others to develop their own variations. We did not intend to describe 'model programs' for literal replication. Yet our descriptions needed to be detailed enough to illuminate particular practices, and conceptual and theoretical enough for generalizing across schools. The resulting accounts of school practice presumably will be useful to practitioners, as well as to the scholarly community interested in attaining a deeper understanding of at-risk students and their schooling.

Finally, it was assumed that a better understanding of students was essential to a better understanding of the dropout problem. We believed it was important to present students' own words, to try to view the world of school through their eyes, and to present their point of view. In addition, we deemed it necessary to interpret their less conscious behavior, attitudes and beliefs from a conceptual or theoretical framework. It was our goal at the outset to go beyond superficial descriptions of students, schools and teachers, and, if possible, to develop and utilize theory about the education of at-risk youth.

Another set of assumptions concerns the need to provide a 'balanced' methodological approach. While something can be said for research methods fashioned after an experimental design, we determined early on that nothing approaching the ideal was possible. The schools we selected were not prepared to have researchers set up tightly controlled research designs. Nor were they open to the possibility that they would become the subject of invidious comparisons reflecting unfavorably on the school or individuals within it. They were understandably cautious about the inconvenience and interference our study might create. We were able to convince schools to allow us extended observations and interviews, and to collect quantitative data on a number of variables schools already had available — failure rates, achievement scores, dropout rates, as well as limited pre/post-test data from students.

This research was based largely upon previous research (Wehlage, Stone and Kliebard, 1980; Wehlage, Stone, Lesko, Naumann and Page, 1981; Wehlage, 1983; Wehlage and Rutter, 1986; Wehlage, Rutter and Turnbaugh, 1987). Conclusions from this work provided initial hypotheses and areas of enquiry for the study. We began with the hypothesis that programs for at-risk students are effective to the extent they succeed in the social bonding process; i.e. the fundamental problem for educators is one of reversing the process of alienation that leads students to drop out. This hypothesis was pursued with both quantitative and qualitative techniques throughout the study.

Qualitative Procedures

One or two project members were assigned to each school and made three one-week visits during the 1986/87 school year. In some cases, additional visits were made to selected sites. The qualitative methodology was a constant-comparative description and analysis of selected school experiences of at-risk students during our visits throughout an academic year. Observations occurred in classes, teachers' meetings, informal teacher-student interactions and peer-group interactions. In addition, formal and informal interviews were conducted with staff and students through the course of the year.

Meetings of the five research staff members were held periodically to discuss, probe and critique our written accounts of school visits. These meetings were crucial to the methodology. As the data began to accumulate, researchers were challenged to compare their findings with those of others. When an account was discussed, members commented freely on ambiguities in the descriptions and challenged claims and interpretations. Collectively, questions were developed for follow-up visits to help gather additional supporting data for claims. Researchers were constantly reminded to check with the participants under study to see whether they would agree with claims and interpretations. This procedure often led to refocused questions for subsequent visits, not only in the school under discussion, but at other school sites as well. Much of the rigor of our methodology is found in the collective process of persistent, tenacious questioning of each report.

Upon completion of the visits and data collection, the methodology entered a second stage. This involved writing a case study of each school in which a more definitive description and intepretation were offered. Again, the procedure called for group discussions in which each staff member articulated the basis upon which he/she made certain claims. The process of discussion and criticism in response to written descriptions and analyses produced focused accounts of each school. When the case studies were completed to our collective satisfaction, each was submitted to the staff at the corresponding school to correct errors of fact or inference.

The fourteen case studies became a refined database from which we drew the accounts and quotes supporting our main findings in this volume. Through our dialogue over written reports and case studies, each researcher came to know all of the schools well enough to use a wide range of data in supporting or countering claims and generalizations. The theory articulated here was developed through the process of consensus: researchers had to be satisfied that claims could be sufficiently supported based on their understanding of the entire data base.

Quantitative Instruments

We sought to measure student growth through two instruments. One, the Wisconsin Youth Survey, is concerned with a set of personal and social attitudes previous research and literature suggest are associated with students' decisions to drop out. It was developed through a number of studies at the University of Wisconsin to measure the effects of school interventions on at-risk students (Wehlage, Stone and Kliebard, 1980; Wehlage, Rutter and Turnbaugh, 1987). In addition to developing this instrument through the study of alternative schools, it was administered to 270 sophomores in three Mid-western high schools representing a broad spectrum of academic achievement and social contexts. About 50 per cent of these students in this sample were minorities, mostly black.

The Wisconsin Youth Survey was administered in a pre/post-test design at each of the research sites, usually by classroom teachers, and was normally completed by students in about forty minutes. The survey contains eighty items; nine are about student demographic characteristics, and the remainder measure attitudes and beliefs.

The construct scales and reliability coefficients for each scale are:

Sociocentric Reasoning (.68); Social Bonding to Peers (.72); Social Bonding to School (.76); Academic Self-Concept (.64); Negative Teacher Behavior (.76); Perception of Opportunity (.69); Acceptance of Conventional Roles (.69); Locus of Control (.75); Self-Esteem (.70).

The second instrument, the Degrees of Reading Power (DRP) test, was chosen to assess reading achievement. This instrument was selected after a review of those available because it was considered the best for use with students of widely different levels of reading ability. It is a criterion-referenced measure of reading using the cloze principle. A series of paragraphs are presented and students must understand the meaning of the paragraph in order to select the correct missing word. The test is designed to be progressively more difficult and thereby determines the most difficult prose a student can read with comprehension. The test has different forms and is intended to be given on a pre/post-test basis to measure growth in achievement. Test scores indicate achievement, or the degree of reading difficulty a student has mastered.

We measured gains in writing skill and performance by obtaining two writing samples. Students wrote essays in response to common writing prompts at the beginning and end of the school year. The prompts asked students to write on the topics of rating rock music lyrics and mandatory drug testing, two current issues thought to be of interest to large numbers of youth. The prompts asked students to take a stand on the issue in a short essay. Several guiding questions to stimulate students' thinking were included in the directions. Teachers in the schools administered the writing tasks as part of a normal classroom assignment.

Student essays were subjected to a holistic scoring procedure. In this process, the two sets of essays were duplicated with all identifying characteristics (for example, grade, school, name) deleted in order to eliminate bias associated with gender, race/ethnicity or school. The essays were randomized, and three experts developed appropriate criteria for scoring this type of essay. These criteria were, in turn, discussed and elaborated upon by a panel of fifteen scorers who developed an inter-rater reliability of 85 per cent or higher. The scorers were all writing teachers with previous experience in holistic scoring of essays. These fifteen teachers read and scored approximately 1500 writing samples over a period of four half-days.

Additional data indicative of student change were gathered by examining school records for changes in grades, attendance and behavior for a random sample of thirty students in each of the programs. One of the major problems in studying at-risk students is their mobility. Since many students move in and out of school during a year, we selected a sample of thirty students in each program who remained in the school the entire academic year. This procedure provides a basis for determining effects on students who remain in the programs for one full school year.

Limitations

The empirical and theoretical findings in this volume are limited by the range of programs initially chosen for study. As already noted, they were chosen to represent programs for different sub-populations of at-risk youth, for different programmatic approaches and for some indicators of their likely success. Our assumptions and hypotheses influenced our selection of schools, and those chosen for the study showed evidence of what we initially believed was important in school programs. If we had been able to widen the range of schools selected to include some with characteristics not hypothesized to be important, our data and findings may have been different. Given the limitations of resources, we chose those we believed to have the best chance of enlightening us about the schooling of at-risk students.

Our resources also limited further the amount of time we had to study each school. Readers will note we have carefully avoided calling our study an 'ethnography'. Three weeks in a school, even a small one, is insufficient to understand in depth the nature of students' and teachers' experiences. This study cannot claim the depth of knowledge gained by intensive ethnographic studies of schools. However, this lack of depth is balanced to some extent by including fourteen schools, using multiple observers and combining qualitative and quantitative procedures.

We have chosen to highlight the positive practices, some of which appeared more in some of the schools than in others. From the beginning we were committed to emphasizing the strengths of each of these schools, rather than ranking them or describing some as failures or less successful schools. This stance prevented us from making certain comparisons across schools, but it had the strength of allowing us to maintain good relations with practitioners who were being apprised of our descriptions and interpretations.

Robert Stake, in *Quieting Reform* (1986), documents the difficulties and dangers of using quantitative analysis to measure the effects of human service programs on youths. In this thorough analysis of efforts to evaluate Cities in Schools, Stake points to the persistent inconsistency between testimonial support of students, teachers and outside evaluators regarding the beneficial effects of the program on many youth, but the absence of quantitative indicators of program success.

Stake explains this discrepancy by noting the tendency of social science to search for parsimonious, context-free generalizations. Evaluation design in the Cities in Schools study was pre-specified rather than emergent and applied to programs that 'consistently resisted regularity, uniformity and operationalization of impact'. He examined inconsistencies between practitioner and evaluator perceptions of program goals, and inherent difficulties in trying to quantify large amounts of interview and experiential data.

Stake's analysis underscores the importance of a cautious interpretation of our own data. Development of our instruments preceded our visits to the schools. Our measures, too, were applied uniformly to a diverse set of programs committed to a wide range of goals. Although our qualitative assessments of program impact reflect our emerging understanding of these interventions, our quantitative data are necessarily limited by our initial perceptions and expectations for all programs and for all at-risk youth.

Collecting data from and about at-risk youth is inherently difficult. Many of these students are transient; consequently, their school records are often incomplete, sometimes even missing. In addition, school systems deal with at-risk youth in different ways. Sometimes schools delete non-attending students from the rolls quickly; others maintain enrollment and keep records on a student for an entire year even though he or she is not attending. Grading systems, credits required for graduation and the rationale behind different forms of disciplinary action vary widely among school districts. It is difficult, to say the least, to make comparisons across schools and programs.

There were also technical difficulties gathering reliable pre- and post-test data with at-risk youth. Because of transiency, in some programs few of the same students were in attendance at the beginning and at the end of the school year. In programs where students remained across the school year, motivation for them to perform well on a post-test for researchers from the University of Wisconsin-Madison was extremely low. Some expressed openly their frustration with taking yet another test. This meant that even when observational and interview data had built a case for a strong program, if students did not take a post-test seriously, the quantitative data failed to validate the program's effectiveness.

We believe the quantitative data presented in this volume is best interpreted within the context of the qualitative data. Supporting Stake, we suggest that only by acknowledging both scientific and experiential knowing can we begin to understand the effect of schools on at-risk youth.

References

AYRES, L. (1909) *Laggards in our Schools*, Philadelphia, PA, Russell Sage Foundation.

BACHMAN, J., GREEN, S. and WIRTANEN, I. (1971) *Dropping Out: Problem or Symptom?* Ann Arbor, MI, Institute for Social Research.

BISHOP, J. (1987) *Why High School Students Learn So Little and What Can Be Done About It*, Ithaca, NY, Cornell University, Center for Advanced Human Resource Studies.

BRYK, A. and DRISCOLL, M. (1988) *The high school as community: Contextual influences and consequences for students and teachers*, Madison, WI, National Center on Effective Secondary Schools, University of Wisconsin-Madison.

BRYK, A., HOLLAND, P., LEE, V. and CARRIEDO, R. (1984) *Effective Catholic Schools: An Exploration*, Washington, DC, National Center for Research in Total Catholic Education.

CATTERALL, J. (1987) 'On the social costs of dropping out of school', *The High School Journal*, 71, 1, pp. 19–30.

CERVANTES, L. (1965) *The Dropout: Causes and Cures*, Ann Arbor, MI, University of Michigan Press.

CHUBB, J. (1987) 'Why the current wave of school reform will fail', *Public Interest*, 86, winter, pp. 28–49.

CHUBB, J. and MOE, T. (1986) *Politics, Markets and the Organization of Schools*, Washington, DC, The Brookings Institution.

COHEN, P., KULIK, J. and KULIK, C. (1982) 'Educational outcomes of tutoring: A meta-analysis of findings', *American Educational Research Journal*, 19, 2, summer, pp. 237–48.

COLEMAN, J. and HOFFER, T. (1987) *Public and Private High Schools: The Impact of Communities*, New York, Basic Books.

COMBS, J. and COOLEY, W. (1968) 'Dropouts: In high school and after school', *American Educational Research Journal*, 5, 3, pp. 343–63.

CONNELL, R. W., ASHENDEN, D. J., KESSLER, S. and DOWSETT, G. G. (1982) *Making the Difference: Schools, Family and Social Division*, Boston, MA, G. Allen & Unwin.

CUSICK, P. (1973) *Inside High School: The Students' World*, New York, Holt, Rinehart and Winston.

DAVIES, L. (1984) *Pupil Power: Deviance and Gender in School*, Lewes, Falmer Press.

DAYTON, C., WEISBERG, A., STERN, D. and EVANS, J. (1988) *Peninsula Academies Replications: 1986–87 Evaluation Report*, Berkeley, CA, Policy Analysis for California Education.

EARLE, J., ROACH, V. and FRASER, K. (1987) *Female Dropouts: A New Perspective*, Alexandria, VA, National Association of State Boards of Education.

ECKERT, R. and MARSHALL, T. (1938) *When Youth Leave School*, New York, McGraw-Hill.

EKSTROM, R., GOERTZ, M. E., POLLACK, J. M. and ROCK, D. A. (1986) 'Who drops out of high school and why?' *Teachers College Record*, 87, 3, spring, pp. 356–73.

ERICKSON, F. (1987) 'Transformation and school success: The politics and culture of educational achievement', *Anthropology and Education Quarterly*, 18, 4, December, pp. 335–56.

FINE, M. (1986) 'Why urban adolescents drop into and out of public high school', *Teachers College Record*, 87, 3, spring, pp. 393–409.

FINN, C. (1987) 'The high school dropout puzzle', *Public Interest*, spring, pp. 64–74.

FORHAM, S. (1988) 'Racelessness as a factor in black students' school success: Pragmatic strategy or pyrrhic victory?', *Harvard Educational Review*, 58, 1, pp. 54–84.

FORDHAM, S. and OGBU, J. (1986) 'Black students' success: Coping with the "burden of acting white"', *The Urban Review*, 18, 3, pp. 176–206.

GHORY, W. and SINCLAIR, R. (1987) 'The reality of marginality: Current state of affairs for marginal students', paper presented at the annual meeting of the American Educational Research Association, Washington, DC, April.

GIBBONS, M. (1984) 'Walkabout ten years later: Searching for a renewed vision of education', *Phi Delta Kappan*, 65, 9, pp. 591–600.

GIBBONS, M. (1974) 'Walkabout: Searching for the right passage from childhood and school', *Phi Delta Kappan*, 65, 9. pp. 591–602.

GOODLAD, J. (1984) *A Place Called School: Prospect for the Future*, New York, McGraw-Hill.

GRANT FOUNDATION (1988) *The Forgotten Half: Non-college Youth in America: An Interim Report on the School-to-Work Transition*, Washington, DC, Grant Foundation.

GREGORY, T. and SMITH, G. (1987) *High Schools as Communities: The Small School Reconsidered*, Bloomington, IN, Phi Delta Kappa.

GULICK, L. H. (1910) 'Why 25,000 children quit school', *World's Work*, 20, 4, pp. 13, 285–13, 289.

HESS, A. and LAUBER, D. (1985) *Dropouts From the Chicago Public Schools*, Chicago, IL, Chicago Panel on Public School Finances.

HIRSCHI, T. (1969) *Causes of Delinquency*, Berkeley, CA, University of California Press.

HODGKINSON, H. L. (1985) *All One System: Demographics of Education, Kindergarten Through Graduate School*, Washington, DC, Institute for Educational Leadership.

INTERCULTURAL DEVELOPMENT RESEARCH ASSOCIATION (1986a) *Coca-Cola Valued Youth Partnership Dropout Prevention Program: 1985–1986 Interim Report*, San Antonio, TX, IDRA.

INTERCULTURAL DEVELOPMENT RESEARCH ASSOCIATION (1986b) *Texas School Dropout Survey Project: A Summary of Findings*, San Antonio, TX, IDRA.

KLIEBARD, H (1986) *The Struggle for the American Curriculum: 1893–1958*, Boston, MA, Routledge and Kegan Paul.

KOLSTAD, A. J. and OWINGS, J. A. (1986) 'High school dropouts who change their minds about school', paper presented at the annual meeting of the American Educational Research Association, San Francisco, April.

KOMINSKI, R. (1988) 'Current and potential race-sex differences in the US educational structure', paper presented at the annual meeting of the Population Association of America, New Orleans, April.

LESKO, N. (1988) *Symbolizing Society: Stories, Rites and Structures in a Catholic High School*, Lewes, Falmer Press.

LEVIN, H. (1972) *The Costs to the Nation of an Inadequate Education*, report to the Select Committee on Equal Educational Opportunity of the United States Senate, Washington, DC.

LEVIN, H, (1987) *Towards Accelerated Schools*, Stanford, CA, Center for Educational Research at Stanford (CERAS).

MCDERMOTT, R. (1987) 'The explanation of minority school failure, again', *Anthropology and Education Quarterly*, 18, 4, pp. 361–364.

MCNEIL, L. (1986) *Contradictions of Control: School Structure and School Knowledge*, New York, Routledge and Kegan Paul Inc.

METZ, M. (1988) *The American High School: A Universal Drama Amid Disparate Experience*, Madison, WI, National Center on Effective Secondary Schools, University of Wisconsin-Madison.

MOLL, L. C. and DIAZ, S. (1987) 'Change as the goal of educational research', *Anthropology and Education Quarterly*, 18, 4, pp. 300–311.

MOORE, D. and DAVENPORT, S. (1988) *The New Improved Sorting Machine*, Madison, WI, National Center on Effective Secondary Schools, University of Wisconsin-Madison.

NEWMANN, F. (1988) 'Can depth replace coverage in the high school curriculum?', *Phi Delta Kappan*, 69, 5, pp. 345–8.

NEWMANN, F. (in press) 'Student engagement and high school reform', *Educational Leadership*.

ARCHBALD, D. and NEWMANN, F. (1988) *Beyond Standardized Testing: Assessing Authentic Academic Achievement in the Secondary School*, Reston, VA, National Association of Secondary School Principals.

NEWMANN, F. M. and RUTTER, R. A. (1983) *The Effects of High School Community Service Programs on Students' Social Development*, report to the National Institute of Education, Madison, WI, Wisconsin Center for Education Research.

NEWMANN, F. and THOMPSON, J. (1987) *Effects of Cooperative Learning on Achievement in Secondary Schools: A Summary of Research*, Madison, WI, National Center on Effective Secondary Schools, University of Wisconsin-Madison.

NODDINGS, N. (1984) *Caring: A Feminine Approach to Ethics and Moral Education*, Berkeley, CA, University of California Press.

OGBU, J. (1974) *The New Generation: An Ethnography of an Urban Neighborhood*, New York, Academic Press.

OGBU, J. (1978) *Minority Education and Caste: The American System in Cross-Cultural Perspective*, New York, Academic Press.

OGBU, J. (1987) 'Variability in minority school performance: A problem in search of an explanation', *Anthropology and Education Quarterly*, 18, 4, pp. 312–334.

PAGE, R. (1984) 'Perspectives and processes: The negotiation of educational meanings in high school classes for academically unsuccessful students', doctoral dissertation, University of Wisconsin-Madison.

PARNELL, D. (1986) 'Shaping the environment', paper presented at the Annual National Convention of the American Association of Community and Junior Colleges, Orlando, April.

PENG, S. (1983) *High School Dropouts: Descriptive Information from High School and Beyond*, Washington, DC, National Center for Education Statistics.

POWELL, A., FARRAR, E. and COHEN, D. (1985) *The Shopping Mall High School*, Boston, MA, Houghton Mifflin.

RESNICK, L. (1987) 'Learning in school and out', *Educational Researcher*, 16, 9, December, pp. 13–20.

RODRIGUEZ, R. (1982) *Hunger of Memory: The Education of Richard Rodriguez: An Autobiography*, Boston, MA, D. R. Godine.

RUMBERGER, R. (1983) 'Dropping out of high school: The influences of race, sex and family background', *American Educational Research Journal*, 20, 2, pp. 199–220.

RUMBERGER, R. (1987) 'High school dropouts: A review of issues and evidence', *A Review of Educational Research*, 57, 2, summer, pp 101–21.

SEDLAK, M., WHEELER, C., PULLIN, D. and CUSICK, P. (1986) *Selling Students Short: Classroom Bargains and Academic Reform in the American High School*, New York and London, Teachers College Press.

SINCLAIR, R. (Ed) (1983) *For Every School a Community: Expanding Environments for Learning*, Boston, MA, Insitute for Responsive Education.

SIZER, T. (1984) *Horace's Compromise, The Dilemma of the American High School*, Boston, MA, Houghton Mifflin.

STAKE, R. (1986) *Quieting Reform: Social Science and Social Action in an Urban Youth Program*, Urbana, IL, University of Illinois Press.

TINTO, V. (1987) *Leaving College: Rethinking the Causes and Cures of Student Attrition*, Chicago, IL, University of Chicago Press.

WAGGONER, D. (1987) 'School holding power in the United States in the eighties', paper presented at the 16th Annual International Bilingual-Bicultural Education Conference, Denver, 31 March.

WALLER, W. (1932/1961) *The Sociology of Teaching*, New York, Russell and Russell.

WEHLAGE, G. (1983) *Effective Programs for the Marginal High School Student*, Bloomington, IN, Phi Delta Kappa, (PDK Fastback No. 197).

WEHLAGE, G. and RUTTER, R. (1986) 'Dropping out: How much do schools contribute to the problem?', *Teachers College Record*, 87, 3, spring, pp. 374–92.

WEHLAGE, G. and LIPMAN, P. (1988) 'Integrating school and community: The Annie E. Casey Foundation's new futures initiative for at-risk youth', Madison, Wisconsin, National Center on Effective Secondary Schools.

WEHLAGE, G., RUTTER, R. and TURNBAUGH, A. (1987) 'A program model for at-risk high school students', *Educational Leadership*, 44, 6, pp. 70–3.

WEHLAGE, G., STONE, C. and KLIEBARD, H. (1980) *Dropouts and Schools: Case Studies of the Dilemmas Educators Face*, Madison, WI, University of Wisconsin, Report to the Governor's Employment and Training Office.

WEHLAGE, G., STONE, C., LESKO, N., NAUMANN, C. and PAGE, R. (1981) *Effective Programs for the Marginal Student*, Madison, WI, Wisconsin Center for Education Research.

WEIS, L. (1985) *Between Two Worlds: Black Students in an Urban Community College*, Boston, MA, Routledge and Kegan Paul.

WHEELOCK, A. (1986) *The Way Out: Student Exclusion Practices in Boston Middle Schools* Boston, MA, Massachusetts Advocacy Center.

WILLIAMS, P. A. (1987) *Standardizing School Dropout Measures*, Madison, WI, Center for Policy Research in Education, University of Wisconsin-Madison.

WILLIS, P. (1977) *Learning to Labour: How Working Class Kids Get Working Class Jobs*, New York, Columbia University Press.

WILSON, W. (1987) *The Truly Disadvantaged: The Inner City, the Underclass and Public Policy*, Chicago, University of Chicago Press.

WITTE, J. and WALSH, D. (1985) *Metropoliton Milwaukee District Performance Assessment Report*, Madison, WI, Study Commission on the Quality of Education in the Metropolitan Milwaukee Public Schools.

Index

Figures in italics denote tables

Absenteeism 51–2, 150, 176–7, 249
  of teachers 149
  see aslo truancy
academic achievement 29, 55, 56,
    124–6, 197, 221
  at Alcott 99, 100
  at Croom 91, 92
  and extrinsic rewards 180–1
  at Media Academy 13
  at New Futures 95, 96
  and program effectiveness 2, 155,
    158–9, 160, 165–7, 172–3
  at Sierra Mountain High 154
academic self-concept 155, 160,
    167, 257
  and program effectiveness
    169–70, 172–3
accountability 71, 135–6, 137, 143,
    · 194, 224
  and dropout rates 234–5, 237–9
adjustment 121, 122–4, 194, 205
admissions criteria 145–6
alcohol abuse 10–11, 26, 65–7,
    171, 242, 247, 248
Alcoholics Anonymous 23, 66
Alcott Alternative Learning Center
    22–3, 53, 131–2, 140–1,
    142–3, 206
  drugs 65, 99, 100
  matching 99, 100, 101–3
  outline 2, 54–5, 242
  program effectiveness 157–60,
    161–3, 166, 172
  teachers' role 135–8

vignettes 7–8, 9–12, 60–1
alienation 68–70, 112, 116, 218,
    220
  at Croom 92
  at Loring-Nicollet 108
  at NA-WAY-EE 108
  at Plymouth C.Y.C. 103, 104
  at Urban League Street Academy
    248
alternative schools 5, 222, 224,
    225–8
aspirations 50, 154
  at Croom 92
  at Lincoln 244
  at Media Academy 12–13, 86, 87
  program effectiveness 160, 167,
    170–3
attachment 117, 133, 176
attendance 37–9, 206, 218, 221,
    229, 253, 257–8
  at Alcott 100
  at Croom 130
  at Loring-Nicollet 69
  at Media Academy 188
  at New Futures 96, 98–9, 145,
    164
  program effectiveness 2, 5, 155,
    158, 163–4, 166, 168, 172–3
  at School-Within-a-School 81, 82,
    83, 250
  at Sierra Mountain High 76, 77,
    78, 81, 154, 250–1
  at Urban League Street Academy
    109

at Wayne Enrichment Center 123, 130
autonomy 134, 144–8, 215, 223, 227, 231–2
Ayres, L. 31–2, 37

Baton Rouge 70
Bear River High School 76, 151
behavior problems 29, 40, *50*, 120, 211, 218, 253, 257
  at Alcott 60–1, *100*, 102, 242
  at Catholic schools 45
  causes 65, 136–8, 196–7
  at Media Academy 209
  at Plymouth C.Y.C. *104*, 105–7
  program effectiveness 155–6, *158*, 161–4, 166, 172–3
  at School-Within-a-School 81, *82*, 83, 205, 250
  at Sierra Mountain High 77, 78, 81, 154, 200, 251
  at Wayne Enrichment Center 123
belief 118, 133
Boston Middle Schools 37–8, 47
Bryk, A. and Driscoll, M. 148–50

Cardinal Principles of Education (1918) 208
Casey Foundation 236
Catholic schools 41–2, *43*, 44–7, 63
census data 73–4
Center School, The 53, *54–5*, 67–8, 246–7 *see also* NA-WAY-EE
Cervantes, L. 35–6
characteristics of dropouts 35–7, 48, 51
church, decline of influence 130, 236, 245
cigarette smoking 20, 67, 153, 162
class, social 2, 32–4, 110, 126–7, 149–50
  of dropouts 36, 49, 221
cocaine 65
Coleman, J. and Hoffer, T. 41–5
college 12, 63, 206, 210
  drop-outs 120–1, 130–1

collegiality 138, 142–3, 144, 149, 194, 232
commitment 23, 142, 200, 204, 212, 217–18, 220
  and social bonding 117–18, 120–1, 133, 176, 177
community partnerships, 222, 235–9, 240–1
community service 212
Conway, Earle (principal of Sierra Mountain High School) 76, 78, 141, 206, 214
cost-benefit 239–41
counter-culture 76, 129, 245
course failure 26, 39, 111, 116, 228–30
  at Alcott 99, *100*
  at Croom 91
  and dropouts 26, 36–9, *50*, 51, 221
  at Plymouth C.Y.C. 103, *104*
  at School-Within-a-School 81
  at Sierra Mountain High 76, 77, 79
coverage 179, 184–6, 223
credit deficiency *50*, *55*, 56, 75, 111, 125, 167, 203
  at Croom 91, 93
  at Loring-Nicollet 69
  at New Futures 95, *96*
  at Plymouth C.Y.C. 103, *104*
  at School-Within-a-School 61, 64, 81, *82*, 145, 250
  at Sierra Mountain High 77, 79, 152, 154
  at Wayne Enrichment Center 110, 123
crime 29, *50*, 67–8, 118, 221, 239–40
  at Alcott 10–11, 99, 102
  at Media Academy 188
  at NA-WAY-EE 247
  at School-Within-a-School 83
  at Sierra Mountain High 77
  at Urban League Street Academy 248
Croom Vocational High School 57, 59, 72, 123–4, 130, 145, 205

curriculum 180–1, 182, 192, 210, 214–15
  matching 91, *92*, 93–5
  outline 2, 14–16, 23–4, 53, *54–5*, 243
  program effectiveness *157–60*, 162–4, 166, 169–71
  school membership 116, 196
  self-governance 140, 147
curricula 2–4, 39, 11–12, 148, 191–2, 241
  at Alcott 132
  at Croom 23–4, 180–1
  cultural background 52, 68, 129
  and employment 180–1, 210
  and engagement 176–7, 192, 194, 198–9, 207, 223–4, 232
  flexibility 144–7, 154
  innovations 184–6, 195, 197, 207, 209, 212–18, 233–4
  at Lincoln 244
  at Loring-Nicollet 108, 245
  at Media Academy 23–4, 86, 88–91, 139, 142, 189–90, 209
  at NA-WAY-EE 108, 246–7
  at New Futures 95, 97–9, 132, 190–1, 248–9
  at Plymouth C.Y.C. 103, 106
  program effectiveness 172–4
  reforms needed 26–7, 31–4, 75, 182, 227–8
  response 200, 208
  at School-Within-a-School 83
  at Sierra Mountain High 78–9, 251
  at Urban League Street Academy 248
  at Wayne Enrichment Center 110, 251–2
Cusick, P. 176

Danforth Foundation 253
decentralization of large schools 231–2
Degrees of Reading Power (DRP) *55*, 56, 69, 155, *158*, 165, 257
delinquency 32, 76, 77, 78, 118–19, 215, 242

demographics *54–5*, 57–8
difficulty as impediment to school membership 121, 124–6, 194
Doyle, Dr. Edward (principal of Croom) 215
Driscoll, M. 148–50
dropout rate 5, 28–9, 46–7, 52, 228–9, 249
  accountability 234–5, 237–8
  in Boston 37–8
  at Catholic schools 41, 42, *43*
  at communal schools 149, 150
  economics 1, 239–41
  and grade retention 230
  history 30–7
  in Milwaukee 38–41
  program effectiveness *159*, 197, 253, 255
  and race/ethnicity 48, 73–4
drug abuse 9, 26, 64–8, 70, 171, 200, 215
  at Alcott 10–11, 65, 99, *100*, 102, 142, 242
  at Croom 93
  and dropouts 221, 226
  at Loring-Nicollet 204
  at Media Academy 187–8
  at NA-WAY-EE 247
  at New Futures 16
  at Sierra Mountain High 66–7, 78, 153
  at Urban League Street Academy 248
  at Wayne Enrichment Center 251
Eckert, R. and Marshall, T. 32–4, 37
educational triage 40
El Tigre 89
employment 112, 198, 202, 222, 235
  credentials 180–1, 206, 219
  at Croom 2, 14–16, 93–5, 130, 171
  at New Futures 98
  opportunities 210–11, 220, 223–4
  part time *55*, 57, 109, 171, 250
  at School-Within-a-School 57, 83

at Sierra Mountain High 153–4
skills needed 23–4, 59
training 75, 208–9
engagement 25, 135, 176–95, 211,
    223–4, 241
  and curriculum 216, 218, 232–4
  defined 177–9
  and dropout prevention 192, *193*,
    194–5
  and employment 210, 220
  examples 186–92
  impediments 179–86, 196–9, 238
  at Media Academy 209
  and program effectiveness *158–9*,
    163, 167
  promotion 147–50, 212–13
  and school membership 120–1
  at Sierra Mountain High 79,
    203–4, 206
  and size of school 143–4, 228
  and social bonding 118, 133,
    203–7
entrepreneurship 138–40, 144, 148,
    216, 223, 232
  and program effectiveness 172,
    194
epilepsy 65, 102
'Essentials of Living' 102
ethnicity *see* race/ethnicity
experiential learning 125, 172, 174,
    191–2, 212, 227–8, 241
  at Croom 23
  at Media Academy 23, 86, 88–91
  at New Futures 23, 97–9
  at School-Within-a-School 83–5,
    146
Explorer Scouts 131
expulsion for profanity 137
extended teacher role 45, 115,
    135–7, 149, 174, 194, 234
extrinsic rewards 179, 180–1, 194

family backgrounds and problems
    25–9, 40, *50*, 51, *55*, 56–7,
    121
  at Alcott 99, *100*, 101
  in Catholic schools 41–2, *43*, 44,
    47

at Croom *92*, 93
of dropouts 35–7, 221, 226, 235
at New Futures *96*, 97–8
at School-Within-a-School *82*, 83
at Wayne Enrichment Center
    251–2
see also single parent homes
Finn, C. (Assistant Secretary of
    Education) 28–9, 35
flexibility 144–7, 194, 217, 231–2
Fremont High School 2–3, 12–13,
    89, 91, 217, 244–5
  see also Media Academy
funding 217, 225–7, 234
  by Casey Foundation 236
  of Media Academy 139
  of Minneapolis Federation 3, 245
  of New Futures 139, 249

gang membership at Croom 93
Gaston, Carolyn (principal of New
    Futures) 139, 147, 168, 215
gender 49, *54*, *87*, 106, 111, 229
General Education Diploma (GED)
    75, 93, 109, *159*, 243, 249
grade point average (gpa) 71, 180,
    218, 228
  program effectiveness 155, *158*,
    163, 166, 173
The Green and Gold 89
Gulick 31
Gutierrez, Mrs. Beverly (principal
    of Alcott) 9–12, 22–3, 99, 101,
    131, 140

Harbor Bay Teleport 13–14, 88
health *50*, 221
  at Alcott *100*, 101
  at New Futures 3, 95, *96*, 97–9,
    248–9
High School and Beyond 36, 41,
    43, 47, 49, 148–9
Hirschi, T. 118–19
Hodgkinson, H.L. 48–9
Hoffer, T. 41–5

incongruence 58–60, 154, 173, 197,
    203

and school membership 121,
126–30, 162, 194
Intercultural Development Research
Associates (IDRA) 239–40
involvement *see* engagement
Iowa Test of Basic Skills 7, 99
isolation 18–19, 112, 154, 173–4,
197, 220
at Alcott *100*
and school membership 121,
130–2, 162, 194, 218
at School-Within-a-School 61–2
at Sierra Mountain High 77, 200
at Wayne Enrichment Center
168–9

jail 11, 65
Jefferson County Open High School
212

King School (Milwaukee) 39

Lincoln High School (pseudonym)
2, 53, *54–5*, 57, 143, 244
program effectiveness *157–60*,
163–4, 166, 169–70, 172–3
locus of control 155, *160*, 167, 169,
173, 257
Loring-Nicollet 56–7, 108, 129,
204, 206
outline 5, 53, *54–5*, 245
programme effectiveness *157–60*,
162–3, 166
punkers 68–70
lsd 65
Lutheran Church 245

Madison Memorial High School,
James 3, 61, *158–9*, 250
see also School-Within-a-School
magnet schools 39, 40, 226
Management Information System
(MIS) 228–9, 234, 238
marijuana 65–6, 153
Marshall, T. 32–4, 37
matching 75–6, 110–12, 207–13,
224, 226
at Alcott 99, *100*, 101–3

at Croom 91, *92*, 93–5
at Loring-Nicollet 108
at Media Academy 86, *87*, 88–91
at Minneapolis E.R.C. 109
at Minneapolis Federation 107–9
at NA-WAY-EE 107–8
at New Futures 95, *96*, 97–9
at Plymouth C.Y.C. 103, *104*,
105–7
at School-Within-a-School 81, *82*,
83–5
at Urban League Street Academy
108–9
at Wayne Enrichment Center
109–10
Media Academy 53, 56–7, 67,
127–8, 140, 147, 219
curriculum 181–2, 209–10,
216–17
engagement 186–90, 192, 195
Harbor Bay 13–14, 88
matching 86, *87*, 88–91
outline 2–3, 12–14, 23–4, *54–5*,
244–5
program effectiveness *157–60*,
164, 166–7, 170
school membership 114, 190, 196
teachers' role 139, 142, 212
Milwaukee Public Schools 38–9, 47
Minneapolis Education and
Recycling Center 56–7, 109,
205
outline 3, *54–5*, 246
program effectiveness *157–60*,
166, 175
Minneapolis Federation of
Alternative Schools 3, 107–9,
245–8
Minneaoplis High School Diploma
109
mobility *50*, *55*, 57, 61–2, 226,
229, 258
at School-Within-a-School *82*, 83
motivation 9, 177–81, 209,
212–13, 216, 219

narrowness of school learning 179,
181–3

National Association of Secondary
School Principals 253
National Dropout Prevention
Network 253
National Longitudinal Survey of
Youth Labor Market
Experience 36
Native Americans 26, 49, 63, 68,
128–9, 253
at Alcott 242
at NA-WAY-EE (Center School)
53, *54*, 107–9, 246–7
NA-WAY-EE (The Center School)
107–9, 128–9, 206
outline 3, 246–7
program effectiveness *157–60*,
162–3, 166, 172
see also Center School, The
Nevada Union School 76, 151–3,
161
New Futures School 53, 57, 62–4,
67, 132, 146, 168, 236
attendance *96*, 145, 164
curriculum 23–4, 182, 190–1,
214–15
foundation 139
matching 95, *96*, 97–9
outline 3, 16–18, *54–5*, 143,
248–9
self-governance 140, 147
social bonding 196, 206
Nike missile base 15, 91, 243
nihilism 163

Operation Fresh Start 84
opportunity, perception of 155, *160*,
167, 169, 257
optimism of teachers 135, 137–8
Orr Community Academy 59, 125,
143
outline 3, 53, *54–5*, 249
program effectiveness *157–60*,
163–4, 166, 169–70, 172–3
Two Majors at a Time 3, 249

pedagogy 125, 129
innovations 103, 197, 207, 209,
212–13

at Media Academy 209
at NA-WAY-EE 247
at Plymouth C.Y.C. 103
at Sierra Mountain High 78
persistence of teachers 135, 137
personal problems 25–6, *50*, 51,
235
phenobarbital 102
Plymouth Christian Youth Center
53, 57
matching 103, *104*, 105–7
outline 3, *54–5*, 247
program effectiveness *157–60*,
164, 166, 170, 175
policy-makers 1, 4–5, 52, 73
recommendations for reform
222–39
poverty 9, 58–60, 118, 221,
239–40
at Alcott 99, *100*
at Media Academy 12
at NA-WAY-EE 247
at School-Within-a-School *82*
see also Socioeconomic Status
pregnancy, teenage 13, *50*, 75, 145,
224, 236, 237–9
at Alcott 99
at Croom 93
as dropout factor 26, 221, 226
at Lincoln 244
at New Futures 3, 16–18, 62–4,
95, *96*, 97–9, 132, 248–9
and program effectiveness 168
at School-Within-a-School 64, 83
at Urban League Street Academy
248
at Wayne Enrichment Center 110,
130, 251
prison 11, 65
profanity 66, 137
program effectiveness 154–6,
157–60, 161–2, 171–4
punkers 26, 68–70, 76, 127, 129,
163
at Loring-Nicollett 108, 245

race/ethnicity *50*, 51–3, *54*, 111,
149–50, 200–1, 229

and course failure 39–40
dropout rates 2, 41, 48–9, 52,
73–4, 221
employment 13–14
incongruence 126–9
at Media Academy 12, 86, *87*,
188
at New Futures 95
at Plymouth C.Y.C. 103, *104*,
105–7
and retention in grade 37–8
reform of schools 32–4, 224–39
remediation 208, 216
resistance 196–7, 199–203, 213,
217, 225
Resnick, L. 181, 182–3, 207, 218
respect 115, 120, 135, 156, 161,
200, 204
retention in grade *50*, 65, 99,
229–31
as dropout factor 26, 37–9, 47,
221
Ropes Course 19–22, 24–5, 61

School Age Maternity Program 64
school membership 5, 112, 113–33,
186, 200–1, 241
at Catholic schools 45–6
components 176, 177
and cultural background 68
and curriculum 216, 218
and drop-outs 47, 192, *193*,
194–5
and drugs 67
impediments 121–32, 196–8
adjustment 122–4
difficulty 124–6
incongruence 126–30
isolation 130–2
importance 114–16, 237
limitations 203, 216
at Media Academy 114, 190, 196
and policy reform 223, 224
and program effectiveness 154–6,
157, 162–3, 167
promotion 147–50
reciprocity 119–21

at Sierra Mountain High 78,
115–16, 162–3
and size of schools 143–4, 228,
231–2
and teachers' role 134–5
theory and research 116–19
school phobia 7, 26, 131
school problems 26–7, 36–7, *50*,
51, 116, 235
at Catholic schools 41–2, *43*, 44
School-Within-a-School 18, 91,
140, 200, 201-3
curriculum 145–6, 182
drugs 65
employment 57, 83
engagement 191–2, 204–5
family problems 57, 60–1, *82*,
83
matching 81, *82*, 83–5
outline 3, *54–5*, 250
pregnancy 64, 83
program effectiveness 156,
157–60, 162–3, 164, 166, 172
race/ethnicity 53, 86
ropes course 19–22, 24–5, 61
social bonding 24–5, 114–15,
162–3
truancy 60–1, 62, 70–2
self-esteem *50*, 154, 191, 198, 257
at Alcott 8, *100*, 101
at Croom 91, *92*, 130
at New Futures *96*, 249
and program effectiveness 155–6,
160, 167–9, 172–4
at School-Within-a-School *82*
at Sierra Mountain High 77
at Wayne Enrichment Center 251
self-governance 134, 138, 140–4,
147–8, 194, 232
sexuality 67, 204
Sierra Mountain High School 68,
125, 151–4, 199–200, 214–15
collegiality 142
drugs 66–7, 78, 153
engagement 79, 203–4, 206
flexibility 146
matching 76, 77, 78–81
outline 3, *54–5*, 250–1

program effectiveness 156,
157–60, 161–3, 166, 172
race/ethnicity 53, 54, 86
school membership 78, 115–16,
162–3
self-governance 140–2
truancy 70, 78
single parent homes 25–6, 42, 50,
51, 55, 56–7, 130
at Alcott 60–1, 242
at Lincoln 244
Single Parent Program 64
size of schools 143–4, 147, 150,
194, 231–2
social bonding 134–5, 176, 197,
223, 255, 257
and academic achievement 124
at Croom 169
without engagement 203–7
and program effectiveness 155–6,
157, 162–3, 172–4
and school membership 117–22,
133
at School-Within-a-School 24–5
at Sierra Mountain High 154
social interaction 27, 44–5, 107,
207
social services 1, 131–2, 167, 171,
222–3,
socioecentric reasoning 155, 157,
162–3, 169, 173, 257
sociocultural characteristics 58–73
socioeconomic status (SES) 25,
48–9, 53, 54, 56, 74, 126
matching 86, 87, 96, 104, 107,
109
see also poverty
Stake, Robert 258–60
substance abuse 50, 64–7
at Alcott 100, 102
at Croom 92
at NA-WAY-EE 108
at School-Within-a-School 82, 83
at Sierra Mountain High 76, 77
see also alcohol abuse, drug abuse
suspension 10, 39, 51, 66, 103, 137
as dropout factor 26, 37–8, 47,
221

effects 229–31
systemic school reforms 222, 224,
228–35, 240–1

TALENT, project 36
Tinto 120–1, 130–1
Title IX 62
Title XX 64
tolerance 204–5, 206
tracking 198, 207–13, 226, 233
Tribune 139
truancy 37–8, 50, 61–2, 69–72,
111, 150
at Alcott 2, 10, 65, 102, 141, 242
as dropout factor 26, 221
at School-Within-a-School 60–2,
70–2
at Sierra Mountain High 70, 78
at Urban League Street Academy
248
Two Majors at a Time 3, 249
see also Orr Community Academy

Unemployment 9, 57, 236–9
of dropouts 1, 221, 239–40
United Way 245
Urban League Street Academy
(Minneapolis) 53, 67, 108–9,
129, 206, 245
outline 3, 54–5, 248
program effectiveness 158–9, 164,
166, 175

vandalism 67
violence 9, 102, 106
vocational training 32–3, 208, 216,
227–8, 241
at Croom 2–3, 14–16, 91, 93–5,
243
and employment 210, 224
and engagement 191–2, 199
at Media Academy 88–91
at School-Within-a-School 83–5,
202, 250
and tracking 209, 233
at Wayne Enrichment Center 251
voluntary organisations 130, 236
volunteer work 145, 191, 211, 250

Walkabout educational model 212
Wayne Enrichment Center 123,
  125, 130, 205, 211–12, 215–16
  admissions 145–6
  employment 57
  matching 109–10
  outline 3, *54–5*, 251–2
  program effectiveness *157–60*,
    162–4, 166, 168–9, 171–2

and race/ethnicity 53, *54*
and school membership 162–3
welfare 1, 29, 51, 236–7, 240, 244
Wisconsin, University of 256, 259
Wisconsin Youth Survey 155, 169,
  174, 256

youth policy 222, 236
youth services 237–8